The Unplayable Lie

The Untold Story of Women and

Discrimination in American Golf

Marcia Chambers

Foreword by Amy Alcott

GOLF DIGEST

POCKET BOOKS

New York   London   Toronto   Sydney   Tokyo   Singapore

Published by:

NYT Special Services, Inc.
An Affiliate of the New York Times Company
5520 Park Avenue, Box 395
Trumbull, CT 06611-0395

and

POCKET BOOKS, a division of Simon & Schuster Inc.
1230 Avenue of the Americas, New York, NY 10020

Chambers, Marcia.
    The unplayable lie : the untold story of women and discrimination in American golf / Marcia Chambers ; foreword by Amy Alcott.
        p.   cm.
    ISBN 0-671-50155-0
    1. Golf for women—United States   2. Sex discrimination in sports—United States.   I. Title.
    GV966.C43   1995
    796.352 ′ 024042.54—dc20   95–13598
                                                                          CIP

First NYT Special Services, Inc. and Pocket Books trade paperback printing June 1996

10 9 8 7 6 5 4 3 2 1

POCKET and colophon are registered trademarks of Simon & Schuster Inc.

GOLF DIGEST/TENNIS, INC. and logo are trademarks of Golf Digest/Tennis, Inc., A New York Times Company

Book design by Laura Hammond Hough

Printed in the U.S.A.

For Stan

❧ Acknowledgments ❧

Many people were essential to the creation of this book. First, those who provided special help with historical and comparative material: Pat Moran, of the United States Golf Association, helped me locate historical materials on women and golf from the USGA library. I was also aided by golf writers on both sides of the Atlantic: Peter Dobereiner, Liz Kahn, Ross Goodner and John Huggan. The National Club Association has kept me informed about legislative developments and their policies over the last six years. Lisa Fitzgerald, a reference librarian at the Yale Law School, assembled a state-by-state compilation of the laws affecting private clubs that provided the basis for the Appendix.

I was helped immeasurably by a group of enthusiastic staff at NYT Sports/Leisure Magazines: Bitsy Farnsworth, Ann Lockhart, Kathy Stachura, Betsy Van Sickle, and Amy S. Lee, associate editor of *Golf Shop Operations*, who helped especially in the chapter on public courses. Mary Rung directed the swift production of this book with grace and humor. I want to thank Jerry Tarde, the editor of *Golf Digest*, for giving me the opportunity beginning in 1989 to explore the world of private country clubs; Lisa Furlong, the managing editor, for sending me to the Women's Golf Summit in 1993 where I gathered information and made useful contacts for this book, and especially Bob Carney, Director of Special Services, who has been involved in the project throughout and who provided thoughtful commentary on the manuscript.

My editor Cecilia Hunt brought to this book style, energy and organization. I learned enormously from her editing. My agent Wendy Lipkind offered guidance and judgment and a sympathetic ear. And Donna Ruvituso, Senior Managing Editor of Pocket Books, directed me through the process of publishing my first book.

I want also to thank the numerous members of clubs who provided a greater understanding of club life. The list is long and most would prefer not to be named but one who deserves public recognition is the late William Roach, founder of Mill River Country Club. Another is Susan Pappas, who brought together a group of top corporate executives to discuss these issues. I also want to thank friends at the Manchester Country Club in Vermont, and colleagues at the Yale Law School.

There are several others: Lesley Oelsner, my former colleague at the *New York Times*, Rita Jensen, my former colleague at the *National Law Journal*, my step-son Kenneth, whose analysis was always on target, my brother-in-law Rik Kabel, who on more than one occasion retrieved my computer copy, my sister Jan, who never lost her sense of humor, my sister-in-law Nancy, who went forward without hesitation as my West Coast gumshoe, and my mother Rachel, who provided love and support throughout.

I am grateful to the women and men attorneys, too many to name individually, who have represented many of the women in this book. Finally, I am deeply indebted to all the women, beginner to expert, amateur to professional, whose stories this book is about.

My husband, Stan, helped guide this project from start to finish and was in many ways a collaborator. He offered thoughtful comments about the book's organizational structure as well as its writing. I am indebted to him for his moral support, his fine sense of humor and his ability to convey to me his lifelong love of the game of golf. He was and is a total partner. I could not have done it without him.

❧ Contents ❧

III Other Voices, Other Venues

IV Turning Private Clubs Around

❧ About This Book ❧

In my twenty-five years as a reporter, I have covered some difficult stories: the shootings of Mafia leaders Joe Colombo and Joey Gallo, the trial of the kidnappers of Patty Hearst, the "Son of Sam" murders, the Bernie Goetz subway shooting in New York City. And I have investigated organizations where secrecy was institutionally entrenched.

Learning about women's experiences on public courses and in professional golf was relatively straightforward, but nothing has been as difficult as the story of the inner workings of private golf and country clubs. One reason is that privacy is part of club credo, and clubs want it to remain that way. Disclosure exposes the club to public scrutiny and that means other people poking around club business. Clubs prefer insulation. That is why club spokesmen rarely speak for the record, even to verify or correct a fact. Policies may change but will be unannounced. I have done my best to describe club life accurately, but there may have been changes in individual cases of which I am unaware.

Much of the material for this book came from court documents, where club views are a matter of record. Much also came from legislative records and from other written sources. I also conducted interviews with those involved with golf at a managerial or policy-making level.

But the largest part of the reporting came from women in strained relationships with private clubs, and getting their story for the record is often almost as difficult as getting the views of private club management, but for very different reasons. They don't invoke doctrines of privacy. Simply put, they are afraid of going public while trying to change club policies.

I get telephone calls each week from women seeking advice. Many women do not identify themselves, let alone their club. Their lives are tied to their country club. What's in it for the wife who shakes up that world? Her image may change from amiable team player to troublemaker, a woman under seige at her own club. Is it worth it?

Many women in these pages have struggled with their decision to go public. Usually they have agreed to public disclosure when repeated efforts to change club policies have failed or when they file a lawsuit. Sometimes they agree to be identified only to change their minds later on. These are not "deep throat" informants exposing wrongdoing in their companies, or à la Watergate, in government. These are women feeling woefully mistreated on the fairways of some of America's most exclusive clubs.

I believe that some day these women, along with the professionals and those on public courses, will be treated fairly. The question is how soon? I hope this book will hasten the process.

MARCIA CHAMBERS
Guilford, Connecticut
February 1995

❦ Foreword by Amy Alcott ❦

When Marcia Chambers asked me to write the foreword to *The Unplayable Lie* I was flattered—and somewhat torn.

I was flattered, because while I have never considered myself an activist, I had always hoped that my accomplishments on the golf course would serve as an inspiration to women. I also hoped my record would be a demonstration to those men who believe that women don't belong in the game, or that women don't feel the same passion for it. Marcia's invitation to me indicated that perhaps I had succeeded in some form of action.

I was concerned, because golf—in its somewhat antiquated and clearly male-dominated state—has been very good to Amy Alcott. Golf is a game I truly love—for its places and courses and its people and organizations. I didn't want to seem either unappreciative or unaware.

And so I found myself in the predicament that many women in golf (and in business, for that matter) and women you'll read about in this book find themselves. How does one say, Yes, this is a wonderful game. Yes, this is a wonderful course. Yes, this is a wonderful club. And still say, But no, it's not perfect, and no, we can't ignore our problems, and no, we can't put off making changes. We can't.

The Unplayable Lie will open your eyes. A friend of mine says good golfers play with blinders on, and believe me, that single-minded focus is an advantage on the course. But it has caused us to ignore inequities and unfairness that other sports—baseball, tennis, basketball—have faced long before. You will read stories in this book that are not only tragic but simply unbelievable in 1995. One woman is chased around the course by a posse in golf carts. A widow is forced to join the same club twice and still not given a membership of her own. Corporate executives are excluded from play on weekends. A governor who can't play an all-male course in her own state until three o'clock on Sunday afternoons. A woman declared "male" for a day so that she could play in a competition.

Sometimes the issues are complex: Private clubs' rights vs. individual fairness. The question of single-gender clubs. Reasonable men and women can disagree. And they do, within the same club, the same women's committee, even the same family. (I have no problem with single-gender clubs, except for the way they are used to lend support to discriminatory policies at family clubs and the mind-set they continue to perpetuate.) What's more, too many of these situations are not so complex. They're simply archaic.

Harry Cavanagh, the attorney who helped to extend access for women in the Phoenix area, talks in Chapter 8 about the need for open discussion. "Somebody has to take on this dialogue," Cavanagh says. "[Men] will say . . . 'Why are you doing this?' But as they are saying that, they're starting to get the message: Whether you like it or not, it is going to happen. Why not listen. And as they listen and you get talking to them, they get more and more reasonable."

Whether you are male or female, a dyed-in-the-wool golfer or just a curious, occasional player, *The Unplayable Lie* will take you out of your comfort zone. It will move you and infuriate you. It will propel you into conversations you would rather avoid, but need to be a part of, for the sake of all young golfers, both male and female.

In the end it will improve.

AMY ALCOTT
February 1995

PART I

Whose Golf Course Is It, Anyway?

A Cultural Backwater

Rosa Parks was told to go to the back of the bus. I was thrown off the bus.
—Millie Rech, who was banished from her country club when she was divorced

Golf is booming in the United States. What used to be a sport accessible only to the wealthy at exclusive country clubs is now accessible to millions, and its popularity is at an all-time high.

Women, playing for both recreational and business reasons, comprise the fastest-growing segment of the golf population. They now make up roughly five million of the 24.8 million golfers. And a huge number of them are teenagers, the next generation of career women, says the National Golf Foundation. Overall, women account for about 37 percent of all new players since 1993.

Yet many women golfers find themselves subject to forms of discrimination and prejudice unparalleled in almost any other part of their lives. At many country clubs they cannot hold a property right in the membership, even though their money may be paying for it. They have no right to vote in club affairs, no real say in the governance of club life. Desirable weekend tee times are often unavailable to them simply because they are women, even if they have paid the same membership fees as a man. And when they wish to top off a round of golf with lunch, they may find that the only place open is a men's grill, to which they are denied entry. Even at the public courses they may find that no matter how good their game, they are treated unfairly.

Women now run their own companies, go to war, become doctors and lawyers and bankers. But the golf world and, especially, the world of the private country club have not dealt with these changes. The women who inhabit the private country club world, in particular, find themselves in a cultural backwater, constrained by arcane rules left over from a largely forgotten age. These old conventions are frustrating, especially for the new breed of working women, married or single, in business or the professions, women who expect the same rights on the golf course as they have elsewhere.

Unfortunately for today's women golfers, the sport they love, which has been growing here for a century, has always been deeply connected with the country club world of elitism and exclusion. Golf began in this country as one of the several enjoyable outdoor pastimes of the very rich. It did not develop as a sport of the people, as did baseball or, later, basketball, or even football, which had its roots in colleges and universities. Golf developed as part of the world of private leisure, first on the estates of the very wealthy and soon after at the private country club with its spaciousness, its acres of woods and grass.

Unlike most other sports, though, golf in the United States has had women participants from the beginning. The wives and daughters of members were always at the private country clubs where golf was played, because their main social life was there, and some went on to become competitive golfers as well. Several participated in a national women's championship as early as 1895. The first winner came from Shinnecock Hills Golf Club, on Long Island, New York, which is coincidentally the site for the centennial celebration of the men's United States Open Championship in 1995.

But for most of these women, most of the time, their role at the club was virtually always as guest or "associate," not as a full partner in the enterprise. If a woman had a son, he was embraced, taken in with great enthusiasm as a teenager. Daughters were not. Membership was unavailable to them unless they married, and then it was transferred to their husbands. Divorce spelled expulsion for either a mother or a daughter. Father and son remained. Unmarried women need not apply.

At the country club, golf joined such other elite sports as hunting, riding, shooting, and sometimes cricket, as part of the leisure life of the affluent. But of all these activities, only golf really caught on widely

4

and spread throughout society, carrying some country club attitudes with it. As early as 1895 there was a public course in Van Cortlandt Park, in the Bronx, New York, and by the 1930s there were seventeen public courses within forty miles of Times Square. The Depression took its toll, of course, but by the mid-thirties Chicago had ten municipal courses, and there were several in Los Angeles and San Francisco.

After the Depression and World War II, public golf grew at a remarkable rate. Today there are nearly nine thousand public courses, including resort golf courses that cater to vacationers. Indeed, far more courses nowadays are public than are private, and many resort and upscale golf courses offer women a respite from the degree of discrimination they often encounter at the private club.

Within the private country club world today, there are some 4,500 courses. What was once a province restricted to the very rich has opened to the middle and upper middle classes. The country club has become a place for all the family, a literal home away from home that can be used by husbands and wives, parents and children, with restaurants, bars, swimming pools, tennis courts, lockers, and other amenities.

To an important degree, the world of golf has also become a stable feature of corporate culture in the United States. Many of the exclusive private country clubs are populated by men who make their living as corporate executives, from middle-level managers to the top CEOs of Fortune 500 companies. For them golf is a social and recreational activity, but it is also a way of entertaining clients, returning favors, and rewarding successful employees. The culture of the golf club world has always been heavily dominated by the males who are leaders in corporate and community life and who often assume leadership roles in their local country clubs as well.

But there is a world of difference between the modern corporation, which must respond to the issues of the day, and the insular, gated, and protected private country club that allows an escape from those issues. Removed as such clubs are from mainstream life, they have retained bylaws that are surprisingly similar to those they had when they were founded. Often today one finds private clubs whose values seem frozen in the social milieu of the mid-1920s, when many clubs were started. That was a different America, a place where women were just beginning to emerge as persons with equal claims to citizenship. The 19th Amendment to the Constitution, which gives women the right to vote, was not ratified until 1920.

When the first country clubs began, in the late nineteenth century, they were established by and for white male Anglo-Saxon Protestants. They were exclusive, of course. They rejected Catholics and Jews and Italians. The question of a black member was never even considered; it would have been unthinkable. The bylaws of many private country clubs specified "Caucasians Only."

Not surprisingly, many of these prohibited groups started their own exclusive clubs, allowing in others like themselves and treating the rest of the world as outsiders. Sometimes they even made distinctions within broad ethnic categories, as when certain Jewish clubs accepted German Jewish members but kept out Eastern European Jews.

This has begun to change. These days many formerly all-WASP country clubs have a few Jews, Catholics, or Italians. Even black males are now admitted, an advance that few black executives ever thought possible but that came about after Alabama's Shoal Creek, the host of the 1990 PGA Championship, was criticized for having no black members. So the old barriers are slowly, slowly crumbling, not always for altruistic reasons but often to avoid unwanted legal complications.

But the old clubs still share one brand of exclusion in common: the exclusion of women, married or single, as full, voting, and shareholding members. This form of exclusion of women seems to know no religious or ethnic boundary.

The world around the country club has changed dramatically, of course. The civil rights movement of the early sixties, the social upheavals of the late sixties, the movement for gender equity in the workplace have transformed the society. If the world of golf were starting fresh, without the cultural weight of old traditions, a different set of policies might have evolved. But golf is still responding to the roles set for men and women in a bygone era. This is one reason that, increasingly, legislatures and courts are stepping into this terrain, passing laws and making judgments that may redefine the rights of country clubs and their members.

Many of these clubs' members, men and even some women, resist having these issues thrust upon them. They feel that because these are private clubs, the courts and legislatures should stay out of their affairs. Their policies are "internal matters," they say. But the issue of fundamental fairness for the women associated with these clubs can't be sidestepped.

In some of the most elite private institutions of our society, those conflicts are now being played out over who has the right, and when, to use a long club to hit a little ball into a barely bigger hole. They are being played out not among strangers, but among friends and colleagues, even husbands and wives, parents and children, those with whom we have our most intimate relationships. That basic expectations such as recognition and respect are undercut for the sake of such seemingly trivial pursuits says much about human nature and our fundamental relationships: male to female, husband to wife, parent to daughter or son.

What goes on in the small world of the private clubs wouldn't matter very much to anyone except its members if it weren't for the fact that the world of golf engages so many influential people, people who are the leaders in their nation, their cities, their towns, their companies. These are people who are among the best-educated in the country—legislators who make state and national laws, executives who manage large and small corporations, judges who sit on state and federal courts. In the past their private and public lives were separate, but now they are becoming blurred. The discriminatory aspects of the club world, the belief that some are entitled to withhold rights and privileges from others—even when the "others" are wives, daughters, mothers, and female colleagues—inevitably have some impact on all of us. When wives and daughters find advancement in their careers curtailed by restrictive policies aimed at them, then they rightly ask, Is it fair?

Some of the leaders of private country clubs, a disproportionately influential group, still support and practice behavior that many others in society believe to be unjust. The story of their treatment of women is sad, funny, and instructive. It reveals much about why discriminatory practices are so difficult to change, particularly when they are intertwined with marriage, friendship, social lives, and power.

The men who control country club life and support such policies may say it's simply tradition, that it has always been done this way, that it is simply an instance of exercising their First Amendment right of association. They are used to the idea of all-male sporting activities. Many of them were raised in all-male prep schools and colleges. What they are less likely to say is more to the point: these traditions serve their interests and they like it this way.

Despite these inequities at private clubs and the occasional "chill" in the air at public courses, a diverse group of women are taking up the game. Many find the game intoxicating. Few other competitive

sports take place in such open territory, and every golf course is different. Each has its own length, texture, easy holes and hard holes, features
that give it what golf-course architects describe as its "signature." The
golf course can be a place where one can bask in the warmth and beauty
of nature while also deeply immersed in a sporting competition with
others.

Golf is also a game for a lifetime. Most sports are part of our
youth and succumb to the inevitable as we age, but golf can be enjoyed
throughout life. It may simply require a higher handicap.

The handicap, which allows golfers of unequal ability to compete on equal terms, is undoubtedly the feature that most distinguishes
golf from other sports. Any golfer who plays with some frequency can
submit scores to a state handicapping association and, after the scores
are adjusted in various ways, will get a handicap that expresses, roughly, how many strokes that player will need to be given if he or she is to
shoot a round of golf in par. Par itself is a bit mystical, but essentially
means what an excellent golfer would shoot if he or she played very well
and took two putts on every hole. Golf is traditionally played at eighteen
holes, and if Player A has a handicap of, say, fourteen and Player B has a
handicap of twenty, A will have to give B six strokes, one each on the
three hardest holes on the front nine and similarly on the back nine, and
then they will be able to play quite evenly.

The system assumes a basic honesty among the competitors—
that they will not turn in fraudulent scores—but assuming that, this system allows people of unlike abilities to compete on equal terms. Try this
in any other sport and it tends not to work or feels artificial, but in golf it
allows a boss to compete with his salesmen, a client with his supplier,
even (dangerously) a husband with his wife. When added to the natural
beauty of golf courses and the lifetime of playing, handicapping gives
golf a rare advantage over other forms of sport competition.

For these reasons, more than one in every ten Americans play
the game, and as many as two million try it for the first time each year.
Successful women are a large part of this current growth. They have a
maddening variety of golf courses from which to choose, including
desert courses and mountain courses, seaside courses and inland courses, short courses and long courses. One of the fascinations of golf is that
it can be played in such an incredible variety of settings on very different
surfaces, with different types of grass and sand.

They can also choose between public and private courses. The "public" in "public courses" refers not to ownership, but to who is allowed access. Public courses form the largest category of golf courses in this country, nearly 70 percent of the more than 13,440 golf facilities in the nation, and they include municipal courses, privately owned public courses, and expensive resort courses. The private courses range from the ultra-private and very exclusive to still-private but easier-access family courses. The only private courses women can't join are the all-male courses described in Chapter 3.

It is the elite private courses of the country that have been the scene of most of the legal battles over women's rights. This raises the natural question: Why put up with restrictive rules of membership and access at private courses? Why not stick to public places? It's a fair question, and not as easy to answer as it might have been years ago.

In the past there was a greater gap between the public-course world and the private-course world than there is now. The private-course experience was restricted to persons of at least moderate wealth, and public courses, with their heavy play and low budgets for maintenance, often had to use rubber mats for teeing grounds and other cost-saving devices that reduce the enjoyment of the game. There were exceptions, but generally the gap between public and private was great.

Now it is far less so. The gap has been closed from both directions. On the private side there are still elite clubs, but they are joined by a number of country clubs that are less exclusive and less expensive. And on the public side, golf entrepreneurs have come to realize that there's a vast amount of consumer dollars ready to go into golf at public facilities, if they have decent courses and policies. So although you can still find the fairly primitive local nine-hole layout, you also have extraordinary new resort courses where they no longer worry about skin color or gender, where, as one person put it, their only color concern is green—as in dollars.

At the same time, public courses are not immune from the gender biases that operate in golf's private world, but when gender bias creeps in it is more as a matter of male attitude and belief, and seldom a matter of club rules and bylaws. Public courses officially are not allowed to discriminate. But that does not mean there aren't drawbacks. Women golfers complain about rangers and starters who treat them poorly. They grumble about slow play by men, often resulting in six-hour rounds; they mutter about the amenities. They hate queuing up at 3:30 A.M. to get a tee time at the local public course.

Not all public courses are in this category. One remarkable woman, Nancy Oliver, saw the potential of upscale public golf courses for executive women and launched the highly successful Executive Women's Golf League. Her leagues and others like it are now giving thousands of women players a positive golfing experience. A fuller account of public courses and especially the EWGL is given in Chapters 13 and 14. Still for a variety of reasons, including the desire to entertain clients, many of these women want the kinds of amenities that only a private club can provide.

"Then they call me up," says Ms. Oliver. "They are astonished. They say they spoke to the membership committee of the club or to the president or to someone and that person has told them they can't join because they are women. They say I led them down the primrose path but I forgot to tell them about the big bad wolf."

But the big bad wolf has been around a long time.

Golf and the American Woman

When women in America first began to play golf, they were allowed at many of the big clubs to use the links only at certain hours on certain days when it was thought that their presence would not incommode the Lords of Creation.

—Genevieve Hecker in *Golf*, the official USGA Bulletin,
January 1902

Golf came to America as a "gentlemen's game." It moved from private estates to actual golf clubs in the late 1880s. Women were part of that move, but their participation was severely circumscribed. It was defined through their relationship to men. Consider the rules at Pennsylvania's Merion Cricket Club, a historic club that built its first golf course in 1895. Women were eligible to play there only if they bore certain relationships to the male member:

> Eligible women of the household means and includes only women who reside permanently in the home of a member or subscriber and who have one of the following relationships to the member or subscriber: wife, unmarried daughter, mother, unmarried sister, unmarried woman relative, mother-in-law or unmarried sister-in-law.

Other clubs had similar rules. Note that there could be no such thing as an unattached female presence. Women on their own were not included. But the women who were included took up the game with relish.

From the time golf first arrived in America, writers extolled the game's virtues for women. "As a game for ladies there can be no doubt that it must become a favorite and popular one. It has the advantage of giving plenty of moderate and healthful exercise, without any of that other exertion that tennis may call forth and which every young lady is not equal to," said an 1890s article in the magazine *Outing*.

Among the many women players, some went far beyond mere exercise and aspired to be champions. Beatrix Hoyt of Shinnecock Hills Golf Club, granddaughter of Salmon P. Chase, Lincoln's secretary of the treasury, and later Chief Justice of the U.S. Supreme Court, was only seventeen when she entered her first championship. She went on to win the Women's Amateur Championships in 1896, 1897, 1898, and then she retired at age twenty-one. One author of the day described her swing in the 1898 championship: "Her drive was a low, round swing and most beautiful follow-through to be imagined. In short mashie approach shots, or in playing out of a difficult lie, Miss Hoyt is absolutely deadly."

What appears clear from the first decade of golf clubs in America is that by 1900 both men and women were enthusiastic about the game and both sexes played the game with zest. Within the short period of a decade, the country had produced a group of champion women players, some playing better than most men. The difference between men and women players was that the women were constrained by a social corset that bound them more than their awkward golfing garments.

Social convention held them to be adornments of their spouses, allowed to play only on Sunday afternoons. They were thought of as colorful additions to the country club setting, but not as achievers in their own right. Country clubs were social clubs, as well as places to play golf, and their well-appointed clubhouses provided drinks, dinner, and social activity for their wealthy members. Women had their place, but it was circumscribed.

As golf historian Herbert Warren Wind put it, "The early golfers liked to find pretty women lounging on the verandas of their clubhouses, but they were not in favor of women playing the game." Men saw them as pretty baubles, elegant accoutrements to a man in a man's world. This was the view held by the vast majority of the men who ran the clubs and set their policies.

But play golf women did. Their records show them as competitors who could be recognized as champions in their own right. Thus from early on in golf we have women in two very different roles: as luxurious adornment to the men in their lives and as successful competitors and achievers on their own. Adornment was by far the dominant role.

❧ *The Early Clubs* ❧

The first country club to claim the title was The Country Club, of Brookline, Massachusetts, which was founded in 1882. To this day known simply as The Country Club, as though there were no others of equal stature, it exemplifies the rich sporting life enjoyed by the wealthy at the turn of the century. Golf was a relative latecomer there, joining horse racing, polo, and shooting in 1893.

An early account shows the game was thought suitable for both sexes: "If golf is indebted to The Country Club for its advancement," wrote George H. Sargeant in 1899, "it has paid the debt in kind; for while not all the country club members are interested in racing, or polo, or shooting, golf is a game in which young and old, men and women, may play with equal zest. Golf has proved a financial tonic to more than one country club in America."

St. Andrew's Golf Club, then located in Yonkers, New York, opened in 1888. A mid-twentieth-century account shows how women's position had improved. "Some of the older members can remember when the ladies were not permitted to enter the club through the main entrance, and the quarters assigned to them were somewhat less than palatial. . . . While technically referred to as guests, today women are permitted liberal use of the clubhouse and the course. On Saturdays and Sundays they are allowed to play (accompanied by a member) in the afternoon."

Still, the St. Andrew's women had to remember their place. "Although there has never been any written law against it, the members of the club have always indulged in a silent hate for the Saturday night party or the ostentatious blowout that might tend to disturb the peace and quiet of the household. When one is trying to concentrate on a game of cards or backgammon or trying to make up his mind about whether to double two no trump or bid three hearts, he prefers silence.

For this reason parties are few and far between. The fair sex has not been totally barred from the premises, but there is no case on record where one has been permitted to invade the sanctum sanctorum or to break bread in the main dining room. The ladies have their own little reception room and private dining room and this is the extent of their participation in club affairs.

"Some years ago several ladies were congregated in their own quarters and enjoying some unusual levity when one of them suddenly remembered that they might have been too noisy. Going to the door she cautiously opened it and inquired of the first man in sight: 'I hope we have not annoyed you gentlemen?'" If she expected to hear that it was perfectly all right, she was disappointed, for the frank member bluntly spoke his mind: "But you ARE disturbing us, my dear lady, and I hope it won't occur again."

Shinnecock Hills Golf Club was a different story.

Although it is hard to tell for sure, because we must rely on the club's own historical account, it appears that from the first, Shinnecock's women played the game seriously and were taken seriously by the membership: "Although the social activities were almost as important as the golf, this pioneering club had a great influence on the development of the game in America. The women, with their unbounded enthusiasm, played an important part in this respect, too."

Perhaps it was the bracing air off the waters around Long Island, but golf flourished and women's golf flourished at Shinnecock Hills. The first U.S. Women's Amateur Championship in 1895 was won by a golfer from the club, Mrs. C. S. Brown, with the admittedly inauspicious score of 132 for eighteen holes. She represented Shinnecock Hills at the championship played at the Meadow Brook Club, then in Hempstead, New York.

But in the very next year Miss Beatrix Hoyt, also of Shinnecock, cut 37 strokes off that score, shooting a 95 as medalist for a qualifying field of eight. Miss Hoyt won the championship, her first of three straight, by beating another member from Shinnecock in the finals. She "retired" shortly thereafter. In the words of the club's official account, "She lived past eighty and, hopefully, died secure in the knowledge that she had single-handedly turned women's golf from a pitty-pat sport into a game of skill."

By the 1900s women's championships were being contested on some of the fine private courses in the East. And these were not merely local events. H. L. Fitz Patrick, a sportswriter of the day, wrote of the championship at Ardsley Country Club in Ardsley-on-Hudson, New York, in 1898, "Unexampled was the widespread interest in the championship. There were competitors on the links who had journeyed one thousand five hundred miles or more to play. Chicago, Pittsburgh, Baltimore, Cincinnati, St. Paul, and Scranton each sent starters, not to speak of the numerous clubs represented from the Boston, Newport, Philadelphia, and New York groups." A women's national amateur competition had taken root.

So there were good players by the turn of the century, but how they ever hit the ball is the wonder. There they were in long dresses past their ankles, with lots of petticoats under their skirts. Their sleeves were of the leg-of-mutton variety, and their hats were reminiscent of the Easter parade.

Many of their attitudes were adopted from their sisters abroad. Women in England, as Mabel E. Stringer, an early British journalist and golfer, wrote, played golf for some time under great clothing constraints: "I can remember when the sleeves were so voluminous that we always had to have an elastic strap round the left arm, or we should never have seen the ball at all."

This versatile elastic strap was named after an American golfer named Miss Higgins. "It was indispensable on account of the width of the skirts. The strap was slipped round the knees when the player was addressing her ball, and was the most useful as well as the most unsightly of the many inventions to counteract the vagaries and inconsistencies of la mode. . . . "

The clothing of the day reflected the friction a woman might feel between her role as adornment and her role as competitive athlete. For the most part, as Caroline F. Manice, an amateur champion, pointed out in a 1904 article, adornment won out. "To look as well as one can is a part of one's payment for one's social keep, in golf as otherwhere. When a woman is dancing, dining, or driving, she frankly wants to look well."

On the other hand, Frances Griscom, a great amateur of the day, believed women were far too busy and too happy on the course to care how they looked. "I do not believe," said Miss Griscom, "when a woman gets in a game of yard golf that she ever thinks twice about her appearance. The game simply takes her out of herself. If it does not, she is not a good player."

The twenties brought bolder women. Still concerned with

style, they made a huge leap for comfort in playing competitive golf. Skirts crept to mid-calf, giving women golfers greater freedom to hit the ball. Golf clothing became fashionable. Women's magazines of the day show mid-calf suits and begin to showcase plus fours or knickers (loose-fitting short pants gathered at the knee) with matching jackets. Women still cared deeply how they looked on the golf course.

❧ *Women Amateurs in the Early Part* ☙ *of the Century*

Beatrix Hoyt was only the first of many women players who excelled at the game. Another fine early player was Margaret Curtis of Manchester, Massachusetts, who won the national Amateur Championship three times (1907, 1911, 1912), and who with her sister, Harriot, established the Curtis Cup trophy, competed for by British and American women amateurs since 1932.

There were other splendid amateur players—Alexa Stirling, Maureen Orcutt, Virginia Van Wie—but there were three women so outstanding, each in her own way, that they deserve more than passing mention. They are Dorothy Campbell Hurd, a Scots transplant; Marion Hollins, a champion golfer and also a successful businesswoman and golf-course entrepreneur; and, of course, Glenna Collett Vare, who was the dominant American woman golfer in the first half of the twentieth century.

DOROTHY CAMPBELL HURD

In 1909, when Dorothy Campbell came to the U.S. from Scotland for the first time, she was twenty-six years old. That year she won the women's national championships of four countries—the United States, England, Scotland, and Canada—and upon her emigration to this country the next year, she immediately became our newest golfing star. She not only played the game like a champion, winning the national championship a second time in 1910; she also wrote about it, penning a column that appeared often in *The American Golfer*.

She had helpful advice for her American competitors. She noted equipment deficiencies and had a suggested remedy: "The contents of many women's club-bags are recruited from the ranks of the cast-off clubs of their fathers, brothers, or husbands, which are, in most cases, quite unsuitable and much too heavy . . . the rejected weapons of several people. It would be a good plan if more orders on club-makers were given as prizes to owners of long handicaps instead of the often useless silver pin trays, scent bottles, etc. In this way players would be able to acquire a really suitable set of clubs. . . . "

Years later, as Dorothy Campbell Hurd, she won her third U.S. Women's Amateur Championship, and she was one of the very few women of her time to score under 70 on a regulation course. She exemplified the type of golfing woman the men could deal with. As one account put it, she was "a womanly woman" whose interests ranged far beyond golf and who enjoyed being a grandmother and managing a household.

Marion Hollins and the Women's National Golf and Tennis Club

As we know, men had their own all-male clubs. Might women also have a course of their own? They might and they did. The founder of the first women's club in the twentieth century was Marion Hollins. She was not only a ranking golfer, having won the women's national championship in 1921; she was also a champion horsewoman and, most important of all, an influential socialite who could assemble powerful and well-placed women. She called her club the Women's National Golf and Tennis Club, on Long Island, New York.

Marion Hollins's dream was to bring out the best in women's golf, and to do that, she felt, women had to have a course of their own, one that would test women without sacrificing length or hazards. Before the course opened on Memorial Day 1924, Miss Hollins had attracted some four hundred members, many prominent socially and in the world of golf and tennis. Establishment names were everywhere. Among the officers were Mrs. Winthrope Aldrich, Miss Eleanor Mellon, Mrs. Childs Frick, Mrs. Howard F. Whitney, along with President Hollins and the then-reigning American champion, Miss Edith Cummings. Members paid $1,000 a share with annual dues of $150.

Many of the women came from the metropolitan New York area, but the roster also included women from San Francisco and other major cities in the United States. Many of the women's husbands belonged to the Piping Rock Club and the newly built Creek Club on Long Island. The need for a women's club had become apparent after a number of new clubs opened on Long Island and women were told they would not be allowed to play on weekends and holidays.

Women's National was a course designed for the great women amateurs of the day. Miss Hollins visited England and Scotland and studied golf courses there. Architect Devereux Emmet designed a course that was not excessively long yet challenged the women with clever placement of hazards. Among the great women players, besides Edith Cummings, who signed on as members were Alexa Stirling; Lillian Hyde, a five-time champion of the Women's Metropolitan Golf Association; Rosalie Knapp, who later became Mrs. Joseph Dey, Jr.; and others. Joyce Wethered began her 1935 tour of America with an exhibition at the club.

The Women's National Golf and Tennis Club lasted a relatively short seventeen years. Like many clubs of the day, it didn't survive the Depression. But Marion Hollins had not been an active force in the club's later years, for she had moved her home and her allegiance to the Monterey Bay in California, where she discovered and built (with the famed architect Alister Mackenzie) a great golf course and real-estate development at Pasatiempo. She struck it rich in oil, and her profits fueled the Pasatiempo estates through the Depression years, when it thrived as a social and golfing mecca with the continuing infusion of her money.

But by 1938 Pasatiempo Estates Development was in deep financial trouble and Miss Hollins was forced to sell. Two years later she severed all connections with the place. She had lost her entire fortune in just ten years and died, four years later, in nearby Pacific Grove, California, at the age of fifty-one. Pasatiempo remains as a ranking course, open to the public, and a testament to Marion Hollins's vision.

Although efforts to establish all-women clubs have been very rare, it should be noted that Women's National was neither the first nor the last. Back in the beginnings of American golf in 1892, at Morris County Golf Club in New Jersey, there was a board consisting of all women! In a reverse mirror image of other clubs, Morris County bylaws made women the regular members, men the associate members. Unfortunately, this arrangement proved short-lived; the men soon took over.

And if we look beyond our border to the north, we find an all-female club in existence there to this day. Like Women's National, the

Ladies' Golf Club of Toronto was founded in 1924, and for similar reasons—its founder, Ada Mackenzie, a top amateur, was barred from her home course on weekends.

The club has about 650 women members, who hold the memberships and have the preferential starting times. Until recently, the men were not allowed in the dining room. Men's hours on weekends are before 8:30 A.M. and after 3 P.M. Things are easing up a bit for the men, we're told. By 2020 men just may get equal rights.

GLENNA COLLETT: THE UNANNOUNCED FEMINIST

Golf historians are virtually unanimous in characterizing Glenna Collett, later Glenna Collett Vare, as the outstanding American woman golfer of the first half of the twentieth century. After an up-and-down start as a teenager, she won her first national championship in 1922, at the ripe old age of nineteen. And it was not a fluke: that same year she won two other leading tournaments, the North and South and the Eastern championships. She won the national again in 1925 and remained the dominant woman golfer in the years between, winning an incredible fifty-nine out of sixty matches in 1924.

But her major golfing feat was yet to come. In 1928, 1929, and 1930 she won the women's national three years in a row. Then, in 1931, she married a Philadelphian, Mr. Edwin H. Vare, Jr. Her brilliant tournament play subsided a bit, but she remained highly competitive and, in 1935, as a married mother of two children, capped her career by winning a sixth and last U.S. Women's Amateur Championship, defeating a rising teenage star, Patty Berg. This is a championship record second only to Bobby Jones's, which explains why she was often referred to as "the female Bobby Jones."

Again, like Dorothy Campbell Hurd before her, she was both golfer and housewife, golfer and mother, recognized and popular among both women and men. According to golf writer Herbert Warren Wind's assessment, besides being intelligent, good-looking, and a long hitter, she was "gifted with a conquering graciousness. Men liked Glenna because she was a woman first and a woman golfer second."

Now, this of course raises a question. Was it required that the great male golfers of the time, Bobby Jones, Gene Sarazen, or Walter Hagen, be "a male first and a male golfer second"? Did Glenna Collett herself have any views on the subject?

Fortunately, one of her many accomplishments was a revealing autobiography, *Women in the Rough,* in which she announced some of her opinions. It helps to remember that when she wrote it, she had won only two of her six national Women's Amateur Championships, was only twenty-four, and was at that time still single.

In comparing women and men golfers, she is clear: "Women lack the strength to play golf as well as men, and there the matter rests." She goes on to note that if a "golfing Amazon" should appear who can hit a ball 250 yards, "there is no reason why she could not tee it up with any man in the world and expect to win." (That day has come, incidentally, in the person of England's Laura Davies, who averaged more than 250 yards on the LPGA Tour in 1994. The problem is that the men have improved also, and Laura would now face men who can hit it 280 yards or more.)

Glenna noted the difficulty golf fans might have because of name changes brought on by marriage, and then makes her own recommendation: "For the sake of keeping golf records straight, if for no other reason, the powers that be should rule that girls who have won golf fame under their maiden names keep them, in competition at least."

In the closing pages of her autobiography she returns to the subject of the women's game compared with the men's. She recalls the extent to which women's clothing may interfere with the swing and the pressures on women to look graceful—"the age-old feminine duty never to look ridiculous if she can help it."

Then she turns to what it means to feel the pressure to be, as Wind put it, a woman first and a woman golfer only second. She addresses the question of whether women can concentrate as well as men when they are on the course, why women sometimes show "tournament nervousness," scoring well on one nine and poorly on the next.

> In the midst of a match the woman golfer will think of and dwell on many things that have not the slightest bearing on the game. Did she order the roast for dinner? Heavens, no! And there goes a slice. Why did she invite the Browns for Friday, when the cook is off? . . . she tops her mashie. . .
>
> A man would consider such things trifles, of no importance, or else easily remedied. But a woman cannot forget trifles. Her life is made up of trifles. . . .

And later, speaking of handicaps for the "ordinary woman":

> She does not have nearly so many opportunities to play.
> The busy broker can slam his desk shut at 3 P.M., call a
> crony, and drive to the links, where they quiet their con-
> sciences by pretending to discuss business affairs. In fact,
> it is a male proverb that many big deals are made on the
> golf-links.
> Women have not yet figured out a method of running
> the household from the links. You cannot well take the
> cook and maid and children's nurse with you for a four-
> some—deciding the menu on the first green, planning the
> spring housecleaning as you proceed along the fairway of
> the five-hundred-yard dogleg hole, and deciding Junior's
> program while blasting out of a trap.

Glenna, ever the woman first, was gentle in her judgment about
this state of affairs. She ends her book with this poignant paragraph:

> I do not wish I were a man, except sometimes, when my
> drives only come within a full shot of my opponent's. I
> envy him his spirit of freedom, his independence of trifles,
> his disdain of convention, his disregard of appearances,
> and his childlike conviction, if he is a golfer, that golf is the
> most important thing on this bunkered sphere.

◈ From the Thirties to the Nineties ◈

Women's golf has seen vast changes since Glenna Collett Vare won her
last championship in 1935. In Glenna's day we could speak of a "national championship" without distinguishing between amateurs and professionals, because there were no professionals. The top women players
began their own professional association in 1948, as the men had done a
third of a century earlier. Stars such as Babe Didrikson, Betty Hicks,
Louise Suggs, and Patty Berg, supported by the Wilson Sporting Goods
Company, formed the Ladies Professional Golf Association. (It would

have been called the Women's PGA, but that title was held by another group that had started a magazine under the name.) The LPGA is thriving today, although in tough competition for the commercial and advertising dollar with its rival men's organizations, the PGA Tour and the Senior PGA Tour.

As the professional tour grew, the leading amateurs joined it, and by the 1960s virtually all the leading women players were on the professional tour. Stars like Mickey Wright, Kathy Whitworth and JoAnne Gunderson (better known now as JoAnne Carner—"Big Mama") have replaced Dorothy Campbell Hurd and Glenna Collett Vare, women who made their name in golf but did not earn income from it.

Golf itself has blossomed as a sport, in part because of the growth of television coverage. And the women's game has grown with it. There are now thousands of courses, both public and private, and it appears to be the fastest-growing participant sport in the nation. And, of course, since the days of Arnold Palmer and the emergence of golf on television, the game has become a popular spectator sport as well. Its TV ratings don't rival those of the National Football League, but they are very solid, and they have special appeal to the "high end" of the TV advertising market.

What have these changes meant for the average woman player? Many more are exposed to golf in one form or another than was true before World War II, when, for women at least, it was still largely a game for the privileged. As the golf boom expanded during the latter half of the century, it began to include more and more women in both its public and private sectors.

As public courses grew (and they comprise about two-thirds of all courses), they naturally reflected some of the biases and prejudices of the social world around them, but especially in the aftermath of the civil-rights movement they could not openly invoke discriminatory rules for membership and access to the course. For the most part, public courses have tried to develop in "user-friendly" ways to capture the growing part of the golf market represented by women. But it has been different in the world of the private country club.

Despite the growth of clubs and their appeal to the broad, middle and upper-middle strata in the society, a trend starting as early as the twenties, the private country club has remained remarkably similar in its operating rules to the clubs that were in place early in the century.

The growth of clubs, and their expansion to the suburbs, did not bring with it changes in governance.

In the family country club, men held the shares and the voting rights, as well as the key committee positions. Their wives or daughters could play in the ladies' 18-hole or 9-hole groups on Tuesdays and Thursdays, and often at other times during the week. Husband and wife would often play "social" golf on Sunday afternoons, but other than that, women were not around much on the weekends. After all, as housewives, they could play during the week. It is perhaps understandable that, growing up in these settings and absorbing the values they embody, men experienced these practices as not only the traditional ways but the right ways.

These rules and practices were not invoked in every single private club, but they fairly describe the vast majority of the clubs in the country. The big surprise is that they continued to be invoked as the clubs moved into the sixties, seventies, even eighties.

But while the clubs and the men who ran them remained the same, the world around them changed. The civil-rights movement of the 1960s led to new legislation and fundamental changes in some of our main institutions. Title VII of the Civil Rights Act of 1964 barred sex discrimination in the workplace; Title IX of the Education Amendments of 1972 did the same thing for educational institutions receiving federal financial assistance. During the same period, elite colleges such as Yale and Princeton opened their doors to women students. Many women have become professionals in law, business, and medicine. Where before there had been a trickle into the executive suites, now there was a deluge.

Many of the women who received their education in the late sixties and early seventies are now in midcareer, with responsible positions in business and the professions. They are unwilling to abide by social conventions carved out in another era, before women even had the right to vote. As working women, they don't like being told that morning weekend tee times are open to retired males and teenage boys, but not to them. And they are taking action to assert their rights.

Unlike the worlds of employment and school, where gender equality is an established principle (even if often not followed in practice), the private country club is a world apart. Legislatures and courts strive to protect not only the value of equality, but also the values of privacy and freedom of association. Because of those values, private clubs were exempt from the Civil Rights Act of 1964.

In the past, courts were reluctant to step into the world of the private club. These days, courts are upholding new state laws aimed at eliminating discrimination in private country clubs, specifically legislation that centers on clubs with commercial features, such as leasing out facilities, taking business tax deductions for entertaining at clubs, and offering meal service to nonmembers. This is an arena for litigation absolutely on the cutting edge of the law.

The State of Michigan, for example, has passed a law flatly barring discrimination in access to facilities in private country clubs. One of the results has been a lawsuit brought by a group of male members of the Detroit Golf Club. This case shows how the battle of the sexes has come full circle. What starts in most states as a claim of right on behalf of women, with the men in a defensive position, has led the group from this club to use the courts against their own club. It is a tale for the 1990s.

In their complaint, these men trace "the history of spousal golf" at the Detroit Golf Club, showing how what began as a custom of bringing their nonmember spouses for Sunday-afternoon outings in the 1920s has "evolved into a supermembership 'right' with spouses and adult children enjoying complete access to the course with no financial responsibilities whatsoever." These men are suing their own club for forcing them to subsidize women and adult children who they say have equal access to the golf course.

This case demonstrates just how divisive these issues can become, as members are divided against other members, their own clubs, the other sex, and sometimes their own sex.

So private country club life has become rancorous at many clubs in the last few years. But as contentious as it is, it could be worse. Just to keep things in perspective, consider the following series of modern vignettes from Scotland and England, the countries from which American golf drew its models.

One day a woman golfer entered the clubhouse at Royal Troon Golf Club on the Scottish seaside, the site of six British Opens in which American male professionals compete. "I entered Royal Troon in golf shoes and inquired if spikes were allowed in the clubhouse. The steward retorted: 'Spikes are, ladies are not.'"

Royal St. George's Golf Club in Sandwich, England, an exclusive all-male bastion, once erected a sign on its property that banned "dogs and women." But while Royal St. George's would not countenance a female member, paradoxically it is a place where women can play. How did this come to pass? Peter Dobereiner, a British observer of the game's customs, reports that Royal St. George's does not specifically ban women. It simply does not recognize that they exist. "It is self-evident that what does not exist cannot be asked to pay a greens fee. So women play happily at Royal St. George's (on certain days) and by long convention, they go along with the fiction that they do not exist."

A few years ago a problem developed, however, when one Miss Fiona MacDonald was selected to play for the all-male Cambridge University golf team. What to do? She was, after all, a she. When Cambridge played its annual match against St. George's, how could Miss Fiona MacDonald tee it up? The committee of elders of St. George's brooded and brooded. Their solution? They declared her an honorary man for the occasion. And so she played, and from the men's tees, at that.

So it appears the more conservative British males pretend women do not exist. The more enlightened crowd tends to view women "as a subspecies to be barely tolerated, as long as they keep their place," says Mr. Dobereiner.

The clubhouse of the Royal and Ancient Golf Club of St. Andrews, Scotland, an imposing and austere building, sits grandly behind the first tee of the Old Course, where many historians believe golf was born in 1522. The course is public and women's tournaments have been played there, four Ladies' British Open Amateur Championships on the Old Course. But the Royal and Ancient clubhouse, gray, square, and slightly forbidding, is for men only. No woman has ever been proposed as a member. That doesn't stop the club from serving as the governing body of golf for all countries except the United States and Mexico, where the U.S. Golf Association presides. The R&A sets rules for golfing standards, both in course play and in equipment standards, presumably for both sexes.

The British male attitude at the Royal and Ancient is probably best captured by the following incident, which is believed to have occurred during one of the Ladies' British Open Amateur Championships. During a cloudburst, the officials of the Ladies' Golf Union huddled together on the side of the clubhouse, because they were barred from entering. They were standing under their umbrellas when a club lackey appeared round a corner.

The women golf officials, wanting to believe that chivalry had proved stronger than prejudice, thought to themselves that the men inside at last had taken pity and were going to invite them in, if only to the trolley shed.

"Ladies," said the emissary, "I have a request from some of the members. Would you mind putting down your umbrellas? They are obscuring the view of the course from the smoking room windows."

The Royal and Ancient is hardly alone. Scores of clubs follow similar policies. Dunbar, one of the most respected clubs in Scotland, practices routine discrimination: women cannot always play when they want to or attend the club's annual meeting or vote. These facts came to light through a Scottish newspaper article last year.

I know the son of a member of Dunbar who is himself now a member of the club. He told me that his wife, a scratch golfer, plays better than do 95 percent of the men in the club. She knows the rules, she plays fast, she would be a good member, and she would be good on the council. He asks his father why, other than her sex, she should not be admitted. His father doesn't really have an answer except that it has always been this way.

Says Mr. Dobereiner, "The British do not appreciate change, especially from the ladies. Golf has been soaking in male chauvinist piggery for 500 years and so it cannot be eradicated overnight."

❦ 3 ❦

Eveless Edens: The All-Male Club

*We love our women, we just don't want any fussin' with
'em.*

—Hord Hardin, former chairman of
Augusta National Golf Club

From a purely numerical perspective, the all-male club in the United
States is utterly insignificant. There are about twenty such clubs in the
country. Although they represent less than half a percent of all private
clubs, they are enormously influential, and they are quintessentially private.

These are the clubs often devoted solely to golf and where, with
minor exceptions, women are excluded from the daily life of the club,
period. At some they are not allowed on the golf course, in the clubhouse, or anywhere on the premises. These clubs have few amenities for
women, often no bathroom or place to change clothing, because there
aren't any women. Not all these clubs date from the early part of the
century. Preston Trail Golf Club in Dallas, Texas, opened its doors in
1965, and Wolf Creek Golf Club in Kansas City, Kansas, opened in 1973.
In both cases, women were invited into the club on opening day to see
where their husbands would spend their leisure time, and then were
banned. Other clubs may make an exception on Sunday afternoons,
mostly for wives of members. All-male clubs permit no women mem-

bership. Wives do not even have the limited subordinate rights of wives and daughters at private clubs with family memberships.

These clubs are important far beyond their minuscule numbers, because they help reinforce those attitudes and beliefs about women that permeate the private clubs, elite and not so elite, that do allow women on the premises. These attitudes have filtered down over time and they help answer the question of why men in family-oriented private clubs hold the shares, the membership, the vote, the right to govern. And it is not surprising to find that attitudes so deeply rooted in the culture of the private golf club seep into the world of public golf as well.

The males who inhabit these clubs don't think of themselves as male chauvinists, or as anti-female, or as opponents of women's rights. On the contrary, they see themselves as normal, upright, very successful citizens. And they are! They see the all-male golf club as a sanctuary, a place of rest and renewal.

The exclusion of women is justified by them on several grounds. First, it is perfectly legal, a First Amendment freedom to associate with whom you choose. Second, since it is part of leisure activity, it really isn't hurting anybody—unlike discrimination in the workplace, which costs people money and jobs. Third, it's fun and relaxing to be away from the real or imagined demands and expectations of wives, girlfriends, and other such suspect categories. Finally, it's sport among friends, a special form of bonding that must be experienced to be appreciated.

These clubs are truly the last bastion of male exclusivity. Well, maybe not the last. There are still secret societies that are part of formerly all-male elite universities like Yale and Harvard. These societies have provided a lifelong support system for their members, for both business and pleasure. Many of them are now admitting women, some twenty years after their colleges did so.

These are the golf clubs that even women executives as well as the top women amateur and professional golfers are not allowed to join. These women may receive an occasional invitation to join a member for a round of golf, but it can't become a general practice. No matter how good a golfer, how successful a corporate executive, how sociable a person, being a woman trumps all other qualities. Though dressed up in nice language, there is only one message: Not Welcome.

The following is a list of the all-male golf clubs that have come to my attention. Some permit limited play by women family members and women guests, generally if accompanied by a member. It is almost certain that I don't have them all. Some clubs are so private you can't find them or get anyone to talk about them.

> *Colorado:* Bear Creek Golf Club
> *Connecticut:* Connecticut Golf Club
> *Florida:* Adios Golf Club and Gator Creek Golf Club
> *Georgia:* Augusta National Golf Club
> *Illinois:* Bob O'Link Golf Club, Old Elm Club, and Butler National Golf Club
> *Kansas:* Wolf Creek Golf Club
> *Maryland:* Burning Tree Club
> *New Jersey:* Pine Valley Golf Club
> *New York:* Garden City Golf Club
> *Ohio:* Sharon Golf Club, Pepper Pike Club, and The Golf Club
> *Oklahoma:* Oak Tree Golf Club
> *Pennsylvania:* Laurel Valley Golf Club and the Squires Golf Club
> *Texas:* Preston Trail Golf Club and Ridglea Country Club

৯ How Some All-Male Clubs Got Started ৾

Larry Wein, a major New York City building and land developer, was a very wealthy man. He once owned the Empire State Building. One day he went to play golf at the Birchwood Country Club in Westport, Connecticut. He and his foursome found themselves waiting for every shot. Impatient, he asked to play through, whereupon one member of a female foursome shouted back, "If you don't like it, why don't you build your own course?" In 1969, he did. It is now called the Connecticut Golf Club and is located in Easton, Connecticut. It is the exclusive preserve of wealthy businessmen.

The Sharon Golf Club in Sharon Center, Ohio, was started in 1966 by a group of eleven millionaires from Akron and Cleveland who longed for quicker play. The move to start the course was led by General Tire president Jerry O'Neil. Women have never played the course and never will, they say. Still, the Sharon Golf Club was the site of the 1972 United States Golf Association Senior Amateur Championship and continued to be used as a sectional qualifying site for the U.S. Open Championship until as late as 1993—even though the USGA in 1990 adopted antidiscrimination rules for clubs that host its events.

Preston Trail Golf Club was the brainchild of four wealthy Dallas golf enthusiasts, John Murchison, Stuart Hunt, Jim Chambers, and Pollard Simons. It seems that the foursome became weary of waiting for tee times at busy Dallas Country Club and Brook Hollow Golf Club and decided to build their own course.

When Preston Trail began operation in 1964, it not only banned wives from the golf course, it also officially banned them from entering the clubhouse during the Byron Nelson Classic, a PGA Tour tournament that has since gone elsewhere.

Among its members, past and present, are Lamar Hunt, the international oilman sportsman; Herman Lay, the potato-chip king; Bob Strauss, the Democratic Party national chairman; Lanny Wadkins, the PGA Tour player; and Mickey Mantle, the baseball player.

❧ Augusta National Golf Club ❧

The great golf champion Bobby Jones dreamed of building a golf club that met his standards for golf, privacy, and friendship. He wanted a place where kindred spirits met to enjoy the game of golf. By all accounts Bobby Jones was a wonderful player and a wonderful man, with broad vision and good values. But he was a man of his times, and for him, kindred spirits did not include women, even though he often played in mixed foursomes with leading players of the day. One was British amateur Joyce Wethered, whom he said had the best golf swing he had ever seen.

In 1931, he and cofounder Clifford Roberts discovered a 365-acre tree nursery in Augusta, Georgia, and with a group of male friends purchased the land that would become the famed Augusta National Golf Club, surely one of the two or three most famous golf courses in the world. Charter members included E. F. Hutton, the investor; W. Alton Jones, president of Cities Service; Eugene Grace, head of U.S. Steel; and Gene Tunney, the boxing champion. Later General Dwight D. Eisenhower joined. Augusta became Ike's vacation spot when he became president.

Traditionally, Augusta's policies have been set by one person, a chairman, who runs the club like a benevolent autocracy. Augusta has had five since it first opened its doors in 1932. Under Hord Hardin, a lawyer and its chairman from 1980 to 1991, the club admitted its first black male as a member, Ronald Townsend, president of Gannett Television.

Hardin acted a month after a near economic disaster occurred at the PGA of America's annual tournament at Shoal Creek in Birmingham, Alabama. A group of top corporations, including IBM, pulled their lucrative television ads after learning that Shoal Creek didn't admit blacks at the club. Nearly five years after Shoal Creek, there are reports that Ronald Townsend is no longer the sole black member at Augusta, that the club had admitted another black male. Characteristically, Augusta officials would not comment.

Why did Augusta act so quickly to get a black male in its midst? Because some of the CEOs at Augusta began wondering whether they would have to resign from the place they so loved because of Augusta's policies. They pressed for change and got it. So far these same CEOs have not expressed similar concerns over women not being members.

Come each weekend of the golf season, top Fortune 500 executives and their guests and clients jet to Augusta National from points across the globe. They are well-known business executives, including, says *Fortune* magazine, John Akers (ex-IBM), Robert Allen (AT&T), Harold Poling (ex-Ford Motor), Stephen Bechtel (Bechtel), Edward Brennan (Sears), Warren Buffett (Berkshire Hathaway), Charles Knight (Emerson Electric), Hugh McColl, Jr. (NationsBank), Thomas Murphy (Capital Cities/ABC), John Reed (Citicorp), and Jack Welch (General Electric). For its size, Augusta National may have more CEOs than any other club in the U.S. On the weekend at the Augusta airstrip, you may find a woman guest. But no woman executive is there as a full member of the club.

Two years after Augusta National opened, the First Annual Invitation Tournament began. By 1938 it officially became the Masters. It is the only major golf championship played each year at the same place and same time, the first full week of April. The coming of the azaleas means millions of dollars for Augusta National. For that one week in April, the course is open to the public. Millions of fans also watch the Masters golf tournament on television, while CBS, its longtime network, earns its highest golf ratings of the year. In 1994, the Masters reached over 7.5 million homes on their Sunday broadcast.

Reportedly Augusta takes in upward of $10 million that week, some $6 million from pro-shop sales alone, the rest from television rights, ticket sales, and a cut from the food and drink concessions. The tournament's expenses are minimal aside from some $2 million in prize money. The Masters is produced by an army of volunteers who gladly work for the glory.

In the three days of practice rounds, before the tournament is open only to long-term ticket holders, men and women flock to a gigantic pro shop where the Masters emblem is emblazoned on anything with a price tag. It, too, is open only for Masters week. Women stand in line to buy fifty-dollar golf shirts, and they buy with abandon, unaware or unconcerned that they are personally subsidizing Augusta's narrow social policies.

The television coverage of the course during the tournament shows women everywhere, a once-a-year phenomenon. CBS-TV, which has typically remained silent about Augusta's social views, jumps to Augusta National's command, in part because its contract is renewable annually. Witness CBS's reaction when Augusta's current chairman, Jack Stephens, ordered the irreverent and entertaining Gary McCord off the Masters broadcast for 1995 because the year before he had compared Augusta's slick greens to skin stripped with "bikini wax." He had also described some mounds on the course as resembling "body bags."

The network caved in to Stephens's demand. Given the money involved, we can see why. But it shows Augusta's ability to control its image through contract and other ways and how CBS cooperates through self-censorship. The television media in general has assiduously avoided reporting on Augusta's social policies or, for that matter, any other exclusive club's policies. That is true even today.

Interestingly, Augusta's bylaws do not specifically exclude women. But so far, in the six decades Augusta has had to think about it, the club just hasn't gotten around to extending a membership invitation to any kindred spirit who is female. This is not an oversight, I suspect.

Cadillac and Travelers Insurance, the Masters' long-term sponsors, seemed pleased in 1990 when Augusta admitted its first black, which was a significant step because the club had long been one of the nation's most visible bastions of all-white golf. It had taken until 1975 for the Masters to invite its first black golfer, Lee Elder.

But Cadillac and Travelers have emitted no discernible discomfort about the lack of women members. I suspect that this is because Cadillac and Travelers feel privileged to be sponsors. That's why they hate it when reporters like me call them and ask them why they accept Augusta's policies. Internal club rules, they say.

Internal and unwritten rules means no women members. But wives and daughters of members may play the course as long as they are accompanied by a member—a husband or father. The same rule applies to *any* nonmember guest who plays the course, according to an Augusta official.

As for professional women golfers, they could easily wind up in the Ladies Professional Golf Association's Hall of Fame without ever having competed at one of the great golf courses in the world.

Not wanting any "fussin' with 'em" (women) cost the United States its first effort at making golf an Olympic sport in 1996. It began when the Atlanta Committee for the Olympic Games, led by its chief, Billy Payne, sold the idea of Olympic golf to Augusta National.

All the leading golf institutions in America, the United States Golf Association, the PGA Tour, the PGA of America, and the LPGA put their reputations on the line to back the idea, even though all these organizations knew full well that Augusta had a long history of excluding minorities and women. Augusta was nonetheless a world-renowned course—what better place to launch golf as a worldwide Olympic sport?

Well, not for everyone. The Atlanta City Council objected to Augusta National as a venue because of the club's membership history. And when Anita DeFrantz, the U.S.A.'s representative to the International Olympic Committee, who happens to be black, learned of the deal the good old boys had cooked up, she let it be known that in her view Augusta did not represent the modern Olympic ideal of brotherhood. Augusta had an image problem. It resembled an old plantation. And neither Payne nor Augusta could overcome it. Ultimately the deal fell apart.

There is a sad irony here. An Olympic event would have forced Augusta to open its course to great women golfers from across the world. To my knowledge, leading women players have never been invited to hold a competition of any sort at Augusta. Some women pros told me they have never been invited to play a round.

Despite criticism from a number of women's groups, who

deplored Augusta's membership policies toward women, the LPGA backed the Olympics at Augusta. It, more than any other organization, understood what opening Augusta's greens to its women pros would mean.

"When I went before our players to gain their approval of our becoming a part of the Olympic effort, we had a very interesting discussion," Charles S. Mechem, Jr., the LPGA commissioner, told me. "All of us, to a person, felt the best way for us to make a statement was to go to Augusta and play it. Once we had done it, you'd never be able to take it away. And that is why we were so supportive. And we took a little heat from a few women's groups who said, 'How could you do this?' I am convinced we were right; I'm just sorry that we did not have the opportunity to make our point."

An Olympic event might well have spurred Augusta's chairman, Mr. Stephens, to change its policies on women. After all, the reason he said Augusta agreed to host an Olympic golf event was "our desire to help advance the game of golf worldwide." Advancing the game worldwide through the Olympics would have meant including golfers of both sexes.

❧ Burning Tree ❦

When I was nine in 1954. . . . I asked my father, a lawyer and a former member of Congress, why are all the people at Burning Tree Club men?

My father explained that no women, no girls could ever go to Burning Tree because the men there were naked. Naked all the time. For weeks I tried to picture cabinet officers and senators striding down the fairways. Did golf bags chafe the senatorial thighs? How careful did Ike have to be when teeing off?"

—Recollections of Constance Casey,
The *Washington Post*, April 19, 1992

There's another tale they tell at Burning Tree Club in Bethesda, Maryland, that the only time a woman ever stepped on the course was when an airplane crashed there and an injured passenger found herself on the eighteenth fairway. She was quickly removed.

Burning Tree—founded in 1922—has never had a woman member or a woman guest. Women are not permitted in the clubhouse, on the course, or even in the galleries. They are barred completely except at Christmastime, when they are permitted to lay down their money at the pro shop for gifts for their men. Yet it is a golf haven to presidents (Eisenhower, Nixon, and Ford played there) and vice-presidents (Dan Quayle was said to be a frequent player). President Clinton, who ran into trouble when he played golf at an all-white club in Little Rock, Arkansas, is now more careful. He does not play at Burning Tree. At least that's what we hear. But cabinet members, senators, and representatives regularly play golf at Burning Tree, men who in the public halls of Congress enact laws barring discrimination against women.

These men regularly play at a course whose members bar golfing female colleagues from the House, the Senate, and the courts. That means that Supreme Court Justice Sandra Day O'Connor, a long-time golfer, and Supreme Court Justice Ruth Ginsburg, a recreational golfer, may not play there. Retired Senator Barry Goldwater once said he would quit the club if women were ever admitted. And Senator Sam Nunn resigned from Burning Tree only in 1990, when he considered running for president.

Burning Tree and other private clubs in the state are governed by a unique Maryland "open spaces" law that gives a lucrative tax abatement to clubs as long as they agree not to sell their land for development. An amendment to the law says country clubs may not discriminate on the basis of race or gender or religion.

For eight long years, the five hundred men of Burning Tree fought to have it both ways: to keep women out and to keep their tax break. In 1989, however, the U.S. Supreme Court let stand a Maryland appeals court decision that stripped Burning Tree of its massive tax benefits unless it altered its all-male bylaw.

Soon after the court's decision, the membership met to vote: admit women or pay back taxes for its property to 1986, taxes based on a new assessment of $500,000. The choice was whether the presence of women was worse than a retroactive tax bill of $1.2 million plus future tax assessments for the members, who now would pay taxes on the real market value of the golf course. The men voted to pay the higher taxes; to keep the club all-male.

The course has hosted its share of dignitaries from other countries, including royalty and prime ministers. Its membership is now racially diverse. Burning Tree continues to welcome the usual crew of admirals, generals, senators and representatives, judges, and lobbyists, along with CEOs like Robert Allen, chairman of the board of AT&T. There is exactly one category that is excluded. Women. All others can tee it up, as long as they are male.

Maybe they do play naked.

❧ Butler National ❧

Butler National in Oak Brook, Illinois, site of the PGA Tour's Western Open for more than fifteen years, gave up its prestigious and lucrative tournament because it did not want to admit women to its club.

Butler National, a relative newcomer to the world of all-male golf in that it opened its doors in 1974, does not admit women as members and does not admit women as guests. Even when it hosted the Western Open, it only allowed women volunteers, concessionaires, and Western Open employees on the course during the week of the tournament.

I can't help wondering if the menfolk there feel happier now that the tournament is gone. Maybe they feel they've done the world of maledom a service by restoring the club to its true, all-male values. Then again, maybe they miss being in on the excitement of this historic tournament.

❧ Pine Valley Golf Club ❧

Being invited to play golf at Pine Valley Golf Club, rated the No. 1 course in the nation by *Golf Digest*, is like getting an invitation to dinner at the White House. You drop everything and go.

Pine Valley began as an all-male national club in 1913 in the borough of Clementon. In 1929, in an act of kindness, the New Jersey state legislature created the borough of Pine Valley, whose boundaries are co-extensive with the boundaries of the Pine Valley Golf Club.

The club owns all land in the borough and leases its eighteen houses, often to officers of the club. To be eligible to rent a home in the borough, a man must first be admitted to the club. No woman can own property in the borough because she cannot be a member of the club. No admission, no rental. The renter leases his land too; he does not own his property.

In short, Pine Valley is itself a legally incorporated municipality with all the powers of a borough and an exclusive private club as well, lawyers say. Pine Valley has its own "police force," whose assignments include keeping unwanted golfers off the golf course. Tax dollars collected by the borough are used to benefit the club; and presumably the male citizens of the borough deduct their municipal taxes accordingly. All borough officials are either members or employees of the golf club.

Pine Valley is a national club, with some one thousand members, most of whom live elsewhere in the United States or abroad. Many are corporate leaders who fly in for the weekend. One has to be invited for membership, and once in, a man pays a nonrefundable initiation fee and annual dues. In 1990, the fee was $15,000. No member has ever proposed a woman for admission. Any member who did would probably be laughed out of the club.

Members generally invite guests for a weekend, and the men stay in suites on the grounds. The club is located in the Pine Barrens in the southern tip of New Jersey, not far from Philadelphia. You have to know how to get there, because, like most private clubs, Pine Valley does not trumpet its whereabouts.

Pine Valley permits women to put spikes to ground on Sunday after 3:00 P.M. if the woman is accompanied by a member. That means that New Jersey governor Christine Todd Whitman, who plays golf, presumably would have to wait until 3:00 P.M.

In 1990, Pine Valley took steps to stave off encroaching laws whose aim is to permit women to initiate business at private clubs in the same way men have always done. "We want to remain all-male," a club official told me several years ago. The club defends its policies on the ground that its members have the right to associate with whom they please. Pine Valley does not hold outside functions like weddings or parties at the club. Its dining room is open only to members and their personal guests. It does not have swimming pools or tennis courts; it does not lease out its facilities.

To keep the club purely private and out of reach of state or federal regulation, it now requires members to sign a pledge that they will not engage in business activity at the club and that no portion of their dues or other expenses will be paid directly or indirectly by their employer. The Everglades Club in Palm Beach, one of the most exclusive in all Florida, served a similar letter on its members.

Violate the pledge and the member is out. When the new policy pledge was sent to all Pine Valley members, many of whom are Fortune 500 executives, all but one signed. As at Burning Tree, these males are willing to pay for the privilege of keeping women out. Although a borough, Pine Valley doesn't tend to emphasize its municipal functions. Rather, it views itself as a social and recreational club, a mecca for serious golfers.

Provided they are serious male golfers.

Caroline Pierce, an English professional on the LPGA tour, and no doubt a better golfer than most of the men at Pine Valley, recently received an invitation to play the course. She would love to do so, she said. "But the member who invited me told me the only time we could play was after 3:00 P.M. Sunday. Not the best time for me."

❧ The Olympic Club ☙

All-male clubs have no women members and are not considered family-oriented. Looking at San Francisco's Olympic Club, a world-class facility with a huge membership—some 3,400 members in 1988, one-quarter of whom were women—one would not think of it as all-male.

Certainly the men in the club did not consider Olympic all-male. The 850 wives and daughters, like women in most private country clubs in America, could be found at the two adjoining golf courses, where they attended various social events and were permitted to play golf or tennis. They had what the club called subordinate rights.

But Louise H. Renne, the San Franciso city attorney, who knew Olympic's policies firsthand because her husband was a member of Olympic and she was a spouse, never had a doubt. From the legal perspective, women could not be full members. They had no vote. Examining the club in light of the legal cases and court decisions that had marked women's emergence into the working world, Ms. Renne believed that the club was discriminating against women on the basis of gender.

Here then is a good example of the gray areas in the distinction between all-male and family clubs. In both types of clubs the men hold the membership and usually the vote. Given the huge membership, it looks as if Olympic were a family club; but there was never any doubt when the legal action began just how unwelcome women were.

In 1987, in her formal capacity as the chief city attorney of San Francisco, Ms. Renne began an inquiry. It came a few days after the Olympic Club hosted the 1987 U.S. Open, an event that drew thousands of people to the facility. She sent a letter to the club's president. The subject: discrimination. Ms. Renne pointed out that Olympic leased public land for its world-famous golf courses, specifically 17.35 acres, three pivotal holes on the club's Lake and Ocean courses. Discrimination against women would constitute a material breach of the lease, she said.

The club's chief attorney, Robert F. Kane, a former state judge and ambassador to Ireland, conceded early on that the club discriminated against women. That was the club's prerogative. "If a club is private then one should be able to associate with whomever you wish, all blacks, all Jews, all Catholics, all men, all women, whatever." The club proclaimed it was entitled under the Constitution to the freedom of association.

But George Riley, then the lead city attorney on the case, argued that in weighing the harms of discriminatory policies at private clubs against a person's or a club's rights of association, the harm outweighs the rights. States and cities were entitled to enact laws to end such policies, he said.

"When the Olympic Club was founded . . . women were denied the right to vote, to serve on juries, to hold public office and to control certain property. The law has long since changed. Yet in 1988, the San Francisco Olympic Club was clinging to a practice of unequal treatment and opportunity that belongs to another century," Mr. Riley said.

And so began Olympic's long, difficult, and costly battle with the city of San Francisco, a battle that cost the club upward of $1 million in legal fees, produced enormous acrimony within the membership, and prevented the club from earning substantial revenues by hosting major golf championships for five years. Olympic's Lake course, opened in 1924, is rated among the top ten in the country.

From the city's point of view, Olympic had a long history of bigotry. For more than 100 years, membership in the club was open to "only white male citizens of the United States." In 1968, the club dropped this explicit racial restriction. Yet even though the club has a huge membership, nearly 3,400 members, it was not until 1988, after the city filed its lawsuit regarding women, that Olympic admitted its first two black men.

Olympic had also had a rigid policy against Jews, one that lasted well into the 1960s. Lawyers familiar with the club's history say that if an applicant had a Jewish-sounding name, he was asked if he was German or Jewish. If he said he was Jewish, his sponsor would be pressured to make him withdraw his application. This all happened behind the scenes, of course—little fights, very important, but never disclosed. By contrast, the fight over admitting women became big news in the Bay area.

The case of Pamela Sayad vividly illustrates their policies. She was the daughter of a member. Once a member's daughter entered adulthood she could not then join the club unless she was married and her husband was approved, even though she had grown up at the club. Sons held special memberships leading to full voting rights; daughters did not.

A native of San Francisco, Ms. Sayad was the founding law partner of Sayad & Trigero. Her father, Sam, had become a club member in the mid-sixties, and she, her mother, her sister and brother all used the club's facilities. After her father's death, she applied for a full membership in her own name, as had her brother before her. She wanted to use the club to play tennis, entertain business clients and to socialize with friends she had known since childhood.

In March 1987 she submitted an application for admission. An Olympic member proposed her, another seconded her, and five other members gave her references. The club, however, refused to act on her application. Donald Bering, then the president, candidly admitted that he knew of no reason why Ms. Sayad should not become a member of the club other than her sex.

Sometime after Ms. Sayad was rejected in 1987, Ms. Renne asked the club to change its policies. The club's board then voted to admit women. But a renegade group of men emerged, dedicated to keeping the club all-male, and the vote was overturned. That led to the protracted lawsuit between the city and Olympic.

The club's decision to settle the long and expensive litigation came in July 1991, after California's highest court upheld a lower court ruling ordering the club to give Mr. Riley a list of applicants rejected from 1980 to 1989. That same month a federal judge said the club's insurance carrier was not required to pay the more than $1.3 million in legal bills the club had run up in fighting the city's lawsuit. The club could see the handwriting on the wall.

In the end, to avoid an acrimonious and potentially embarrassing and expensive trial, the club settled. In 1992, the club formally ended 132 years of all-male rule and admitted women as full members. The city agreed to sell Olympic the 17.35 acres of city land on its golf courses and Olympic went back into the business of hosting major golf tournaments. And Pamela Sayad? She is now a member in her own name. She would like to meet other women in her category, but meeting them is difficult because Olympic, understandably fearful of the public record, does not publish a club directory.

❦ 4 ❦

The Grass Ceiling

It's time. We're all in the same board rooms, we're all in the same meetings at work.
                    —Barbara J. Litrell, publisher of *McCall's*

As the nation approaches the twenty-first century, there is one group of women who experience the golf world with a special sense of urgency. These are the new career women, launched into business, industry, and the professions as a result of the sea change that has occurred in American society.

Women lawyers, bankers, publishers, and other business executives are taking up the game in increasing numbers. Beyond mere recreation, these women are looking to the golf course to form business relationships. Many women executives expect to learn how to play, join a club, and have access to their club's facilities. They want to entertain clients and entertain them well. They have the financial backing to do it. They know what their male counterparts have long known, that golf provides a way to create business opportunities.

The growing importance of women in the economy has transformed women's traditional relationship to the game of golf. Defined primarily in relation to their working husbands, women golfers were housewives accustomed to playing golf on Ladies' Days, generally Tuesdays or Thursdays, their established days at the club.

For the woman business executive the game is no longer only leisure activity, and it is no longer defined through her relationship to her husband or to her father. More often than not, the career woman, married or single, wants an individual or corporate country club membership in her own name, with rights equal to those of any other member. She expects the same kind of treatment at her golf club that she now receives as an accomplished manager in her business.

Barbara J. Litrell is one of these women. She grew up in New York City and never felt anything was closed to her. She came to love golf when she was well into a career at the *New York Times*. She has seen how golf is connected to business, to advancement, and to bringing together divergent groups.

Ms. Litrell is unique in having combined her current role as publisher of *McCall's* with that of being a named corporate sponsor of a professional women's golfing event. We met in the Green Mountains of Vermont, where *McCall's* hosts the popular LPGA tournament at the Stratton Mountain golf course. We had an extended conversation about women, golf, and business.

Ms. Litrell took up golf when she was building a career as an advertising executive at the *New York Times*. The year was 1982. She wanted to learn how to play golf because each year the advertising department at the newspaper held a golf tournament and only the men went.

"And suddenly it dawned on us women that there was something going on here that we weren't quite a part of. And so one day I said to a woman who worked for me, 'Mary, we have clients who play golf. We really should learn to do this.' And we went out and took a lesson, and three weeks later we played eighteen holes.

"The men in the office were encouraging, and that helped enormously. There were several men at the paper who would come in on a Monday and say, 'So did you play this weekend—did you watch the women on television?' And they were supportive, and whenever we had outings, they were the best golfers and they would put us in their foursomes and play with us and encourage us. That was super. There was a guy who was probably a six handicap or better and he was the biggest supporter of all of us. And then you had the men who never played golf who started getting excited about it. So it turned the advertising department into a really strong golf thing."

She learned to use golf in the development of her business. At one point in her career at the *Times*, she did all the advertising for the alcohol beverage companies, a heavily male business, she said. "And my whole department was female, and we were all starting to play golf. So we decided one good way to get through to our clients was to hold a tournament. So we held the first New York Times Wine and Spirits Classic. We hosted a tournament on a Monday for about thirty people in the wine and spirits business. I got a couple of our best male golfers and a few executives for the foursomes, so there were good golfers playing along with beginners. We made friends with everyone in the industry that way. It broke the ice."

When she arrived at *McCall's,* her staff knew she loved golf. "In the magazine world it's good for business. So one day my marketing director came in and said, 'You know, *Family Circle* does the tennis cup, maybe *McCall's* should do an LPGA event?' And I did just what you just did. I said, 'Hmmm. That sounds like a great idea.' And we started pursuing it. Within a year we did our first LPGA event here. This is now our third year.

"This event generates enthusiasm. We are very pro golf. We held a clinic for twenty-four women at the Westchester Country Club this year—almost all beginners in the advertising business—and now I have them up to the tournament as guests and they're dying to come. Some women still have reticence. And I will always take a person who has never played on a course before out with me. A few weeks ago I asked one of the women at the clinic if she and her husband wouldn't like to come and play at my home course on Long Island, a public course. And she said she was not good enough. I encouraged her to come on out. So she and her husband came, and the four of us played. She is a total beginner and we just said here's what you do. We got around the course and she played her first eighteen holes. Now you know she's hooked; she'll go for lessons and it will be good for business the next time someone calls and says, You wanna play?

"What we have always tried to do, whether at the *New York Times* or here at *McCall's,* is encourage women to play golf—that it's good for business. And we've actively done things to get them involved with it. When I was at the *Times*, there were two of us who started playing golf one year. And by the end of two years we had twenty-two women in advertising playing golf."

Women wanted to learn how to play golf because everyone was always talking about it. "People wanted to go because they saw we loved it and got excited. And then we would set up golf outings.

"The outings were held at various public courses in Rockland County. And we had twenty-four women at the first outing; they were all beginners. We all got designer shirts that said 'First Annual 1982 Golf Outing.' The first person teed off (we picked the best to go first), and she hit it 150 yards. And after that it was all downhill, but it got them really excited. We always taught them that you had to pick up your ball when you were having difficulty and move along. There were four of us who stayed pretty serious about golf. Every year we and our husbands go to a different resort. We just celebrated our tenth anniversary."

The women formed their friendship at the *Times*. Now they are all in different places. "But we still go to resorts together. It was the kind of thing that ten years ago only men did. Only men went down to Myrtle Beach for four days when we started going. We would have 7:30 A.M. tee times. We would have all the men behind us and we'd hear them—and the management would send a ranger out to follow us and time us. And they would say, 'We have three rules for women here—step aside, step aside, step aside.' It was all this outrageous stuff.

"Now we are much more on the offensive. When we go to the tee at 7:30 A.M., the first thing we say is 'Hi, good morning. What a great day. Do you think these guys are gonna hold us up?' They are immediately caught off guard. So we have learned to take it head-on and defuse it. Whether we are good, bad, or indifferent out there, they get an impression of gee, these women are really hip. We are not intimidated. We just go do it."

Golf provides the setting for getting to know new business associates, but business, she points out, should not take place on the golf course. "Everyone says that all these guys are doing business on the golf course. That is not the case and it shouldn't be. . . . What I find is you invite someone out and you play golf, and you become better friends and you understand each other's personalities. Then the door is open for business."

Then she can make the phone call. "That's the key," Ms. Litrell says. "The key thing is what it does for the relationship. It changes the relationship. It gives you the opportunity to observe someone for four or more hours. You learn all about their families, you learn about their likes and dislikes.

"I found that here, there are people who came to the Stratton tournament that were my clients, but I didn't necessarily know them. By the time they are leaving . . . you know that the next time a business deal comes up that a trust in the relationship has been developed. And you can call, or they will call."

When Barbara Litrell became publisher of *McCall's* in 1991, one of her perks was a country club membership. That's a standard benefit. Men in executive positions are routinely sponsored and accepted. Black executives sometimes have great difficulty. So do women.

It took Ms. Litrell more than two years to find a club in the New York area that gave her full privileges. Along the way, she learned a great deal about how clubs keep the women's issue invisible. "There were very few clubs that allowed women members. But if you call and ask, 'Do you have women members?' the answer is always yes."

Ms. Litrell found that when people knew their club did not allow women full privileges, they didn't talk about it much. "You don't get much information. They just don't discuss it."

Wykagyl Country Club, site of the LPGA JAL Big Apple Classic, is a beautiful turn-of-the-century club located in New Rochelle, New York. Betsy King, one of the great women pros, says it is her favorite golf course. Ms. Litrell spoke to officials there. The club had individual memberships. At lunch one day, the membership chairman asked Ms. Litrell, "'Oh, by the way, are you married?' And I said, yes. And he said, 'Hmmmm.' And I said, 'What's the matter?' And he said, 'Well, your husband would have to be the member.' And I said to him, 'How can you have an LPGA tournament here and have these kinds of restrictions?'"

Had she been single and sought a full membership, she might have been admitted, but at that time the club had restrictions on tee times, she said. As a married woman, her husband would be the member even though her company was paying steep initiation fees for her to hold the membership in her name. So Ms. Litrell said thank you very much, that won't work. She took her money and went elsewhere. Wykagyl has since changed its policies.

"The key thing is that you need to join a club the clients want to go to. I mean I could join a lot of clubs. But I needed to join a club that's prestigious and that a client would say, 'Oh, I want to play that course—there's a tournament that takes place there.'

"And what I found is that these clubs do not have women members. Westchester Country Club is an exception.* Westchester has gender-neutral requirements. That's why I am a member there." Her

---

* Not always. For Nancy Saunders's version, see p. 61.

husband is the associate member. She may tee off at any time on the weekends.

"But a lot of courses do not have women as the full members. A lot of them have associate members or you can be a member if you are single or divorced, but you still have restrictions on eating places and tee times, and that's no good for business. And I swore that if I were going to join a club, it had to be one that had full privileges for the member. It took me a long time to find one."

The Barbara Litrell story is instructive. In just twelve years, she has learned how to play golf as an adult, learned how to use it in business, and with her company has become a leading sponsor of a women's professional tournament. She has also learned to play for leisure enjoyment, has used both public and private golf courses, and enjoys the resort course experience with her husband and friends. Hers is a great success story, though even with her individual and corporate resources it took a lot of shopping around to find the right private course for her needs.

For some other firsthand accounts, I spoke to a group of Connecticut executives, all women, all golfers, all leaders in their companies, all friends or acquaintances, all wanting to take special clients out for a round of golf at their clubs.

To a woman, all said that one of the most grating aspects of life in a private club is being shut out by restricted weekend and holiday tee times. Private club membership is expected of executive women, and since each of them works all week long, getting onto the course on weekends is crucial. It is one reason they may have invested upward of $15,000 for full membership rights.

Pat Yoder, a corporate executive at GE Capital in Stamford, Connecticut, was based in Pittsburgh prior to her current assignment. At the time, she and a friend, a media personality, each belonged to one of Pittsburgh's two most exclusive clubs. Pat's company sponsored her and paid for her membership at the Pittsburgh Field Club. But she could only gain admission, the club said, as an associate member, because she was a single woman. She was the first female member accepted at the club via this route. Her friend belonged to Fox Chapel Golf Club, across the road. Neither club granted women the right to tee off on Saturday mornings, regardless of the nature of their membership.

"When I lived in Pittsburgh, she and I wanted to play on Saturday mornings. Now, how insane is this? The two of us belong to the greatest, best golf clubs in Pittsburgh. And what would we do on Saturday? We would drive thirty-five miles away to a public golf course so that we could play at 8 A.M. And afterward we would say, as we sat in a cart at this public course, 'What's wrong with this picture?' "

Mary E. Green is an executive at Champion International, a paper manufacturer whose corporate headquarters are in Stamford. "I want to take business clients out when I want to. For me that would be about 10 A.M. on Saturday. I don't want to have them have to wait to tee off. That is ridiculous when I am bringing the club three hundred to four hundred dollars' worth of revenues that day."

Mrs. Green does not have a membership in her own name at Woodway Country Club in Darien, Connecticut. She is the wife of a fifteen-year member. As a woman, she has restricted weekend and holiday tee times, after noon on Saturday, 11 A.M. on Sunday, 11:30 A.M. on holidays, even though she works all week and often uses the club for business purposes. At this point in her career she finds the situation particularly galling. "I am bringing in considerable revenues over and above the substantial dues and other fees to pay for this club. But I am not recognized as the member, so I cannot play during prime time."

Nor can she tee off Thursday or Friday between noon and 1:30 P.M., other times reserved for males. "Ladies" at her club have exclusive use of the course until noon on Tuesday, the club's Ladies' Day, and the ladies' nine-holers may tee off between 8:30 and 10 A.M. Wednesday.

Bonnie Axthelm, general manager of MNI, a 3M company, belongs to Silvermine Golf Club, in Norwalk, Connecticut, a club that recently opened its tee times to both sexes on weekends. The only caveat is that prime times are reserved for member foursomes. Ms. Axthelm said that when she moved to Connecticut, she was told a more exclusive club would accept her if she agreed to their terms—even though there was a five-year waiting list. "They told my realtor they were eager to have me. I was ideal. Why? Because I was a woman and I wasn't going to mess up the tee times on Saturday and Sunday mornings. They would get my thirty-thousand-dollar nonrefundable bond and I couldn't play weekend mornings."

Susan Pappas heads the multimillion-dollar marketing-communications firm Pappas MacDonnell, in Southport, Connecticut. She is a "full" member of Brooklawn Country Club, one of the oldest and most established clubs in Connecticut. She is a fine golfer, with a five-handicap. But despite paying full membership fees, she cannot tee off weekend mornings because those times are reserved for men.

Until Brooklawn she had two alternatives: a public course or an easy-access private course. Her experiences at each are instructive. She gave up the public course owing to rounds that lasted five to six hours and because she didn't want to wait in the car queue at 2:30 A.M. in order to get a tee time .

She then moved into an easy-access private club, one that required annual dues but no initiation fee. Two events indicated why this club was untenable, she said.

The first incident occurred when she took her foursome to lunch after the round.

"We are having lunch," she said, "and the owner comes up to us and said, 'Are you a new member?' I said, 'Yes, I am,' and he said, 'That's great. You girls are real nice. If any of you want a job, I'm looking for waitresses.' "

Susan didn't miss a beat. "Only if you can pay me as much money to be a waitress as I am getting paid now," she said.

The second event occurred when she invited another group to play. One of the women in the foursome was particularly attractive, and one of the owners propositioned her immediately. Susan made a silent vow to leave the club. "It was embarrassing to take my clients there."

What she wanted was a fine golf course, the amenities of club life, a hassle-free place to take clients to play golf. She found a sponsor, met with the members of the board, and was admitted to Brooklawn in 1990. Because she is a woman, however, her membership, which included a $15,000 initiation fee, does not entitle her to tee off on weekends until after 1 P.M. on Saturday and 11 A.M. on Sunday. Nor can she play with the ladies' nine-hole or eighteen-hole group on weekdays. "I work then," she says. She is the only woman in her club who has paid a full initiation fee for her membership.

"In this day and age, I am astonished that a sixteen-year-old son of a member, who has paid nothing for his membership, can tee off Saturday and Sunday mornings, and I can't." Daughters of members who have played with boys at the club all their lives learn that when the boys reach age sixteen they can tee off on weekend mornings but the girls cannot. As it stands at Susan's club, teenage boys as well as male guests have greater access to the golf course on weekend mornings than she does. So far she has not succeeded in getting club officials to give her tee times that match her full-fee membership.

At our gathering, she told the group how, on one Saturday afternoon in 1994, she made a blunder. She and her foursome arrived at the club and after warming up hitting balls, the guests decided to skip lunch. The group included Ms. Yoder and Ms. Axthelm, as well as LPGA player Lori Garbacz.

As Ms. Pappas describes it, "We were there at noon and we were not supposed to tee off until 1 P.M. Around 12:45 P.M., with the tee having been open for forty-five minutes and with no one in sight, we made the mistake of teeing off. The next Monday I got a call from the chairman of the Golf Committee.

" 'Susan, I understand you teed off early on Saturday. Can you meet with me and the head of the rules committee at 5:30 P.M. Thursday. We want to explain our position to you.' And I said sure."

At the disciplinary meeting, one official read Ms. Pappas the club's rule saying that women and children cannot tee off on Saturday until after one and on Sunday until after 11 A.M. "That's really insulting," she said to them, "that I am grouped with children." This club, like others that keep women off the course until afternoons, has a frequent bottleneck at the first tee, which promotes slow play and ties the course up all afternoon. The club is now studying possible underutilization of the course during the late-morning hours because it might be the cause.

Another topic of concern to the women is the potential for golf outings where women have a chance to play in company-sponsored tournaments with clients. Barbara Litrell speaks highly of these gatherings in connection with businesses, and so do some of these women.

Charity is a frequent vehicle for such tournaments. A company leases a public or a private golf course and sponsors a charity outing. The company hires a golf-event group to put on what is usually a one-day affair. A tournament for charity permits the sponsoring company to deduct certain business expenses in connection with the event. It helps the charity and it brings together clients and colleagues to provide invaluable contacts in business.

But few women ever play in these tournaments. Why? Either the sponsors don't know the women play golf, or the women don't think they play well enough, or the women are less likely to take time off from work to play golf. Several women said that they would not leave the office even though they know their male subordinates would go in a minute and might well wind up playing with the boss.

One marketing director for a Dayton, Ohio, company, who asked that her name, company, and country club not be used, told me most of her golf contacts occur from participating in charity golf tournaments. Elaborating on the benefits of these occasions, she said, "Somehow after you play golf with them [men], some kind of bonding occurs. You're one of the guys after that."

Susan Pappas agrees about the importance of charity golf tournaments for meeting new business contacts, and about charity tournaments attracting few women players. "I've played in three charity events this year, two Diabetes events, and one MS event. There were two hundred and eighty players at the MS event and six women. There were one hundred and forty players at the first Diabetes event and six women, and one hundred and forty players at the second Diabetes event and two women. I felt like I was from Mars." Many of the men were juniors in their companies. "They would be three to four rungs down from any of the women executives in the tournament," Pappas said. "And yet they had taken off the day."

Indeed, there are so few women at these events, and so few sponsors actually believe a woman will win a tournament, that prizes are rarely selected with the woman in mind. As one woman told me, "When they ask you your size, and you say 'Small,' what comes back is a men's medium. That is the smallest size they have unless they have a tournament with Japanese male clients. Then they will have a men's small."

Connie Bennett, a vice-president for sales at *Business Week* magazine and another participant in our rap session, began to play golf three years ago, primarily on public courses in San Francisco. She played regularly and saw herself improving. Working at *Business Week,* a magazine that is big on golf, she found out that executives are expected to participate in the rituals of managerial life, and golf is one of them.

Many companies have hired outside golf consultants to teach female employees to play. *Business Week* has gone a step further by setting up clinics in major cities for women clients to learn the game. Their teacher? None other than DeDe Owens, head of the Teaching and Club Professional division of the LPGA.

Business Week's new publisher, David Ferm, former publisher of *Golf Digest,* says that many of the company's conferences and meetings are planned with golf in mind. When he arrived at the magazine in late 1993, the company was planning its third annual CEO golf tournament, to be held at the Gleneagles Hotel in Scotland, a three-day working holiday to thank the magazine's top corporate advertising clients for their support. The guests flew to Scotland from the United States, Europe, and Japan. The first two years, only men went. But he wanted his women executives to participate in 1994, and he encouraged them to learn to play. Five women, including Ms. Bennett, were among the first group of women invited to Gleneagles.

"The fact that I got to go is important in that men on my level at the company have always gone on this trip. It's extremely important in my job to be able to participate with CEOs from our company's outside firms; golf is an excellent way to do it. I don't know any better way to get to know a person than to share a round of golf. At Gleneagles I got to know several senior CEOs, and I keep in touch and continue to do business with them. The fact that I played golf with them for three days was invaluable; a unique and special way to interact. This trip let me know what I had been missing."

There was no gender issue at Gleneagles. It is a public resort course that avoids the demeaning treatment women usually receive at British courses. The five women played in mixed foursomes—one low-handicap, two mediums, and one high. "Every foursome had a range of playing ability to keep the tournament fair. We played three different courses. We had a caddie. We walked all day. The wind, the squalls. It was just beautiful."

❦ PART II ❧

Disadvantaged in the Land of Privilege

❦ 5 ❦

Getting In

We call ourselves WORMs. That stands for Wife of a
Regular Member.

—A spouse at Medinah Country Club

The women of Medinah Country Club have an acronym that expresses precisely the status of most women in most of the private clubs of America. At the country club, a woman is whom she marries, because the traditional way into club life for a woman is to be the wife of a member. If the woman also happens to be a stockbroker or lawyer or banker, her professional status usually matters not.

Now, if you are a male—whether WASP, black, Jew, or Catholic— and you are accepted into a club, you will get full rights as a member. But as the spouse of a member, the woman is a guest. Sometimes she is called a family member. As part of a family membership, she generally does not get the same privileges as her husband, even if she is paying the bill. Typically, she will not be allowed to vote or hold a proprietary interest in the membership. Club bylaws won't permit it.

As a full member, the male's status at the club doesn't change when his marital status does. Single, divorced, widowed, it doesn't matter. But for a woman a change in marital status may transform her relationship to the club in dramatic ways, usually to her detriment.

This unequal arrangement took shape as we saw in Chapter 2, at the turn of the century, when many of the great private clubs were formed. Women had not yet gotten the right to vote and few owned property. Club membership was a male privilege, with each male member purchasing a share of the course. If there were 350 members, there were 350 shares. The share was in the man's name. From that share came a male's voting privileges, governance rights, and, as clubs have grown, service on the main golf committees.

Women held none of those rights. Of course there might be women on the entertainment committee or the women's tournament committee, but they were less likely to be on the greens committee, the budget committee, or especially on the governing board of the club, not then and not now in many of the nation's private clubs.

These inequities and their possible solutions have been slow to surface as an issue in club life for many reasons, but a central one concerns the couple's or family's reason for joining a particular club in the first place, assuming the membership wasn't just inherited. Most couples join to enjoy the simple and obvious pleasures of club life. It's a place for them to play golf or tennis and to meet friends and for families to take the kids to the pool. If the woman's work is primarily as housewife and mother, much of her life may center around the club. If the man is in the business world, he may use the club not only for fun and relaxation but to entertain clients.

In short, people join clubs not as an investment or a place to exercise their civil rights, but to enjoy life. Many women members, even if they don't have full rights, experience themselves as members. They may be bothered by some club regulations, but unless the rules are extremely constraining or stifling, it is easier to go along and not make waves.

A woman's claim on this world is called into question, however, when her marital status changes. Then and only then will it really make a difference whose name is on the deed of club membership or what the bylaws may say about who can hold the membership. Indeed, the saddest tales in this chapter concern divorced women and what divorce means for women members. And sometimes, single women and widows don't fare much better.

❧ *Being Single* ❧

Traditionally, country clubs, recognizing only the state of marriage, have had trouble with a woman in any single state: single, divorced, daughter, widowed. Until recently most country clubs did not have a category for single-women admissions. They don't have such difficulties when it comes to men.

One problem single women face is that many married women members don't want them around. A single woman or divorcée, no matter what her ties to the club in the past, is considered a threat. She is not trusted. So married women in these clubs have strong feelings about single memberships, whether for club divorcées or single women professionals.

Ronney Rosenberg's experience illustrates what can happen if you're a daughter who is single. She is a commodities trader at a New York commercial bank. She spends her days in a high-pressure job trading oil and gas commodities. On the weekends she likes to play golf. She practically grew up at Fenway Golf Club in Scarsdale, New York. A Jewish club with some 275 members, the club started in the 1920s. Among its members is former *New York Post* publisher Peter Kalikow.

Ronney had been playing golf at Fenway since she cut down her mother's old clubs when she was twelve. She and her sisters were raised at the club. But when she turned twenty-nine, she knew, her parents' membership would no longer cover her. She was not as yet married, and in the world of country clubs, if you are not married by a certain date, you are either out of the club or severely restricted in your use of its facilities.

This sort of bylaw did not exist for sons. They even received a substantial membership discount: a $5,000 initiation fee as opposed to $12,000 for an outside member under age thirty-nine. Moreover, sons did not have to go through a stringent social evaluation. Had Ronney been married, her husband could have applied under a favorable rate for sons-in-law of members.

At about age twenty-nine, Ms. Rosenberg decided to do what most sons do: she applied for a full membership. She had just been made a vice-president at Goldman Sachs, and she wanted greater access to the course. Her father and her grandfather sponsored her application for full membership. Her grandfather was the member of longest standing at the club, having been at the club for some sixty-five years. She went before the board in September 1991.

"First thing some members told my father was that I should read the bylaws. They said only men over twenty-one may apply. And I was born a daughter. Most of the men on the board were sixty-five or older. They smiled and told me that I should get married. . . . They were not set up to listen to any argument. The president at the time was on his second marriage, and his first wife had been booted out of the club. He wanted to know why I wanted this so much. Wouldn't I be insulting the other associate members, namely the wives, if I did this?"

Ms. Rosenberg said that at the time she petitioned for membership some six other daughters wanted to join on their own, even though the club was not particularly accommodating to single persons. "We wanted to play golf. The message taught by the membership of clubs like Fenway is that although women and men may be held to equal standards in their political, academic and professional lives, they are on unequal ground when they play." Her application was not considered.

Her father helped continue her "special membership." She got to play but only late on weekends, after the men and the couples and the guests had teed off. She is single and thirty-three. Yet her category is widow. She is last, and she knows it.

Not far from Fenway Golf Club in Scarsdale lies Winged Foot Golf Club in Mamaroneck, New York, one of the most prominent clubs in the nation, site of four U.S. Opens and the PGA of America's 1997 championship. In 1991, the club changed its bylaws, which had restricted memberships only to men.

In opening its membership to single women and to daughters, the club agreed to let daughters seek the same full membership rights as their brothers. Two years later it granted these women full access to the golf courses on weekend mornings. But the WORMs' status did not change much. Membership was still in their husband's name, though their starting times had been moved from 1:30 P.M. to noon on weekends.

In a letter to its members in April 1991, the board said it was acting for a variety of reasons: For one thing, New York State was considering legislation to prohibit discrimination in private clubs. For another, some courts in other states were deciding against private clubs that practiced discrimination.

"Aside from these external issues . . . there is the basic issue of whether it is right for Winged Foot to engage in discrimination at this time in our history. The role of women in our society has changed dramatically since 1921, and your Board believes members should be selected on the basis of their individual merit and love for Winged Foot and the game of golf."

The board said it had carefully considered "the legal, public relations, and moral issues" presented by an all-male membership (note the order of the club's concerns) and had decided unanimously to endorse a bylaw change as a "prudent and logical initiative." The club also resolved that no person shall be denied membership on account of gender, race, religion, or national origin.

Whether moved by justice, altruism, or the desire to keep their reputation as a site for national championships, the men of Winged Foot have made life better for single women.

At some clubs when you're single, the membership can come with strings attached. Pat Yoder, the executive at GE Capital, recalls the admission process when she was sponsored for membership at the Pittsburgh Field Club, one of the state's most exclusive clubs.

"You go to lunch with the sponsors, you go to lunch with some members of the membership committee, while they look you over. That all happens before you even do the application. And then there's the application and then all kinds of meetings and a cocktail party and another cocktail party and on and on, forever. The final step is the membership committee.

"One older member said to me, 'And I assume Mr. Yoder is dead?' And I said, 'Not the last time I got a check from him.'" She was finally admitted to the club and her company paid a five-figure initiation fee. Were she a man, she said, this would be a lifetime investment. But she is female. "My membership agreement says that if I remarry I will have to resign my membership."

Like Pat Yoder, a woman we will call Pamela Charles faced a similar problem when she wanted to join a club in the Northeast. Since memberships are traditionally held by the male, clubs don't usually look closely at the females brought along through marriage. But when single females get memberships, the clubs' officers are often concerned that the men they marry will not pass scrutiny.

The man who sponsored Pamela Charles for membership at his

club, an elite but informal sort of place, tells what happened. "I called the chairman of the admission committee and proposed this woman for membership," he said. "I didn't expect any difficulty, but then our membership guy says, 'We are concerned about taking in divorced and single women. They will remarry . . . and the guy they marry may be unacceptable.'"

Of course, at most clubs single male members would not be denied admission for fear of who they would marry. And many a male has married a woman whose appearance and attitudes conflict with country club life.

The sponsor, a New York lawyer, said he was shocked by the raw discrimination he was hearing. He had known the woman for years, and he thought that by 1989 his club was progressive enough to handle a divorcée. "She was not being rejected because of her personality—she was well liked and a good golfer—but because of her marital status. This was discrimination. The chairman tried to talk me out of it. I said absolutely not. I refused to be talked out of it."

The next step was the club cocktail party, the occasion where proposed members meet the rest of the group. "We arranged for the usual admission, the cocktail reception. You know they come in twos and threes. We stand around for ten minutes and we're gone. It's pretty informal. She was admitted to the club."

About a year later, the divorcée remarried. And whom did she marry? Why, she married the local plumber. He did not play golf. But during midweek, while she was at work, he took to lunching at the club. Mostly in summer. He did not have lunch at the grill. No. He would drive his plumber's truck with all the paraphernalia hanging from its sides right up into the country club lot.

And he would take his brown bag lunch at the pool and watch the young women and children swim. It was a sunny, nice place to have lunch, and he felt comfortable there.

"Well," said our lawyer, "I started to get flak. 'What are you going to do about this?' our membership chairman asked me. I got flak . . . oh, my, did I get flak."

Before the matter reached the board's agenda, the couple divorced. The marriage lasted about a year. And what a year it was for her sponsor. When he thinks of it now, he sort of rolls his eyes. He says, with a grin, he thinks his sponsoring days are over.

❧ ❦

Westchester Country Club in New York was progressive. Few clubs had individual memberships for women in the early 1980s, but there a single woman held her own equity rights and held her own vote.

Nancy Saunders joined Westchester in 1981. She is now a partner in the Saunders Company in Greenwich, Connecticut, just on the other side of the New York border. She is sometimes heard on radio, when she does a spot in praise of the *Wall Street Journal*. Ms. Saunders is also a fine golfer. An eleven-handicapper, she can play the best of courses. She loves the game. She was delighted to be a member with full rights, even though her single membership in 1981 did not permit her to tee off on Westchester's championship course until 1:45 P.M. on weekends and holidays.

Then she met David Saunders and they fell in love. He, too, was a member of the Westchester Country Club. He had been since 1974. They married in 1985. Marriage dramatically changed her standing. She was still an executive, still had a fine handicap, still Nancy. But the club's bylaws required that she transfer her membership to her spouse.

Wedding bells for Nancy meant going from a single membership with equity holdings and a vote to a family membership with no equity and no vote. She not only lost her equity share in the club, she never got back any of her initiation fee. As a real-estate executive she knew full well what it meant to abandon equity rights in a prime piece of Westchester property if the club ever decided to sell. "I was now the parenthesis" (the spouse's name now appears after the member's name in the club directory).

Some months later Ms. Saunders quietly set out to change the rules at Westchester. For the results, see page 190.

❦ *Getting Divorced* ❧

Divorce? Widowhood is better, no question.
                                    —Mary Ann Warfield

In the world of country clubs, divorce for a woman often means being pushed out of her country club as well, at a stressful time in her life. No matter that the woman might be the club's golf champion. No matter that she spent endless hours sprucing up the course, putting on events,

representing the club at statewide tournaments, developing friendships.

All those years when the now-divorced woman lived for her
club, she thought she mattered. She thought the club needed her. Now,
to her astonishment, she learns that the club could care less. Nothing
personal, of course. It's just that if old Fred wants a new wife, the old one
gets the boot.

The discarded wife has been cut out at the time she most needs to
belong to the club. Often she is forced to confront another tough reality:
the other women at the club may not want her around either. They
don't like single women near their husbands. "We're considered live
bait," one woman who was thrown out told me.

When she agreed with her then husband to join the club, she
probably didn't stop to think what it meant that the membership was in
his name. Why should she? Probably he didn't dwell on it either, not
thinking of the membership in his name as a big deal. It is just the way
clubs do business. Only after the relationship crumbles does the reality
hit home.

From the point of view of the club, the wife is not a shareholder;
she holds no equity in the club. Her name does not appear on the club's
stock certificate. She has no formal financial involvement in the club,
even if she has been footing the family bill. She may nonetheless believe
that her goodwill, her devotion to club activities, her having been the
golf champion will count for something. She may believe the club will
find some way to keep her. Perhaps a new category of membership
might be created. Something. Anything that will treat her fairly and
with respect. Dream on.

Golf champ Millie Rech spent most of her adult years at the North Hills
Country Club in Manhasset, Long Island. For decades North Hills was
the center of her social world. She was the club's woman champion
three times. She knew everyone. Her father had paid for Millie and her
husband's initial membership. She was married for seventeen years.

Then she went through a divorce. That was eighteen years ago
and she is still bitter. She was the golfer in the family. She lived to play.
"The club becomes your whole world, particularly if you are deeply
involved in the game of golf. If you spend a lot of time practicing and you
are there all the time and it is your life, to just get cut off like that, well,
it's humiliating."

Her friends drew up a petition urging the club to let her stay. She sought her own full membership. Nothing worked. One day when she arrived at the club to play, she was told she could not.

Instead, she was ordered to clear out her locker. "I was told to make way for wife number two, who didn't even play golf," she said. Ms. Rech, now sixty-three, remembers how awful she was made to feel on that particular day. The experience is seared in her memory. The year was 1977.

"I came in from playing one day and a group of girls were sitting around the table talking and this one girl says to me, 'You know, Millie, we were just discussing you and we've decided that you are far too attractive to be around here without a husband.' I almost punched her in the face. I am not a beautiful woman, but they just didn't want me around.

"I told one man I respected at the club that this was ridiculous. He said this was a family club. I said what about all these single men here. I have a family. I have three daughters. 'We don't want that stuff around here,' he told me, meaning single women.

"You are made to feel practically like a prostitute if you are not married. But it wasn't always this way. When we first joined this club in 1960, when it was located in Douglaston, a woman could stay on if there was a divorce. Then the club was more progressive. Then they got a different kind of membership, more traditional Italian, and it all changed." Here was a club that was not just acting out of tradition. It had gone backward.

Ms. Rech is now back on the golf course, a public course she uses near her home. She didn't play for nearly fifteen years. "I was still so angry." I asked her what had made her so angry that she gave up golf for so many years.

"What they do is they do everything they can to encourage you to use the club, you and your children. They encourage you to come into the club and spend money. Swimming pools for the kids. Tennis courts. We have our ladies' auxiliary. We have our ladies' luncheon. So you go there every day and spend money and it becomes your life. And then when the husband says you are disposable, you are swept out with a broom. I never considered myself to be a second-class citizen. . . . I was shocked when it happened."

Just as shocked was Dale Stark Leff, who learned after her divorce that her former husband got the membership, even though he didn't particularly want it. Mrs. Leff, a retail executive and television fashion coordinator in New York City, grew up going to the Meridian Hills Country Club in Indianapolis, Indiana, one of the premier clubs in the city. Her parents were members, and she spent her teenage years there meeting friends, playing tennis and golf.

When she married her lawyer husband in the early 1970s, they became members of the club. When the marriage ended in 1990, she learned that her husband, whom she had brought into the club, held their shares of stock in the club. A year after an amicable divorce, the club's officers told him, not her, that she, not he, would have to go—club rules.

"I'm terribly angry. It's as if I disappeared from the face of the earth. I was a nonentity in the club's eyes. The club never wrote to me, never asked me what I wanted." After the divorce and with her former spouse's permission, she returned to the club for various events, including a party she gave for her mother's seventieth birthday. She would sign his name and reimburse him for costs.

"Then one day the club notified him I was a divorced woman and not a member of the club. My family and I were absolutely disgusted, just disgusted. My mother won't go back there."

When she thinks about it now, Mrs. Leff, who was known at the club as Dale Stark Shumate, still gets upset. This was her social world for years. And in a small city, it is the best place to meet people. Some difficulty came from "the married women at the club who didn't appreciate single women at the club," she said.

As a professional she viewed the club as essential to her business world. "I was professionally and socially hampered when I was thrown out. I had been active in social events and charities. I would invite my friends, many of whom were my clients, to the club. Then I could not do that anymore." Her former husband was also upset, she said. "He was as angry and disturbed as I was. But he gave way to their rules."

And the rules were, after all, on the man's side.

The rules generally are. Be it New York, Indiana, or California, or any number of states in between, divorce generally benefits the man, even if he agrees in a divorce settlement to give his wife the club membership.

That is what happened in the case of Mary Ann Warfield, who for eleven years was a family member at the Peninsula Golf and Country

Club, an old-line club surrounded by ancient sycamores some miles inland from San Francisco. It is a typical country club for families—with Saturday-night dances, tennis courts, and club tournaments.

Mary Ann, her former husband, and their son and daughter were members of the 350-member club. They joined in 1970. Mary Ann was a big hit at the club, because she was one of those women who lived and breathed golf. Her father, a golf pro who lives in Oregon, taught her the game. She entered her first tournament when she was nine. She was the first girl on the all-male golf team in high school, and she earned a letter each year. Her wedding gift from her husband was a set of woods.

As a young woman her handicap had been as low as a six and her dream had been to play on the LPGA Tour. That dream didn't materialize, but at Peninsula she was active in interclub competition. She was the women's club champion for seven years. She was also a real-estate agent who often met clients at the club. Golf and the club were central to her life and her livelihood.

When the Warfields divorced in 1981, there was never any question in their minds that Mary Ann and the two children, Wendy and Brad, would get the golf membership. Her husband wanted it that way because she was the ardent golfer in the family. During the divorce proceedings, she paid the country club bills. When the divorce became final, her lawyer told her to file her divorce papers with the club. "If I had never filed the damn thing, things would not still be going on. My whole life would have been different," she said later. Once she filed her divorce papers, the board told her she was not entitled to her husband's equity membership since he was the shareholder and equity holder of record. At the time, the Warfields' membership, originally purchased for $7,200 in 1970, was worth about $50,000.

The club did offer Mrs. Warfield a redemption fee of $6,129, which represented Mr. Warfield's membership. She refused. It also offered her a special membership. She was now asked to pay $10,000 as an initiation fee for a nonproprietary membership. She would have no equity interest.

"Don't start taking things away from me and then tell me it's okay. I'll get a token membership for which I have to pay more and get less. I already had a family membership. It didn't make sense to me. The only thing different was I was divorced. I told the board, 'I am not that dumb.' The board said, 'That's the way it is, Mary Ann.'"

"I love golf and I had represented Peninsula for over ten years. I play better than most men. And this was their response. I said there is something wrong here. I felt what they were doing was a slap in the face. So I said, Good-bye—I'll see you in court."

When she filed her lawsuit, she became persona non grata at the club. "The club was very important to my business. I suffered extreme backlash from people I thought were my friends at the club. Once I was invited to play, but another woman took my friend aside and said, 'Don't invite Mary Ann. The lawsuit is still going on.' "

Thus began the longest court battle in the nation over a woman's right to her husband's membership in a private club. The club could have changed its ways for a person who represented the club as its champion. It didn't.

Now the lawsuit, which has been up and down the court ladder a handful of times, has taken on a life of its own. The case is now in its four-teenth year. The California Supreme Court took it for review in 1994. Mary Ann Warfield now lives in Sacramento, and she rues the day she ever got involved with the courts. (Warfield's court case appears in Chapter 9.)

Each club deals with divorce differently. At one East Coast club, a woman was permitted to keep the membership provided her former husband did not move back to the area within five years and claim it.

At another club, there is concern that wealthy women, often daughters of members, are getting pushed out in favor of their former husbands, who have inherited the membership under the bylaws. The very women who were helping to endow the club were being pushed out. The club's solution: if the marriage breaks up before ten years, the woman keeps the membership; if after ten years, the man gets it. If a wife's marriage is precarious, she'd better act to end it before the ten-year rule takes effect.

Finally, some clubs have done away with marital status as the basis for membership. At one West Coast golf club, a couple may be married but each person pays his or her own initiation fee and dues. This simplifies matters if there is a divorce because each spouse may make his or her own independent decision whether to stay or not.

So not all clubs are backward when it comes to divorce. Some actually think about individual situations, especially if the woman is well-liked, has been a long-term family member, and just happens to be a superb golfer.

Brooke Knapp of Los Angeles met those qualifications. She is a sportswoman, an aviator, and a golfer with an eight handicap. For years she lived with her husband in a house on the thirteenth fairway at the Bel-Air Country Club, west of Beverly Hills. After they divorced, Ms. Knapp wanted to stay at the club "and continue my lifestyle as I had known it for the past sixteen years." By that she meant she wanted to be a regular member, as her husband had been. She also wanted full voting and equity privileges.

It took the club more than six months to think it over, she said. And then they admitted her as a full woman member. The club has had two or three other women members in the past. When they admitted Ms. Knapp in 1988, she was the only woman member at the time. "I wasn't applying as a test case. It was a natural progression for me, and it seemed that way to the board as well. I probably knew more members than anyone else there," she said.

She said she was delighted the club admitted her. "What's most exciting," she said, was that "when they decided to take in a woman member, they didn't alter the bylaws in any way. Other clubs have invited women and put restrictions on their membership. Bel-Air offered the complete regular membership package. I have the exact rights of any other of the four hundred and thirty-five regular members," she said. In 1988, its initiation fee was $55,000, with monthly dues in the $300 range.

There may have been one other factor that prompted the board to give Ms. Knapp the nod. Although they knew her, liked her, and found her a worthy member, they also knew that Los Angeles had recently adopted an ordinance banning discrimination based on gender, religion, or race in private golf and country clubs. Private clubs had been put on notice.

❧ *Being Widowed* ❧

I've been through this twice. I've paid twice. I don't think I should be put in a position where I have to join Paradise Valley Country Club a third time.

—Dorothy Moller

Widowhood is the final stage of marriage. Unlike divorce, widowhood permits a woman to stay at the club where she has spent most of her adult life.

This is a comforting thought to most widows. They can remain within the social world of the club, and that is heartening to them as they age. They play in their husband's shoes, so to speak. At some clubs their numbers are quite large. At Palma Ceia Golf and Country Club in Tampa, Florida, one of the area's most exclusive clubs, there are roughly two hundred widows.

Often wives are offered a variety of club options when their mates die. The real golfers among them choose a golfing membership. Others accept a social membership, without golf privileges. Still others agree to sell their membership rights, often to the club, for a hefty fee. The club generally gives the widow six months to make up her mind. Sometimes that time is insufficient. One woman who had been at her club for forty years was so morose after her spouse died that she sold her membership. When she felt better and decided to return to the club, she had to pay all over again, and at rather steep prices.

Golf and country clubs typically outline in their bylaws a variety of approaches to widowhood. Sometimes widows pay half price, at least for a while. Or, in rare instances, the widow becomes the full member and finally gets to vote and possibly hold an executive position at the club. More often, widowhood means no vote and no standing at all.

Usually if a woman did not have voting or property rights before her husband died, she won't get them after. The bylaws at many clubs simply do not allow a widow to inherit the membership, quite apart from the wishes of her departed husband.

What if the widow wants to remarry? Watch the fine print here. Some clubs have bylaws that say if a widow remarries, her new husband must first pass club scrutiny and the couple must pay a new initiation fee in order for him to become a member. A man who is widowed does not face the same problem.

Dorothy Moller has been asked to face this issue more than once in the thirty-five years that she has been a family member at Paradise Valley Country Club, one of Arizona's most exclusive clubs. Supreme Court Justice Sandra Day O'Connor and her husband are honorary members there.

Dorothy Moller has been made a widow twice while a family

member of Paradise Valley. The first time Mrs. Moller was widowed she was forced to resign. The second time she was offered a "legacy" membership, but not a full voting membership. If she remarries she pays steep new initiation fees. She doesn't think this is fair.

"The thing that's so annoying is that a man can marry and divorce, or do whatever he wants, and all he does is call the office and say, 'My wife's name is now Jane and not Mary.' And that's all that's involved. If his wife dies, same thing. The club doesn't check, doesn't screen her. Nothing. But reverse it and I'm out again."

Mrs. Moller is an avid golfer who likes to play every day and usually does so either at Paradise Valley or at Phoenix Country Club, another exclusive enclave. She also plays at two clubs she belongs to in Santa Barbara. Her handicap is eighteen. Sparkling, funny, down-to-earth, a woman who has spent most of her life within the social world of country clubs, she hardly seems a likely candidate to sue her club. But here she is in 1995, and that is precisely what she has done.

In 1960, Dorothy and her first husband were invited to join Paradise Valley. They paid a large initiation fee. He died in 1963. "Plunk, I was a widow," she said. As a widow member she paid less dues and had no guest privileges.

She picks up the story. "In 1965 I married Joe Moller, and immediately I was thrown out of the club. I was just out." The reason? Widows who remarry are no longer married to the prior member. If the Mollers wanted to join, it would be up to Joe Moller to seek admission. That's because he would own the shares.

"I loved to play golf. My husband Joe, who had never played golf, immediately took it up, and we started playing together. I had belonged to another club, Desert Forest, and they just transferred my membership over to my new spouse and me. But not at Paradise Valley. So we joined Phoenix Country Club, and soon after our friends at Paradise Valley pushed for our admission. We paid a five-figure initiation fee (which she paid for) and we got back into the club." The year was 1968.

So in a space of eight years, Dorothy Moller had twice joined Paradise Valley and twice paid steep initiation fees for the privilege. In October 1993, Joe Moller died. Soon after, she received a letter from the club saying she could have a nonvoting "legacy" golf or social membership, that she would pay two-thirds of the dues, and that she had six months to make up her mind or she would be out. All in the same letter. "Real class," she says.

Mrs. Moller went to speak to the chairman of the membership committee. "I told him, 'I want a regular membership. I don't know if I am going to remarry or not. But I don't want to give up this option. I've been through this twice, and I don't think I should have to be in the position where I have to join the club a third time.' " (The club's bylaws were amended in 1992 to allow females to join as regular members.)

The club turned down her request for a full membership unless she paid a third nonrefundable initiation fee, this one for $36,500. And there was one other caveat, she says. "Now, get this. They said if they gave me a regular membership and I remarried and then I died, then my spouse would be a member of the club and he would not have been screened." The club next told her she could either become a "legacy golf or social member" with less than full privileges, or her membership would end. Legacy memberships, unlike regular memberships, do not permit her to vote, hold office, or nominate prospects.

She accepted the legacy membership, she said, under protest, but advised the club she would retain her legal options. In January 1995 she sued in Arizona Superior Court, claiming that the state should not provide property tax and liquor license benefits to a club that engages in gender discrimination.

The complaint says that the club's refusal to recognize her as a regular member is "based solely upon her gender and is void as against public policy." And by accepting her initiation fees and dues and then refusing to grant her a regular membership, the club "has been unjustly enriched." Twice. Her lawyer, Amy Gittler, a partner at Brown & Bain in Phoenix, has asked the court to order the club to give her a regular membership and to award her compensatory damages and lawyer's fees.

If Mom doesn't get it, what happens to Dad's membership when he dies? Who inherits it? Generally the father who owns a membership wills it to a son. Most private clubs do not permit fathers to bequeath memberships to daughters, even though the daughter may be the better, more committed golfer. Bequeathing memberships has been one way to assure that only men owned shares in country clubs.

But some clubs are changing. In 1987, Hillcrest Country Club, a predominantly Jewish country club in Los Angeles, whose members have included Groucho Marx, Jack Benny, and George Burns, changed its bylaws to permit members to bequeath memberships to daughters as well as to sons. The club admitted its first regular women members, giving approved women the right to buy a membership, which in 1987 cost $50,000.

Hillcrest and Brentwood Country Club, also in Los Angeles, changed their inheritance bylaws in 1987. Los Angeles had recently adopted an ordinance that barred private clubs from discriminating on the basis of race, religion, or gender, the same ordinance that may have benefited Brooke Knapp at Bel-Air.

A man's membership status at his club is not altered by a change in his marital status. A woman's is. Whether it will remain this way will depend not only on the men but also on the WORMs, the wives of regular members. They are torn between the older values and the new. Many like their role just as it is. When asked to support the goals of single, widowed, or divorced women, they are often reluctant to sign on. Their daughters tell them to change, but many don't want to.

❦ 6 ❦

Getting On

First they wanted to vote. Now they want equal wages. Just wait! Next they'll want to play golf Saturday mornings.

—Conversation of one male golfer to another
Comic strip by Dik Browne.

If the Berlin Wall and communism could collapse in less than a year, might there be hope for an end to men's-only weekend tee times at America's private golf and country clubs? Probably not. The remarkable reality is that communism may be easier to topple than preferential tee times.

Weekend tee times have traditionally been reserved for men and they do not give up that privilege lightly. Social customs run strong and deep and efforts to change the protocol for coveted tee times have set off nasty battles in normally genteel clubs.

Some clubs have opened the golf course on weekend mornings to women rather than see the club's social fabric torn apart. Some have resisted change, creating searing confrontations that have been emotionally and financially costly to all sides. Those who have lived through such an experience say the clash has the capacity to bring out the worst in both sexes.

Men enjoy special tee-time privileges today at many private clubs thanks to tradition. Men owned the shares in the club and they created the rules. Women were seen by men in terms of their social roles in the country club; golf was often considered secondary for them. Wives would have the course mostly to themselves on weekday mornings while their husbands worked; hence the creation of Ladies' Days, the province of Tuesday- or Thursday-morning nine- or eighteen-hole ladies' groups that had exclusive use of the course until noon or 1 P.M. The men often reserved Wednesday afternoons or other weekdays and were free to play unimpeded on weekends. When men and women played together, what better time was there to do so than on a relaxing Sunday afternoon? So began the tradition of letting women on the course on Sunday at 2 or 3 P.M.

These patterns still hold at many private country clubs in America. Clubs did not anticipate executive women or single women who might have an outlook similar to that of their male counterparts. Clubs find it difficult to change their attitudes toward traditional tee times because they are an utterly accepted way of club life. Many women still accept restrictive tee times and make little fuss. These are mostly older nonworking women, often the WORMs, who are shy about asking for voting rights and other privileges. Many older women regard playing on the course as a privilege; younger women are more likely to regard it as a right. If they are new to golf, they are stunned that there exist tee-time restrictions based upon one's sex.

Executive women in particular have found that in asserting what they view as a human right they are defying a deeply ingrained practice in the culture of the private country club. When they move to do something about it, all hell can break loose.

❧ *Showdown at Cedar Brook* ❦

Cedar Brook Golf and Tennis Club in Old Brookville, Long Island, New York, was the scene of a tee-time conflict that escalated to a harassment case and led to what is believed to be the first criminal trial over a tee time in the nation. The year was 1988.

After pressing club officials for weeks, Lee Lowell had finally received permission from the club's management to tee off early one weekend morning. She would be the first woman at the club to do so. She wondered how hard that could be for the men, who were so used to their special weekend tee times. But that system couldn't last forever.

This was America. It was 1988. It would be okay. She was a good golfer.

She and her husband had joined Cedar Brook a few months before. She played there mainly in the summer and autumn months; the remainder of the year the couple lived in Florida and were members of a club that had no restrictions on tee times. She hated the tee-time restrictions at Cedar Brook and had vowed to change them when she joined. One could see why. On weekends the pecking order put women last. First men members teed off. Then men members with male guests. Then honeymooners, of all things. And finally, "Lady members with or without guests." Lady members were spouses.

This day Mrs. Lowell, a former art teacher, faced a special obstacle. She would be playing in a shotgun. A shotgun means golfers begin play simultaneously from all eighteen tees in order to get play moving quickly and to end the round together, usually at a gathering. Had it not rained the previous day and had she gone out with men she knew, events might have turned out differently. As it was, a shotgun meant she would be playing with strangers.

She arrived at the seventeenth tee. "The two gentlemen I was supposed to play with told me they would not play with me." She was bewildered, stunned; she didn't know what to do or say. Being a golfer, she played the hole alone. She then climbed into her cart and went on to the eighteenth tee.

It was there that she first met up with Ronald Forman, the chairman of the men's golf committee. He and a couple of other men were standing in the middle of the fairway, obviously unaware that she had been given permission to play. From where she stood it seemed they were trying to stop play. Mrs. Lowell couldn't understand what was going on. Suddenly, Forman erupted like Mt. Vesuvius. He began yelling obscenities at her and was joined by others. "They kept screaming I could not play," Mrs. Lowell said. Rather than keep to the order of the game and go to the first tee as required, Lee Lowell headed for what she thought was safer ground, the sixteenth tee. It was empty.

Forman and his men revved up their golf carts and went after her. They gunned their carts. That meant that when they floored it, they were trotting along at a solid ten miles an hour. They cursed at Lowell from 150 yards away. Undaunted, she teed off, her drive narrowly missing Forman. As she drove her cart to her ball, Forman walked up to it, picked it up, and put it in his pocket. He continued to curse at her. She fled again, now to the second tee. As she teed it up, a posse of golfers appeared on the horizon, racing toward her in their golf carts. It looked like a group of eight to ten men, including Forman. They stopped and got out in front of her. One of them unzipped his fly and peed in front of her. She coolly observed his penis. "If that's all you've got to show, it really wasn't worth taking out, was it?" she inquired. Then Forman, who would have needed the Green Berets to stop him now, waved the ball he had picked up on the sixteenth hole and threw it at her. "He shook his finger in my face and told me, 'You will never hit another golf ball again.'" Still screaming at her, he kicked her ball off the tee.

Now she was really terrified. She tried not to show it, saying to herself, "Okay, I'll just leave." She took off in her golf cart. But this was not to be. As if in Dodge City, the golf posse, led by the fearless Forman, pursued her up and down the fairways in a frenzied golf-cart chase. You could see their brightly colored trouser legs hanging out the sides of their carts as they careened around turns.

Finally they encircled her. The course appeared to fall silent. "I was alone. But I was determined not to let them run me off," she said. "Yet I was scared. I felt like a child who was afraid of being maimed or hurt. I felt the rage in these men. And Forman reduced me to a child. That's what angers me. I've raised my children, I got myself educated, yet that man diminished me. And where was I? I was in a wealthy county on the fairways of a country club."

She said she felt as if she were being held prisoner. And for a few minutes she was. She glared at the scowling faces. The men were deep into analyzing their next move. How should they resolve what the judge would later describe as Lowell's gender invasion?

While the men were discussing it, she maneuvered her cart away and took off, playing the empty tees, moving quickly from seven to eight to nine and then onto one and five. Afterward, she went to the ladies' room and cried. "I love golf and that's what broke my heart," she said.

A few hours later, the club manager telephoned her at home. She learned that, without ever hearing her side, the golf committee, some of whom had chased her in their carts, had now suspended her for two weeks. The Lowells' life at the club would never be the same. They stayed on, but it wasn't pleasant. Her friends ignored her. "I can't in my heart look at weak women anymore," she says now.

She tried to stay active in the club. She signed up—not surprisingly—for the grievance committee. Learning that, the club's officials disbanded the grievance committee. Her scientist husband was denigrated, too. He would be summoned from lunch to the locker room to find no one there. Both received threatening telephone calls at home. "You better not play or your life is at stake," said one caller.

Having survived the ambush and the humiliation, Lowell took Forman to criminal court. The harassment trial was heard not by a jury but by a judge. But the prosecutor had a heavy burden. She had to prove beyond a reasonable doubt that Forman followed Lowell for ninety minutes, threw a golf ball at her, shouted obscenities at her, and blocked her with a golf cart—all with criminal intent. The judge found Forman's conduct repugnant: "His actions on the golf course in pursuing a lone woman, speaking harshly to her, and bringing the enforcement of golf etiquette to the level of personal intimidation speak for themselves. If the golfing ethics of the membership of the Cedar Brook Club are exemplified by the actions of Ronald Forman, then perhaps it is best that a member with the integrity of Lee Lowell not associate with such an organization." But the judge also said Forman's actions didn't reach the level of a crime and he acquitted him.

Soon after, the club refused to renew the Lowells' membership. Undeterred, she filed a complaint against the club before the New York State Human Rights Commission. It took three years, but in July 1992, the commission ruled in her favor at its first level of inquiry. The commission found "overwhelming evidence" that Cedar Brook had engaged in unlawful discriminatory practices in tee times, at the men's grill, and in refusing to renew the Lowells' membership in retaliation for the complaint she filed. After their ouster, the Lowells joined a resort course, the Marriott's Wind Watch Golf Club on Long Island, where there was no tee-time discrimination. "The best experience we've had," said Lowell. She stayed there for three years before moving to Florida. Her current club has no tee-time restrictions.

She learned plenty from her experience. "I learned that women don't stand up for what is in their hearts and souls. I feel horrible for women because of that. The country club brings it to the fore."

One final irony: In the aftermath of the commission's findings that Cedar Brook discriminated against Mrs. Lowell, the club realized it now fell under the state's public accommodations law. It has since marketed itself accordingly, telling reporters it is a woman-friendly course, with equal access on weekend mornings and a mixed grill. So maybe Mrs. Lowell accomplished something after all for others. For herself, she is still awaiting the financial settlement she feels appropriate. She has rejected offers she found unacceptable. Her case, now ready for the second level, a hearing, is still pending before the commission. It has been seven years since the golf posse took off after her.

❧ *Retaliation in Prince Georges County* ☙

Unlike Lee Lowell, who held a family membership at Cedar Brook and was considered a spouse, Alice Moore holds the membership in her name at the Country Club at Woodmore in Mitchellville, Maryland. Her husband is the spouse, the name found in parenthesis. She is a fine golfer, plays competitively for her club, and is the only female member on the club's board of directors.

She is also one of fifteen named plaintiffs who filed a discrimination complaint with the Maryland attorney general's office, asserting that the club, with 508 members, discriminates against spouses. At Woodmore, *associate members* means *spouses*, and their access to the golf course is restricted unless they hold a full membership, as Mrs. Moore and six other women do.

"My husband and I joined in 1983," Mrs. Moore said. "I am in real estate and wanted to use the club to entertain clients. He is retired. My name is on the certificate. He cannot play golf early Sunday or Saturdays. He doesn't care. We play golf all over, in England and abroad, at public and semiprivate clubs. I play competitive golf. My handicap is about fifteen."

Mrs. Moore became a plaintiff because she was concerned that female spouses, as well as newly recruited female members, were having difficulty getting to play. Woodmore had a history of treating its females poorly.

An independent study the club commissioned in 1992 found that its program for women's golf was deficient. The study found that "women have all but been abandoned by the golf program at the club. Few women play golf regularly at the course, about twenty in the nine-hole group, twenty in the eighteen-hole group. Where else in golf does a club with an excellent golf course that averages 400 golfing memberships produce less than 50 regular golfing women? The answer might be—nowhere else."

At the time the complaint was filed, women's tee times, for spouses or females with memberships in their own name, started at 12:30 on Saturday and 1 P.M. on Sunday. The club also had a men's grill. The club, however, maintained that it practiced no discrimination. Indeed, it viewed its policies as models for other clubs to follow. So it said in a letter to Linda Hitt Thatcher, the attorney and member of the club who brought the complaint on behalf of the fifteen women golfers. She acted after the board rebuffed her efforts for change in tee times and voting and after it turned a deaf ear to the women themselves.

What is remarkable about the board's position is that the club, like many others in Maryland, has a contract with the state that gives the club a huge tax break so long as the club does not sell its land to a developer. To get the tax break under Maryland law, the club may not discriminate against its members.

Mrs. Moore was in a unique position. Elected to the twelve-member board in 1994 for a three-year term, she decided to become a named plaintiff on the complaint. She knew she would be opposing the board, but she had become increasingly frustrated by the failure of the club to institute fairer rules and to come into compliance with Maryland law. For example, a woman doctor who had purchased a membership in her name and paid top dollar for it came into club life in 1994 during a major membership drive to help the club obtain financial solvency. She found she could not play during the morning weekend hours. She wrote to Mrs. Moore for help and received it. She would be "fit in" anytime on Sunday.

After the attorney general's office received the complaint, in June 1994, Mrs. Moore sent out letters in board envelopes informing the membership of the complaint. It did not take long for the board to retaliate. On July 11 she was informed that she had "misappropriated envelopes" and was asked to resign from the board. The same day the board passed a resolution to seek legal counsel to remove her from the board.

Soon after, the attorney general's office notified the club that the law prohibits them from taking retaliatory action against a member once a complaint has been filed with the state. Moreover, the state would move against the club to stop any such activity, the club was told.

So far, says Mrs. Moore, the board has done nothing more against her, though through its staff it has kept tabs on precisely the times her "associate" husband plays golf.

She is philosophical about her role. She points out that a number of new and expensive private clubs in the area have recently opened. "They do not discriminate against women. They are more progressive. The law in Maryland says they have to be. These older clubs are fighting to keep the status quo. It's the good old boy network. The older men oppose it. But someday they'll get the message."

Skirting Medinah No. 3

Speaking of the good old boy network, the one at Medinah Country Club in suburban Chicago was in fine form back in 1989, the year the club's board made a remarkable decision that few knew about.

Medinah No. 3, one of the most magnificent golf courses in the country, had been the site of two U.S. Opens and was selected by the United States Golf Association to host a third U.S. Open in 1990. Each fall, the USGA conducts a meeting for a volunteer group of twenty-five handicapping experts from across the country at the site of the following June's U.S. Open. The group pays their way to the meeting and examines the course for the U.S. Open. Letting them play the Open course is the USGA's way of thanking the volunteers.

The chairman of the USGA handicap committee in 1989 was Judy Bell, its first female officer and arguably the most influential woman in amateur golf. That year marked the first time a woman had been chairman of the handicap committee. A Denver businesswoman who is a fine golfer and has made a tremendous commitment to the game, Judy Bell had been a member of the USGA executive committee since 1987. She is in line to become the USGA's first woman president in its 100 years of existence. (This accomplishment would be marked by ceremony on both sides of the Atlantic. If she becomes the president, she would automatically be the first woman member of the Royal and Ancient Golf Club of St. Andrews in Scotland, an occurrence that might well leave the British speechless.)

Back in September of 1989, she was the object of some unabashed discrimination at Medinah. At the time, Dean Knuth, the senior director of handicapping for the USGA, was in charge of organizing the handicap procedure meeting held at Medinah on October 5. "I had to send Medinah a list of the players about a month before our meeting," said Mr. Knuth. "The club came back and said, 'Well, the problem is, you have a woman listed among the players. Our club policy at Medinah is that women can play the No. 1 and No. 2 courses at any time, but they can only play the No. 3 course on certain days and certain times.' And so it would not be possible for her to play in the pairing on the day the committee was going to Medinah No. 3."

Mr. Knuth was stunned. "I then wrote the club a letter. I said this was inconvenient for us. Judy was a member of the executive committee of the USGA and an official of the U.S. Open at Medinah. We asked the club to reconsider and make an exception to allow her to play. The Medinah board of directors actually discussed it, and they came back and said, 'She's welcome to play Nos. 1 and 2, and No. 3 on a different day.'

"I was again surprised by their response, and I went to David Fay [the executive director of the USGA] and I said, 'I propose we cancel the meeting there and we'll go someplace else.' He agreed and said, 'We don't want to have a meeting there under those conditions.' We then took the steps to go elsewhere, to another very good Chicago club. We would meet there and play golf there and not let anybody play Medinah. And then I got that all arranged. I had even asked for the assistance of the Chicago District Golf Association, and they were trying to help because they didn't agree with Medinah's policy either. They made inquiries and couldn't accomplish the change either with Medinah. So we were all set to go to another course.

"Then I called Judy and explained the situation to her and said we had set up the meeting at another good club. And she said, 'I don't want you to do that. I want the meeting to be at Medinah. I don't agree with the club's policy, but I don't want to make a big issue out of it.' And she added, 'I have business I can do in Chicago during the golf time.'

"She said she wanted the meeting to be held at Medinah because the reason we were doing this in the first place was not for her but for the twenty-five volunteers who were paying their own expenses to come to this meeting. 'I don't want them to lose the opportunity to play a U.S. Open course,' she said.

"I told David, and David said he didn't agree with Judy on that. He said we should go elsewhere. We both thought the Medinah policy was ridiculous. Then David spoke to Judy. Again she directed us not to make a big deal about it. She just forbade us from moving the meeting. So we went to Medinah and she didn't show up until the dinner and the meeting." She did not play Medinah No. 3.

The irony here, of course, is that the USGA was poised to act on behalf of Ms. Bell, an action that would have portrayed Medinah in a deservedly unsympathetic light. But the men of the USGA were stopped by the very woman who was the object of discrimination. Her refusal to move the site allowed twenty-five volunteers to play a U.S. Open venue, something they could not have done otherwise.

Not every woman would agree with Judy Bell's decision. Many women who have confronted discriminatory tee times have done what Mr. Knuth and Mr. Fay did; they work behind the scenes to try to straighten it out, and failing to do so, they act to assert their rights.

❧ *Cheval's Management in a Snit* ❧

Molly O'Dea is one of those women. "Whatever she thinks is right she takes to the end," said her mother, Marion O'Dea, when she heard of her daughter's decision to sue her country club in order to get a weekend-morning tee time.

Molly O'Dea grew up playing golf at New York's Elmira Country Club. The former pro there remembers her as the best golfer of her age at ten or twelve. She began playing when she was four years old, loves the game, and has always been competitive. So it was natural that she would assert her rights when as an adult she found she and a client could not tee off on Saturday morning at her new country club.

An executive at the Xerox Corporation, she says that when she joined the newly built Cheval Country Club in Lutz, Florida, a non-equity residential golf community that boasts such illustrious residents as General Norman Schwarzkopf, she did not know full-paying members did not share equal privileges. Unlike spousal "members," as a full-paying member Ms. O'Dea paid the same fees as a single male.

When she told the club she felt she was entitled to the same access to the course as a full-paying male member who works, the "compromise" it offered was to allow her to tee off the back nine on Saturday mornings. Ms. O'Dea mulled over the offer and looked at the back-nine setup. "The back nine was for fivesomes, the ragtag foursomes, leftovers, and women. Going off the back nine just reinforces that you're a second-class citizen," she said. She didn't have to add that a client might think so, too. She had paid $2,500 plus $175 monthly dues, the same as any other new member, and she wanted to start off on the front nine.

Being discriminated against was something new for Molly O'Dea. At thirty-nine she had not felt it at the Xerox Corporation, where she is now the manager of sales operations for the State of Florida. "At Xerox I was treated fairly. The playing field was level. I worked hard. I advanced. When I try to do business on the golf course, I should be given the same level playing field. At home I never felt it. I grew up in a family where we were not raised in the typical sexual stereotypes: the boys cut the grass and the girls do the dishes. We all cut the grass; we all did the dishes. When Cheval said you can't play golf on Saturday morning because you are a woman, and you should feel lucky that you can play at ten o'clock, I just could not accept that."

A sensible, articulate person, Molly first took the issue to the club president. That went nowhere. The club manager wasn't helpful either, she said. After months passed and nothing happened, she went to see a lawyer, Rosemary E. Armstrong. Ms. Armstrong filed a complaint, the first under Florida's new private-clubs antidiscrimination law. The law says a private club, equity or not, with over four hundred members that provides meals and requires fees may not discriminate against protected classes, including women over twenty-one.

In April 1994, after a seven-month inquiry, the Florida attorney general found that Cheval had violated the law, both in its weekend tee-time restrictions and in keeping separate grills. The state gave the club twenty days to change its bylaws. (See letter, Chapter 15.) It pointed out that the club faced fines of up to $100,000 for the grill discrimination. With no consultation with the membership, the club faxed itself into compliance within an hour.

Following the attorney general's ruling, the club made a series of peevish reforms that illustrate just how wacky things can get when a club digs in its heels. Without consulting with the attorney general's office, which later said that none of these steps was necessary or required, the club threatened to end traditional male-only or female-only club competitions, including the popular member-member and member-guest single-sex tournaments that most clubs sponsor. It disbanded the men's and the women's associations, thereby throwing into disarray all outside competitions as well as those held on its own grounds. It created instead a member-only golf association with a men's and women's division. Finally, it ended midweek Ladies' Day. These were largely vindictive rules designed to punish a recalcitrant membership. In other states faced with similar laws, clubs have managed to find ways to keep sex-specific tournaments and competitions. Some months later Cheval did too.

This dispute, like others, generated a good deal of conflict between the wives of spouses and the single women. The head of the Ladies Golf Association at Cheval, for example, was livid over the matter. She said that management was fair to women, giving them special play days and "the honor of holding tournaments on the weekends, which is unheard of at most clubs."

Gregory Durden, the civil-rights chief who handled the case for the state, said he was surprised by this attitude. "They are parents of sons and daughters who are professional people, whom they raised to be fair and to be equal. It does not jibe. It does not make sense to me."

Meanwhile, at Cheval, Ms. O'Dea, a fifteen-handicapper, teed it up on the front nine on the first Saturday morning she was permitted to play. She reported no difficulty but did observe one ranger on the course eight different times.

"I took it in stride. I kept the ball as a souvenir. A couple of men in the golf shop congratulated me. A third guy who looked miserable walked in and said he had played poorly. 'It's this ladies' thing,' he said. 'Let's not discuss that in here,' the pro said."

❧ The Primary Member ❧

Faced with the prospect of lawsuits or legislation or internal unrest among members, country clubs are grappling with ways to handle women's tee-time and membership conflicts. In the last several years, clubs have come up with what sounds like an equitable gender-neutral solution: allow the couple to decide who will be the primary, or designated, or preferred, member. That member, husband or wife, gets the coveted weekend hours (although the wife might not get the membership). This new designation seems to be catching on at clubs around the country.

One of the first clubs to adopt a plan like this was Lakewood Country Club in Rockville, Maryland. But they had a one-time-only plan, approved by the Maryland tax department, which meant the designated player would retain the privilege for as long as the couple were members. They couldn't trade positions even if they wanted to.

Under this policy, it should come as no surprise that of the club's then 560 members, only thirteen wives got the coveted slot. There was a further complication. When Thomas R. Smith, then an associate editor at *National Geographic*, designated his wife, Mary, an editor at the magazine, as the preferred member, the Smiths had been led to believe that the designated member would have voting privileges. But the golf club changed the language from designated *member* to designated *golfer*. "The executive board said, whoa, watch out. We'll end up with a bunch of women who can vote, and we may even have one on the board," Mrs. Smith recalled.

Some clubs have adopted primary membership policies less onerous than a lifetime decision. Some clubs permit couples to determine a primary member on an annual basis. One club, Carrollwood Village Golf and Tennis Club in Tampa, Florida, changed its membership category after two women family members, Dr. Ruth Hanno and Mrs. Mary Stiegler, an elementary-school teacher, sued for better weekend tee times. (See Dr. Hanno's letter to the club in Chapter 8.) Under the primary-member policy, the second adult would pay an additional initiation fee of $500, plus added monthly dues.

But the primary-member idea at Carrollwood met with great opposition among some working women golfers at the club and in the press as well. The reason, said the working WORMs, was that they couldn't convince their husbands to give up their prime tee times. Some months after the women filed their complaint, Carrollwood dropped the primary-member idea, made wives members, and gave open weekend tee times with no increased fees.

The working WORMs had triumphed. A side benefit: Now couples who like to play together can do so whenever they want.

The problem with the "primary member" or "designated member" idea is that whichever member gives it up experiences the loss as a real deprivation. If both members of a couple work, both may feel the need of weekend tee times, and this plan generally doesn't permit that. The crowding problem this could create doesn't happen often. People are creatures of habit, and most will continue their past practices. The relatively few who really do need weekend tee times will have them. At least that seems to be the experience so far. To single members of either sex it might seem unfair if a husband and wife sharing a membership both tried to play during the crowded weekend morning hours, and some clubs have made adjustments in fees.

Clubs may handle the dual-tee-time issue in a variety of ways: by raising dues for family membership, or lowering them for singles to equalize the burden; by allowing tee times by lot, so that no one can complain of discrimination; by eliminating any sex-segregated events on weekends, and putting them all on weekdays so tee-time availability for all members is at its maximum when the course is most in demand.

A variety of other solutions will occur to creative clubs. But to force one member of a couple to allow the other to prevail on a long-term basis strikes many as simply unfair, perhaps especially because men who have traditionally benefited will simply want to keep on doing so. Wives who know that will be under pressure to acquiesce, and we'll be right back where we started. Whether this system works, and it is one that increasing numbers of clubs are adopting, depends on its flexibility. Can spouses switch with ease within the membership? If the primary membership is based on a monthly, rather than a yearly or lifetime, requirement, it may better serve the needs of the couple. The main drawback is that couples who want to play a round of golf together on a weekend morning cannot.

Of course, the simplest way may be the best: give the husband and his wife each a half vote and let them play whenever they can get a starting time. A few clubs have adopted this approach and report that it works just fine.

❧ *Louise and Karsten Solheim Do It Their Way* ❧

Louise and Karsten Solheim, now the owners of Karsten Manufacturing Co. in Phoenix, Arizona, the manufacturers of the highly successful Ping golf clubs, once went out to play a round of golf at Moon Valley Country Club in Phoenix, Arizona.

The year was 1975 and the time was 2:45 P.M. "Karsten and I were on the first tee. We played the first hole and went on to the second or maybe it was the third. What we did not know was that someone complained. The pro shop sent someone to bring us in off the course. We went. Karsten was quite upset because there was nobody in front of us or behind us," Louise Solheim recalled.

The violation? The wrong they had committed? Teeing it up before 3 P.M. That was the time women were allowed on the course if no man was waiting.

The Solheims did not forget the incident. And when the success of the Pings made them among the wealthiest families in America, they purchased Moon Valley and changed the tee times. Well, sort of. There is still a men's day on Saturday, but only until noon, not 3 P.M. as before. And there is a Ladies' Day on Tuesday. Women can play any time on Sunday.

Is change in the air? Perhaps. Mrs. Solheim observes that women still can't tee off between the hours of 11 A.M. and 2 P.M. on Wednesday, Thursday, and Friday, the days men often take clients out. "It's very difficult for the professional woman who wants to take clients out to lunch at the club. That hampers women," says the wife of golf's most celebrated clubmaker. The fact that they own the club and it still has such rules speaks volumes about the sacredness of tee times.

❦ 7 ❦

Getting Fed

No Girls Allowed
　　—Sign on a boy's treehouse

In 1970 Liz Kahn, one of Great Britain's foremost female golf writers, attempted to get into the Trophy Room at the Royal and Ancient Golf Club at St. Andrews, Scotland, where her male colleagues were headed for a drink.

She was stopped by an attendant.

"Ladies are not allowed in here," she was told.

"How extraordinary," she muttered.

"No, madam, not even the queen," the attendant replied.

Numerous American clubs have modeled their own grillrooms after those of the British. The grillroom is the last place for all-male camaraderie at many clubs and some men will fight fiercely to preserve it. Here is where good conversation can take place, where men recount their golf game, tell jokes, settle the bets in their foursome. On many occasions professional women have been not only barred from the grill but stopped at the front door to the private country club, or evicted from a meeting within, or forced to use a rear door to attend an event. Sometimes their presence indoors has prompted management to move an entire meeting to the outdoor terrace.

These actions diminish and embarrass the woman and her associates. They cause such general discomfort that the male person hosting an event at the golf club may well decide it's not worth the trouble to invite a woman colleague to the next one. Ultimately she stops being included, and that does not bode well for her career.

Charles Mechem, Jr., the LPGA commissioner, knows firsthand what being turned away at the door means. When he was chairman of the board at Taft Broadcasting, he and some of his colleagues went to negotiate a major business deal at a luncheon club in Ohio.

"We had with us our treasurer. We went up the steps, and they refused to let her in. I told them we had a luncheon meeting. I was just beside myself. I had never run into anything like that in my life, though I know now it obviously happened a lot. I wanted to call the police or something, and she said no. Finally they said, 'Okay, but she will have to go around through the kitchen.'. . . And she said, 'Don't make a fuss.' And we went in and had this meeting. I was totally outraged by all this. This kind of thing has bothered me as long as I can remember."

Many private luncheon clubs in the United States have changed their policies and now admit women. But that is only in recent years. In days when it was socially inconvenient to bar women entirely, they were permitted to enter the private club through the side or back door. It still goes on at country clubs.

A friend was playing one day at the Wannamoisett Country Club in Rumford, Rhode Island, and he commented that the front door of the clubhouse was truly beautiful. "Yes," said his partner, "but it's only for the men. The ladies are not allowed in the front door. They have to use the side door."

So old habits are hard to change. And at the men's grill old habits have a life of their own. Even at some clubs where women have been successful in getting the grill opened, or the state has said 'Open it or you will lose a tax break,' that doesn't necessarily mean the grill is used by a mix of men and women.

There are various ways for men to open their grill and still keep it all-male. One way is to apply social pressure. At Lakewood Country Club in Rockville, Maryland, the men's grill has been integrated for five years. But, says Mary Smith, a spousal member at the club, "there are still a lot of the old coots sitting in the corner growling when women come in."

So ingrained is the social conditioning at some clubs that even when women win the right to enter the grill, many voluntarily tend to stay away. At Los Angeles Country Club, one of the premier golf courses in the country, discrimination has long been practiced, against actors as well as the usual categories. (There is also a rule at the club that no woman may play the course unless she is wearing a skirt.) We hear the club's bylaws are now gender-neutral. This means the men's grill is now officially open to women in skirts. But we are told that women rarely, if ever, pass through its doors. Old habits may be as constraining as firm rules.

The men's grill is still a staple at many of the nation's golf and country clubs. If a woman steps into the men's grill, she is evicted. She may also be expelled from the places leading up to the grill or adjacent to it. Over the years I have collected eviction anecdotes from women. One was removed from the veranda outside the grill. Another was banned from the grill but was passed a sandwich through the grill window so that she could dine alone on the veranda.

Women have been banned from a porch or veranda in front of the grill, from a pathway leading up to the grill, from a bench on the path to the grill, or at any other demarcation area that men feel sacred to the premises of the grill. These sorts of rules do not sit well with everyone when the club assesses fees on family members to renovate the men's grill. Women have filed lawsuits and gone to their legislators when they have been forced to pay a bill to benefit a grill they cannot enter.

If the men care so deeply about it, why not let them have it? Don't men have the right to have their own little place, all to themselves? Haven't we given women enough? they ask. Haven't they taken over our men's schools, our golf courses, our lives? Is there no privacy? Is there no way to keep them out?

The answer is that if men do care that deeply, they will now have to go to great lengths to preserve the status quo. They can buy their own golf course and make the club all-male. If they keep their numbers small and select, and the activity strictly golf, they will be able to have a men's grill. If, however, a private country club leases out its facilities, permits business to be conducted and is located in a state that bars discrimination on the basis of gender, the club may well face trouble.

Women want access to the grill not because they wish to impose themselves on a male sanctuary but because they, too, want to be able to entertain guests, both friends and clients. Single or married women, professional or not, say exclusion from the grill harms women on a personal and professional level. When a private country club is designed for families, sooner or later the men's grill may become an embarrassment. This is particularly true if the club hosts an outside professional golf tournament.

❧ *Confusing a Bar with a Urinal* ❧

Let's look at the elegant old Oakland Hills Country Club, site of the 1996 U.S. Open. For the longest time the club had a men's grill. How then did Oakand Hills' men's grill become a men's locker room? Answer: When desperation set in.

At least that's what I think happened when the State of Michigan adopted an antidiscrimination law in 1992 that applied across the board to all private clubs. Faced with the prospect of having to admit the ladies for lunch, the club's grill became a locker room.

The men reasoned that since the men's grill was adjacent to the men's locker room, they would simply extend the premises of the locker room, thereby keeping the ladies out. This small change in nomenclature that bespoke so much might never have become known publicly had it not been for the six women whom the men had permitted into their grill on a daily basis: the female waitresses whom they permitted to serve them.

Overnight the new law brought hardship for these female employees. Once they had earned good money serving the men in the men's grill; now they were told that since the grill had become a locker room, their very gender precluded their employment. They were furious. Their efforts to resolve the issue with the club went nowhere. And so, as often occurs with disputes in the last decade of the twentieth century, the employees hired an attorney.

His name was George Washington. He had never before seen anything like this setup, he said. He filed a lawsuit. He noted that Oakland Hills is the site in 1996 of the most important golf tournament in America, the U.S. Open, a lucrative and prestigious event for the club. He not only observed that the club had a men's grill, but also discovered that there were no women with full memberships among the club's 575 bondholders, and no blacks. (He later learned that at the time the lawsuit was filed one woman and one black had received temporary admission.)

The club's legal committee took some time studying the status of the men's grill–locker room. Meanwhile, then State Senator Lana Pollack, the sponsor of the Michigan legislation, pointed out to the gentlemen of the club that renaming the grill the locker room could cost the club its liquor license.

The lawsuit was eventually settled; there was a monetary agreement and the female employees are back in the grill. But Senator Pollack had the last word: "That they would confuse a bar with a urinal is preposterous," she said.

❧ *Westchester Keeps a Tournament and* ❧ *Loses an All-Male Sanctuary*

One expects that Oakland Hills will resolve this problem before the 1996 Open. In case the good men there are still thinking about it, they ought to know what happened at Westchester Country Club in Rye, New York, in 1992. Westchester has been the site of the Buick Classic for several years, a PGA Tour event that attracts television coverage and thousands of fans to the club each June.

When the Buick Classic arrived in 1992, it was met with picket signs held aloft by members of the National Organization for Women. The signs spoke of discriminatory tee times and the men's grill. Buick was stunned. Stunned.

Women, they knew, bought cars—their cars.

Buick wrote to the tournament's other sponsors, telling them that they would withdraw as chief commercial backer unless the club opened the men's grill to women.

The club decided to end the men's grill, a gesture that drew protests from some five hundred members, who petitioned the board to retain the grill. Faced with such overwhelming opposition, the club confronted a dilemma: give up the Classic and its lucrative financial benefits, which helped to offset the club's expenses, or integrate the grill.

"Westchester Country Club is a private club. The choice to hold the Classic and other outings at the club, however, brings our private rules into the public eye," a letter to the members said. "Your view of whether the men's grill is a discriminatory practice or an expression of freedom should be weighed against the desire of the companies which hold outings at the Club, including the Buick Classic, to avoid the negative publicity that has and could result from sponsoring an event at a club that maintains a men's grill. Some companies may decide not to hold outings at the club if a men's grill is maintained, and may even question paying for club membership fees. Some members may be forced to resign if discriminatory policies come into conflict with their own business policies, associations and community activities."

Their next step was a survey. Of the club's 985 members, 616 persons responded, a large number for a mail survey. Although a majority, 55 percent, felt that in principle the club was entitled to have a men's grill, fully 75 percent voted to keep the Buick Classic and 71 percent favored a mixed grill.

In the end, economics had won out over the social pressure to keep the grill all-male. The prospect of losing the prestigious event, which helped finance the club's activities and generated funds for a local hospital, convinced even the diehards. The grill opened its doors to women. Buick stayed on. The negative publicity ended.

❦ A Woman's Trophy and a Men's Grill ❧

There are many things that hold a woman back in golf that are not common to the two other popular sports—tennis and swimming. I know of no tennis clubs that bar women, and there are no restrictions at all on the use of the ocean.

—Glenna Collett, 1928

The most poignant tale about men's grills did not concern locker rooms or picket lines. After renowned amateur champion Glenna Collett Vare died, in 1989, Metacomet Country Club, the Rhode Island club where she learned to play and where her father was president, wished to create a memorial in her honor.

Mrs. Vare, the acknowledged first lady of women's amateur golf in the U.S., holds the record for winning the most United States Women's Amateur golf championships—six in all—from 1922 through 1935.

She had spent a day at Metacomet when she was fourteen.

"Standing on the broad verandah, perched high on a Rhode Island hill, I watched Dad send a long, raking tee-shot through the air. It drove far down the fairway," she wrote in her book, *Ladies in the Rough*. "Tremendously impressed, I hurried out on the course and asked for permission to play along with him. With beginner's luck my first shot off the tee went straight down the fairway. . . . 'The coming champion!' shouted one sun-browned veteran, who asked me to duplicate my swing. His comments were followed by others of lavish praise and warm encouragement as I moved from hole to hole. I had a natural golf-swing . . . . Dad was elated and my head was bursting with the soaring dreams that only the very young and ambitious live and know. As I came off the course after the first game, my destiny was settled. I would become a golfer."

Many years later Mrs. Vare's two grown children, Glenna and Ned, named after their mother and her brother, may have remembered that passage when as adults they read with pride a proposal from Metacomet to honor their mother.

The club's decision to honor Glenna Collett Vare came shortly after she died. The club president asked the children "for memorabilia from your mother's great golfing career in order to have a permanent memorial in her honor here at Metacomet." The children decided on an early trophy and they were invited to present it to the club at a ceremony on October 30, 1991.

Just before the ceremony, the club's top officials, including a man who had been a golf partner of Ned's for years, took Glenna's husband and Ned for a celebratory drink at the bar in the men's grill. Glenna and the wife of another friend who was there were not invited in. They were left to sit on a bench outside. Glenna was stunned. Ned later said that he went inside in deference to his long friendship with one of the members who was present that night. "I was appalled," he later said, by "its discourtesy, especially as it became prolonged."

Glenna Collett Vare's daughter was upset. "I was angry. I kept thinking to myself, How can I get out of here, how can I get the car keys and go home?" She said later, "No one has ever done anything like that to me in my life. It was so crassly done. It had never occurred to me that I was a second-class citizen. "

As Ned and his sister reflected afterward on the incident, they thought about their mother. "Our mother would never have stood for such treatment," Mr. Vare said. "And had she known about Metacomet's policies toward women, she would not have donated anything to honor such a club. Had my sister and I known about the rules, we would not have donated anything, either. . . . There would have been no ceremony."

The club's president sought to explain, but offered no apology. In a letter to Vare and his sister, in February 1992, then club president Robert Verri asserted that there was no discrimination against women. He said they had their own locker room, grillroom, and card room. Mr. Verri remarked that no member had ever complained about the arrangement, and he added, "we allow our women more favorable tee times than other clubs in the area." The club's president went on to urge the Vare children not to deprive the club of their mother's memory "by removing her trophy."

Vare and his sister thought about it. They then told the club they would give them time to change their discriminatory rules against women, but "our request remains that Metacomet put into writing that it disallows discrimination by sex ." If the club could not do that, then it must return the trophy, the children wrote.

The answer came by registered mail. Without comment, the club returned the trophy.

❧ 8 ❧

Getting Heard

Responsible club leaders will move to implement a true race and gender integration of the game immediately. It is a painless process and in the long run the game will be better off.

—Reed Mackenzie

Ned Vare and his sister tried to work with the leaders of Metacomet Country Club to change its policies. So did most of the women who faced problems getting in, getting on, getting fed. On some occasions they succeeded, often they failed, but for the most part they began their efforts to end unfair practices by working within the structure of the country club.

Their efforts to work from within deserve careful scrutiny. They tell us much about country club life. They are especially important because part of the culture of private clubs is to remain private and out of the public eye. If there is controversy of any kind within the club, it is kept quiet. Again and again as I talked to women for this book, I was struck with how often they thought they were alone in facing these problems, that it was somehow unique to them and *their* situation at *their* club. The result is that they fail to learn from the experiences of women elsewhere.

❧ *Knowing What You're Up Against* ❧

Private country clubs vary enormously, but if they share one common trait it is that the country club stands for retreat and privacy. The country club is a place for sociability, leisure, tranquillity, a relaxed outlook. Many members view life at the club as a retreat from the world, not an occasion for social activism.

The reality may, of course, be different. The club may be riven with factions, may have many members who just want to go their own way. But assuming that the outward appearance, and culture, of the club is one of harmony, and change is being sought by a member, there is a natural starting point for bringing it about. Just imagine what would happen if that member began by finding a tough lawyer, a real barracuda, and threatening a lawsuit. These are moves that will assure ostracism, not support. In the long run it is better to start gently and to start within.

Getting clubs to change is complicated by their organizational form. The permanent staff of clubs, including the manager, is made up of employees who report to a board or to various committees. The board and its committees, in turn, serve for only a brief time. There are many variations, of course, but at most clubs the board members may serve staggered two- or three-year terms, which means that this year's majority on any given issue may become next year's minority. The committees change also. In any case, the boards, as a rule, are not bound by their committees. Often a board appoints a committee to evaluate women's concerns, the committee recommends changes, and the board turns them down. Two other features of board life may influence outcomes. First, the past history of male dominance in such clubs may mean that unless one or more males are enlisted for support, the attitude may be that these are "just the women again." Calls may go unreturned, letters unanswered. The second factor comes into play when there are lawyers on the board. There are conciliators and hard-liners, and outcomes may turn on which view is represented when an issue arises. These facts of country club life may be frustrating in the extreme to anyone who is working for change. Those persons will profit from knowing as much as possible about how the club conducts its affairs, and about positions taken and attitudes expressed by its most influential members.

There was a time when those attitudes would have been common to virtually all the male members. The most stable, historically rooted feature of club life is the culture of male dominion. It is so deeply institutionalized that it is often unnoticed, taken for granted. It is not as bad as the five hundred years of "soaking in male chauvinist piggery" that Peter Dobereiner says is true of Great Britain, but it is still present in the life of most country clubs. It exists in the informal banter of the male foursome. For a putt that falls far short of the cup, "Nice putt, Gladys!" It exists in common practices: if a man's tee shot doesn't make it past the ladies' tee, he may have to buy a round of drinks for the foursome when they get back to the clubhouse. What humiliation—not even up to where the women tee off! These underlying attitudes sometimes find expression in the visible features of country clubs. According to a recent story in the San Jose *Mercury News*, visitors at the all-male Gator Creek Golf Club in Sarasota, Florida, would find flags on the front nine holes bearing "pictures of a woman's breasts, those on the back nine a woman's buttocks."

But it would perpetuate a stereotype to assume that all males adhere to the old value system. Some still do, many do not. The latter may be a silent minority (or majority, as the case may be) because the most vocal and strident male voices may support the status quo. But silent or not, many men are objective enough to see the injustices in some club rules, and those with daughters often show a special interest. They might not have confronted these issues in connection with their wives, but when they see practices that may damage their daughters' careers, they have a newfound stake in changing the rules. Where this is the case, women working for change from within may find support from male members. It would be equally a mistake to assume that women will naturally support the fighter for equal rights. As women, mostly career women, struggle to get full access to the private country club, they make an unpleasant discovery. Often the older women in the club, the more traditional country club wives, have become their enemy. They position themselves as defenders of the status quo.

Sometimes the more traditional woman decides it is time for a change. She may start out full of vigor to get a vote, to sit on the board, to become a full member, to change outmoded tee times. This established wife may actually write a letter to the board or consult the ladies association at her club. She may say, it's time: She is a fast player, a low-handicapper. She deserves this. And then just before the vote, she changes her mind.

"It happened at our club," said Mary Smith, the retired senior editor at *National Geographic* whom we met in Chapter 6. "The women were poised to act. And then they were pressured by their husbands. They sort of gave up." Mrs. Smith has learned a lot about women, she says.

"They are awfully fearful about their marital relationship. I don't think there is any other word for it. They are afraid, afraid of getting male displeasure, bringing to themselves some sort of amorphous dishonor . . . some sort of ephemeral thing, that girls don't act that way."

Women lawyers who take on these cases are often amazed at the timidity of the more traditional woman. Beyond the fear of "amorphous dishonor" there is financial fear. "Many of these women do not work. Their husband is their financial lifeline, and they don't want to displease him," one lawyer said. The younger woman, reared in a more gender-neutral society, married to a man who is no better educated than she, is stunned when other women in the club won't help her get on the course on weekend mornings. At one club in the East, working women seeking open tee times on weekend mornings found unexpected opposition from some *young* married women who understood the gender-bias issue but wanted their husbands to play early on weekends so that they could get home in time to spend the afternoon with their kids.

Many men also feel strongly that they want to play and be home by early afternoon on the weekends. More women playing on weekend mornings might prevent that. There was also expected opposition from older women who wanted their husbands to play with male friends. Perhaps the only lesson from all this is to avoid gender and age stereotypes and try to look at each situation with fresh and open eyes.

❧ Mill River: A Cautionary Tale ❧

That's what the women of Mill River did. This is a cautionary tale, included here to show just how difficult it is to achieve change. Mill River in Oyster Bay, Long Island, New York, is a progressive club, one dedicated to religious and racial diversity. Its policy is to maintain an integrated membership, roughly 50 percent Jewish and 50 percent Christian. In recent years it has become ethnically diverse.

Unlike most private clubs in America, Mill River's men talk about their progress. They discuss the club's advances as well as the club's struggles. They accept interviews; they talk to the press. They invite reporters to look at their policies; they advocate diversity. In this they are virtually unique among country clubs.

Mill River was founded in 1961, the brainchild of William S. Roach, an attorney, who believed in religious integration. Many members had mixed marriages. Prospective members were screened during their interview for prejudice. Over the years the club kept a roughly fifty-fifty ratio between Jew and Gentile. In recent years it has made an effort to admit blacks and Asians. But its social consciousness stopped when it came to women. As in most country clubs in America, the women of Mill River could not vote, could not serve on the board, and were told to leave if they got divorced. There were also those women, "those seven-handicappers, who wanted to tee off on the weekend mornings but couldn't," Roach recalled. While membership at Mill River has included Christians, Jews, blacks, men from Asia and from India, until very recently it did not include the largest minority in their midst: women. And when they were included, it was not without a long struggle.

Women were not permitted in the male grillroom, and women could not tee off on weekends until all male members had gone off. In short, women felt the very segregation and discrimination that the club so fought against when religion, race, and ethnicity were concerned. The most telling indicator of women's status was stunning in its triviality: women were allowed to eat in the main dining room but were not allowed to sit in chairs that had arms. All armchairs were saved for male use only.

The women of Mill River began a quiet push for change in 1989. A woman whose husband had died had remarried, and when that marriage ended in divorce, the woman asked to remain at Mill River. Other club wives were sympathetic. "It started hitting home," said Jeanne Benjamin, a retired career woman and WORM for twenty-five years.

"Our club was a forerunner," said Fran Esernio, a retired accountant from Great Neck, who is married to a former club president. "It has taken a while to extend this policy to the last minority—women."

For more than five years, wives pressed for change from within. At first they spoke to me only on the condition of anonymity. They were frightened about talking to someone outside the club; they worried what their husbands might say.

Said one spouse, "What is intriguing about the voting issue is that the sexes are not strangers to one another. They are our husbands. We eat with them. We talk to them. We sleep with them. We raise their children. We run their households, and we run our own professional lives. It is hard to understand why we cannot vote at the country club." From 1990 to 1994, the men of the club appointed committees to hear the issue. Behind the scenes, great social upheaval was going on with much angst and despair. Much of the male feeling centered on keeping women in subservient positions. "I have two words for all feminists: Drop dead," one male member was quoted as saying. The more progressive men pushed forward. One was a lawyer, William Levine, who wrote to the club's president: "This denial of equal rights for women is a disgrace, it should have been addressed long ago, and the delay can only be, in my mind, attributed to chauvinistic hardheads on the board of governors who want to keep things status quo and disenfranchise half the members of the club. These members should resign from the board and practice their discriminatory policies within the confines of their homes." Eventually, the bylaws became gender-neutral. Single female members could join with full rights, a move that gave them voting and board rights, entry to the men's grill, and access to the golf course on weekend mornings.

The men also voted to permit divorced women to have full membership privileges if the former spouse gives up his membership. She would only be charged 50 percent of the regular dues.

In 1994, Mill River took yet another revolutionary step. It recognized nonmarital relationships as family. It said so-called significant others could become members of the club—just as long as there was only one significant other each year.

But the club still had not dealt with wives, the women who had sought equality in the first place. Art Taylor, the club's president in 1992, said the easy part was admitting women members. "But what about the wives, the largest group in the club without rights? It is easy to achieve new women's membership, but how do you achieve current women's membership? That is the issue we are grappling with."

It is sobering to realize that a club so tuned in to issues of prejudice and discrimination can still find it agonizing to deal with women. It has taken far more years to get this far than the club members ever imagined, and far more rancor than the club has ever before experienced. But this is a club that talks about these issues openly, and that makes them unique in the private club world.

❧ *Finding Allies: Arizona Country Club* ❧ *and Harry Cavanagh*

Arizona Country Club, one of the three most exclusive clubs in Phoenix, is publicity-shy. How it altered its rules is a classic case of change achieved from within. It took a core group of women dedicated to achieving a goal, and a well-respected, low-key male Phoenix attorney with a deep knowledge of the nature and politics of club life who was willing to serve as informal presenter, negotiator, statesman, and, when called upon, press advocate. Sometimes what is needed is one such male, who may be able to convince the husbands of older unsupportive women that it is okay to back change.

The woman who began the quest to change the bylaws and tee times at Arizona Country Club was Margaret Dyekman, a Phoenix businesswoman who, along with three other spouses, had become increasingly frustrated by restricted tee times. Women could not tee off until 3 P.M. Saturdays. Their own Tuesday Ladies' Day was reserved for league play, and if you were not a member of the league, you could not play. Men were not required to join a league to play golf Saturdays, where they had unrestricted use of the course until midafternoon.

Mrs. Dyekman did some research. One Saturday she went to the pro shop. There were more than a dozen tee times available before 2 P.M. that day. Yet two spouses who were there could not play because of the gender restriction.

The first formal step was a letter that the women composed and sent to the board in November 1993. They argued that their daughters were not "afforded the same golfing privileges as our sons," in that their hours on the course were as restricted as their mothers'. "We find this discriminatory practice a continuation of the 'glass ceiling' as described in disparate treatment employment statistics. At our country club, and with our money, we are fostering a 'grass ceiling' rather than offering our daughters an equal chance to excel personally and socially."

They suggested opening the tee to men and women equally, giving widows who play golf the same memberships they had when they were married, and opening the men's grill to women. They contacted officials in other states to learn how they dealt with these issues. They looked to lobbyists, too.

The board quickly set up a four-man committee to meet with the women and to evaluate their concerns. Soon after, Mrs. Dyekman said, the committee made some "very decent recommendations. It wasn't everything, but it was a big step in the right direction. We said, yes. Let's go forward, we'll help communicate, we understand change is difficult, etc. The committee sent its recommendations to the board.

"And then our board turned it all down—all down."

The board's president explained to the women that "the Board does not feel that the Club's current policies are discriminatory as suggested by your letter." Therefore there was no need to change anything—tee times, the men's grill, the problems of membership for widows and daughters. But the board held out some hope—it would consider additional tee times.

In May 1994 the board announced its changes: Women would get an extra half hour to tee off on Thursday during lunch. The men's grill would be open to women on Sundays from 2:30 to 7 P.M. Women could not play golf Saturday before 2:30 P.M., Sunday before 9:30 A.M., Wednesday from 10 A.M. to 2 P.M., and Thursday from 10:30 A.M. to 2 P.M., when men want to have lunch and take clients out for a round. Friday the course was open. When the board offered up only an additional half hour on Thursday during lunch, that got the attention of Harry Cavanagh, a prominent Arizona lawyer. Cavanagh, who represents the Karsten Manufacturing Co., among other top clients, had served on the boards of Phoenix and Paradise Valley country clubs, and his wife, Geri, is a three-time state champion and a scratch golfer.

"That's when I got really involved. They [the men] were saying: No way, see you in hell, and all that kinda stuff. I am not a member of Arizona, but I knew the guys at Arizona. I then met with the presidents of the Arizona and the Phoenix Country Club, which was also having problems. "I said, 'Why don't you start looking at the twelve to thirteen states that have new laws about this and see what they have done? Do you want it forced down your throat or do you want to get ahead of the game and do it sensibly?' And both clubs wanted to get ahead of it. That brought Arizona into line. It will take a little education and staging and all that. Most women don't want to play Saturday morning when the men want to play. The gals that work, they almost have to. They want to network with their people, just like I do. And they are entitled to."

While he was working behind the scenes, a comprehensive story entitled "Fairways, Not for Women" appeared in the *Phoenix Business Journal*. This story laid out the conflict and presented the players. They were an impressive group of people. Right there to the left of the box on restrictions at the three exclusive clubs—Arizona, Paradise Valley, and Phoenix—were the comments of Harry Cavanagh.

"It's archaic" is how he began. "It's a problem for women, and I don't think people in power are recognizing it." With those words he was acknowledging in print that he was lending his very persuasive authority to changing how clubs operate. A member of Paradise Valley since 1955 and of Phoenix since 1947, Cavanagh said the rule banning women golfers from prime tee times and from the men's grills of both clubs was unreasonable. Cavanagh later told me that the greatest resistance he encountered centered not on tee times but on the men's grill. "Oh, the guys on the grill, they were ragging me all over the place. But you need to get somebody who can talk to them to talk to them. That's what has to happen. Somebody has to take on the dialogue. Because they will say, Hell no, god damn you, why are you doing this? But as they are saying that, they're starting to get the message: Whether you like it or not, it is going to happen. Why not listen? And as they listen and you get talking to them, they get more and more reasonable. You may still have some members of the board that will be obstreperous or block it. Hopefully, if you have a reasonable president, then you can get the job done. If you have a bullheaded president, one that's pigheaded and oldfashioned, you may have to wait until you get a new president."

The story in the *Business Journal* also quoted Linda Brock-Nelson, owner of a major car dealership. She owns a home on the Paradise Valley golf course, and her husband is a club member. But she had to join another club nearly an hour away in order to get on a course on Saturday morning. "I'm a working woman, and I have only two days a week I can play. An eight-year-old boy can get on the course any time he wants, but not a woman. It's absurd."

On June 3, 1994, the very conservative newspaper the *Arizona Republic* dropped a bomb. Its long lead editorial left no doubt where it stood. It observed that Sandra Day O'Connor, a member with her husband at Paradise Valley, cannot golf during prime times at her own club, and it went on to say, "Or put another way, male club members can strengthen their business ties with other businessmen during prime times on the golf course and in the grill. But male club members are denied the same opportunity with, say, the new president of Bank of America, Kathy Munro, or other women business and political leaders. Such discrimination is outrageous. It is unacceptable. But unfortunately it is not unusual."

The editorial then set the stage for the next fight. "Several states have passed laws mandating equal access for women at all golf clubs. Others have made tax benefits and liquor licenses for country clubs contingent upon nondiscriminatory membership practices. Paradise Valley, Phoenix, and Arizona country clubs can either revise their own policies or risk having them revised for them. Here's hoping they get with the times and choose the former."

The idea that these clubs would be grist for the newspaper mill in the coming months reinforced Mr. Cavanagh's message that change would be forced down their throats. It only took two months. One Saturday afternoon in late July, Mrs. Dyekman had a conversation with Jay Binsfeld, the club president. She informed him they had commitments from two Arizona lobbyists who had the laws of other states in their briefcases. The lobbyists were ready to roll. "I told him they were ready to show the file to the attorney general. That's how we left it."

The following Monday, the board met and created gender-neutral tee times. Either member of the family would now have the right to be the full member, and that member would have open weekend tee times. For the first time, the twenty women who were full members and the forty women with widow memberships would be able to play weekend mornings. Wives, too, could play, but only if the wife was appointed the primary member. The couple would make that designation. Gender-specific tee times had been eliminated. "There are women who are still upset because they can't tee off early in the day, but that's a couples' issue," says Mrs. Dyekman. She has tabled her legislative plans. But several other spouses who want weekend tee times are thinking about it.

How did this much change come to Arizona Country Club so quickly? First, the women stayed with a major theme—fairness. Despite disappointments, they kept to a schedule. They lined up legislators and lobbyists and editorial writers, and they let the club know they meant business.

Second, they won support from a few good men, led by Cavanagh, who argued their case. They used the media to present their position to the community at large. Third, and perhaps most important, stories in the press got people talking; club members began to hear how others viewed their actions. Altogether an impressive illustration of successful working from within, along with the judicious use of local media coverage.

❧ *Letters to the Board* ❧

The first formal step at Arizona Country Club was a letter to the board. This is typical. When members are moved to act, they will write a letter alerting the club's board to some aspects of the rules or procedures the member finds problematic. I have assembled a small sampling of letters. All the letters relate to situations in this book.

Remember the daughter, Ronney Rosenberg, who couldn't get her own membership in the club she grew up in because she was single and in her thirties? Her grandfather was the club's member of longest standing. Her father, Seymour Rosenberg, a New York City attorney, wrote a letter to the membership of Fenway Golf Club on September 21, 1991. It was an appeal to conscience.

> Dear Member:
> My daughter, Ronney Lynne, has expressed interest in becoming a regular member of Fenway. The Board of Governors has pointed out that the club bylaws would have to be amended to admit daughters (including daughters-in-law) under the same terms that sons (sons-in-law) are admitted.
> My wife and I, as well as my father-in-law, have always supported the academic, social and professional interests of our children, without discriminating based on their sex. . . . Accordingly, I ask that you sign the petition to amend the club bylaws so as to admit all of our children, daughters and sons alike; under the same terms.

Deborah J. Kline, representing a group trying to change policies at Terrace Park Country Club in Ohio, sent a letter to the club's president and its board on April 12, 1992. She asked for changes in the club's bylaws, observing that the rules had been adopted when the club was a men's club.

> We offer several additional reasons why open play is fair and reasonable. The opening of the Ivy Hills Club will create strong competition and an economic threat to Terrace Park. Ivy Hills will not have playing restrictions for family members on weekends. Therefore Terrace Park

stands to lose to Ivy Hills not only potential members, but current members as well. Legal counsel indicates that present members who were not appropriately informed of playing restrictions upon joining Terrace Park, could potentially sue for a refund of their initiation fees.

And she discusses the historic shift in the structure of family life since the 1950s.

> Just as society has changed today, Terrace Park Country Club needs to change by removing these antiquated restrictions prohibiting women from weekend morning play. Less than ten percent of today's families are the traditional family of the 1950s with a male breadwinner and a wife that does not work outside of the home. The majority of families need two incomes to survive and to afford the luxury of a country club membership. And for many families at Terrace Park, membership is contingent upon income from the wife. It is unreasonable to expect today's family to join a club where only one adult is considered the member when it takes the economic contribution of both adults in order to afford the membership.
>
> Representatives of our committee would like to meet with the Board to discuss these changes and hopefully come to an agreement.

Unfortunately, the board did not see fit to change its policies, and Mrs. Kline sought relief before the Ohio State Human Rights Commission. For the results, see Chapter 9.

Carrollwood Village Golf and Tennis Club in Tampa, Florida, is a neighbor of Cheval Country Club. Cheval, you'll remember, is where the club went overboard in reacting to Molly O'Dea's effort to get a fair shake regarding tee times. At the time, Carrollwood was having its own problems. It was denying decent weekend tee times to women family members. One of them, Dr. Ruth Hanno, wrote the following letter to the club's president.

> As we discussed on the phone last weekend, I am very disturbed by the prohibition of women's play on our golf

course on Saturday mornings. I know this issue has been brought up before and small adjustments have been made. However, the restrictions remain and I would very much appreciate your discussing my letter at the next Board of Directors meeting.

As you know, I am a physician and I work during the week. Weekend mornings are prime golf time at any club. I called for a tee time Friday afternoon and was told I could not play on Saturday morning until 11:55. I was told that my husband could tee off at 9:35 without any problem. The only reason for my being restricted from using the golf course that morning was my gender.

She then outlined the reasons for the restrictions, reasons she said that are not valid.

1. Women should be restricted because they play slower than men and allowing them to use the golf course on Saturday mornings would slow down play.

   If the problem is slowness of play, then slow players should be restricted from using the golf course, not women. The ranger could aggressively move golfers along and remove players that are playing too slowly. There are plenty of slow men golfers and plenty of quick women golfers and to make this distinction on the basis of sex is arbitrary.

2. Since one of the nines is closed, the course would be too crowded if women were permitted to play on Saturday morning. If the problem is crowding of the golf course, then the number of tee times should be restricted. Whoever calls first for a tee time should be given the tee time, regardless of sex.

3. Men cannot play on Thursday mornings; this time is reserved for women.

   This argument is irrelevant to women who work. It is obvious that tee times during the week are not nearly as desirable as tee times on the weekends. To restrict women from the coveted weekend tee times and restrict men from a weekday, when tee times are not nearly as desirable, is inherently unfair. Thursday morning is not equal to Saturday morning.

4. This has been a tradition at Carrollwood for over twenty years.

This is no argument. A sexually discriminatory practice should be ended immediately and not continued because of tradition.

She ended the letter by saying, "I hope we can settle this issue by doing what is right and fair." Here was a letter that was not simply a complaint but a response to the reasons she had been given for the club's policies. This is reasoning about the reasons and helping the club take a new view of the issues. When her letter and subsequent meetings failed to work, she and another woman sued Carrollwood. Ultimately the tee-time restrictions were lifted.

Finally, there is this whimsical note from Pat Yoder to the president of the Pittsburgh Field Club, tweaking their awkwardness in dealing with the gender issue. A fitting finale to the use of letters when working from within.

The newsletter states that the Board of Directors reminds all members that the small parking lot adjacent to the men's locker room is reserved for <u>persons</u> using the men's locker room.

This leads to the following obvious questions: Which parking lot have you set aside (reserved) for persons using the women's locker room? Have you built a special lot? ... Since you are implying ... that you are now moving to a "separate but equal policy," I assume you are taking steps to provide separate but equal parking lots. If you are not taking the above steps, then I assume the statement "<u>persons</u> using the men's locker room" implies that the men's locker room is now open to whomever chooses to use it ... male or female. I would like a response as soon as possible since I plan on using the club facilities in the very near future.

She never got a reply.

❦ *The Saga of Holly Hopeful* ❦

When this story began, Holly Hopeful was a person with a real name. She belonged to a club with a real name, in a state with a real name. The story of Holly Hopeful is in many ways the story of this book. It began as a strong story about a vibrant, bright woman, fighting for the simple right to be treated fairly at her private country club.

What gave Ms. Hopeful anxiety about revealing her journey was that the country club in question, which has found reasons to deny her requests for equitable tee-time policies, would be even more hostile if she went public with her complaints. A male supporter who agrees with her position is similarly reluctant to have the issue exposed to public view. So I will call her Holly Hopeful, who lives in Anywhere West U.S.A. and belongs to Stubborn Oaks Country Club, located on the outskirts of town. Here's the story.

Holly Hopeful, an executive and a fine golfer, arrived at Stubborn Oaks Country Club in the late 1980s. Her journey to be admitted to one of her state's best golf clubs was the culmination of a long search for a fine course, as well as an impressive place to recruit and entertain clients. Our golfer is a naturally upbeat woman, intelligent, funny, rational. She is an optimist by nature.

Stubborn Oaks appealed to her because it had a membership category for single women, which she is. Not easy to find in the state of Somewhere, or in most states for that matter. She paid a five-figure initiation fee to join, plus monthly dues.

She was introduced to the club's members. At one point board members asked her if she had read the bylaws. She rightly took this to mean a reference to restrictive weekend tee times for spouses. "I knew the rules were very restrictive but I didn't have much choice. I love to play golf and I need to entertain my clients. I figured I'd just get in and see what kind of change I could make." In fact, the rules forced this leading female executive, along with her clients, guests, and playing partners, to wait to tee off until afternoons on Saturday and Sunday, while her fellow club members who are single males had no such restrictions.

So she moved to change the restrictive bylaws by working within the club, confident that in time they would come to see the wisdom of her views. Here is a rough version of what she thought as she approached the future.

Year One: Do nothing. Get in, be pleasant, meet everyone, be social, play golf.

Year Two: More of the same, but start to figure out who is on what side of the aisle.

Year Three: Provide educational information to the golf committee and other influential folks at the club. These are the tee-time issues. Let's start a dialogue so we can make change.

Year Four: More discussion. Build a constituency. Get others to help bring about change.

Year Five: Make this a members' issue, not a women's issue. Help club leaders become proactive, take steps for change in light of legislation elsewhere.

During her first four years, the men's grill was integrated and the club eliminated some luncheon and tee-time restrictions imposed on women. At one point the board actually gave the spouses a chance to vote on getting weekend tee times. However, this was coupled with the understanding that the club would end its exclusive tee times for ladies on Tuesdays and Thursdays. Not surprisingly, the plan was voted down.

So as Holly Hopeful approaches Year Five of her life as a member of Stubborn Oaks, she is still not able to invite guests or clients to play on weekend mornings, one of her hopes when she joined the club.

Should we feel sorry for her? In one sense, no. She knew the rules when she joined the club. But so did Rosa Parks when she boarded the bus that day in Montgomery, Alabama. The country club tries to keep out people who might try to change it. That's one reason change has been so slow. But Holly Hopeful is not a bomb-throwing revolutionary. On the contrary, she is trying to work within the rules.

She is working so quietly that her name and that of her club are out of this book. The instructive lesson is that private club membership means so much that any whisper of a suspicion that a member will challenge the rules and discuss it in public scares one into thinking that that alone might be a basis for dismissal. The sad fact is that Holly Hopeful still doesn't know what her fate will be at Stubborn Oaks Country Club. She lives in the hope that the club's position will change, but she has no real reason to believe that it will.

9

Getting Fed Up

*I must say that as a litigant I should dread a lawsuit
beyond almost anything else short of sickness and death.*
— Judge Learned Hand

Virtually every woman in this book who has faced unfair treatment at the
country club first tried to fix it from within. Many have spent years writing letters, talking to club officers, trying various approaches to end their
club's unfair practices. In most cases, they failed. When they finally get
fed up, they may well decide to take their club to court. (There is another
alternative: going to the legislature. See Chapter 15.)

The reason going to court should be the last resort for a club
member is that, regardless of the outcome, the member who sues is usually ostracized from his or her social world. Friendships are damaged,
club members take sides. The plaintiff becomes a pariah.

Filing a lawsuit gets members angry also because if it is not settled quickly, the club may incur costs not covered by liability insurance.
When the lawsuit goes on and on, and insurers begin to balk, club
members may well be assessed the lawyer's costs. And for what, they
ask? An early-morning tee time? A divorce settlement that doesn't follow the club's rules? The men's grill?

To husbands and their wives who want to keep the status quo,
these are issues seldom worthy of a court fight. But they are not so trivial
to those getting short shrift.

Lawsuits also expose country clubs to discovery, the process by which one side or another gathers information for the lawsuit. That often means a bitter fight over subpoenas seeking information about membership rosters, forms of corporate payments, and the tax structure of the club (usually a nonprofit with a property tax benefit). Clubs don't take kindly to giving up this sort of information in an adversarial proceeding. It's their business, they feel, no one else's.

Besides discovery, there are the depositions club officers are required to make, the sort of testimony that can take hours or days to complete. These are often people with busy lives and demanding jobs who now find themselves under oath, not for a lawsuit involving their company, but for a lawsuit involving their club. Add possible assessments for costs or damages imposed and it's clear why clubs view lawsuits with horror.

Women starting a lawsuit believe they have done nothing wrong. After all, it is the club that won't budge. They simply want to right a wrong and then get on with things. That is what they naively think in the beginning. They never think that at the end.

❧ Mary Ann Warfield Goes to Court ❧

Mary Ann Warfield, the woman in Chapter 5 who was divorced and was awarded the country club membership as part of her settlement, sued when the club then took it away from her. She had been a family member at Peninsula Golf and Country Club for eleven years, was active in interclub competitions, indeed, had been the women's club champion. And her former husband wanted her to have the membership.

Golf and the country club were central to her life. She felt she had every right to the membership. The club disagreed. Its bylaws said in 1981 that memberships "shall be issued only in the name of the adult male person. Proposals for regular family memberships shall not be approved for females or minors." The bylaws further stated that upon a divorce, the husband would retain the membership. It stood behind those bylaws and refused to reconsider.

On November 1, 1981, Mary Ann Warfield filed a complaint in the California Superior Court. Incredible as it may seem, the case is still going on after fourteen years. At the heart of the lawsuit is a simple question: Is the Peninsula Golf and Country Club a business establishment or not? Why that's the issue takes a little explaining.

Back in 1959, the State of California passed the Unruh Civil Rights Act. Its crucial language is as follows: "All persons within the jurisdiction of this state are free and equal, and no matter what their sex, race, color, religion, ancestry, national origin, or blindness or other physical disability are entitled to the full and equal accommodations, advantages, facilities, privileges, or services in all business establishments of every kind whatsoever."

Does Peninsula possess sufficient businesslike attributes to be included within the Unruh Act's reach? Thus far both a district court and the California Court of Appeals have said it does not. The most recent appellate court opinion is that any business conducted at the club or by the club was incidental to the club's primary purpose, which is social and recreational.

The fact that members or their guests make purchases at the bar, restaurant, or pro shops (the club had two, tennis and golf) does not make it a business. "We find that the provision of goods and services to members merely furthers the recreational and social goals of the Club and is not, under the circumstances, a business-like attribute," the judges wrote.

The court may have been influenced by Mrs. Warfield's rejection of the nonequity membership she was offered by the club. That membership would have allowed her to play golf, bring guests, and participate in club life. The one thing it barred was a proprietary interest in the club. She would get no equity and could not participate in its growth as a full member. She rejected this "second-class" membership, particularly since the value of the family's equity membership was five to six times more than its purchase price of $7,500 in 1970.

The case is now before California's highest court. Her side will argue that the appeals court got it wrong—that since Peninsula has a paid staff of over 100, owns property, provides meals and services to members, and, through them, rents out its facilities for receptions and outings, it has all the businesslike attributes identified in other California cases as falling within reach of the Unruh Act.

The National Club Association and other groups supporting the club's position will argue that California's interest in preventing invidious discrimination in public life, laudable as it may be, does not allow the state to intrude into the kind of private social activity represented by private organizations like Peninsula. They will direct the court's attention to the underlying purposes of club life. They will argue that California law protects its citizens' freedom to associate with whom they choose, and that by forcing private clubs to be gender-neutral in their bylaws and other rules, they are invading that freedom.

Both sides are keenly aware that the case will set a precedent for how all private clubs in California will be viewed. The National Club Association says a win for Warfield would subject every private club in California to the Unruh Civil Rights Act. Such an adverse precedent would affect not only California, the organization says, but other states as well.

Ironically, behind the scenes Peninsula now has single women as full property-holding members, precisely the category Mrs. Warfield sought when the club terminated her family membership following her divorce decree. Since the club has taken this step, why are they still fighting? And fighting hard?

To a small degree the answer lies in the fact that clubs may make changes in the course of trying to settle a lawsuit. But more important, this case has become a political football. Both the California Club Association and the National Club Association, lobbying groups that represent private clubs, have a strong interest in preserving things as they are at private clubs.

Elizabeth Kirby Hart, NCA's vice-president in charge of legal and government affairs, is the organization's chief legal spokesperson. In explaining why the NCA filed a friend-of-the-court brief in behalf of Peninsula, she argued that a ruling by the California Supreme Court in favor of Warfield would "threaten the continued existence of many private clubs."

It is against this backdrop, as well as a strong lower-court ruling, that the California Supreme Court will consider whether Peninsula—and clubs like it—are business establishments under the Unruh Act.

Mary Ann Warfield is long gone from Peninsula Golf and Country Club. But she has learned to live with this lawsuit, a lawsuit that she never imagined would consume her life and leave her in legal limbo for fourteen years. Over those years she has changed. She plays golf less and, these days, at public courses. But she is no less convinced of the essential reason for suing the club in the first place.

"I did something I believed in. . . . I mean I grew up always having felt an equal. You have to understand I played on the boys' high-school golf team. Back then it was boys because girls were not supposed to play golf. I went to the principal. I said, 'I would like to try out for the golf team.' And he said, 'Do you think you can make that team? You go right ahead.' And I made that team. It meant a lot to me. I was treated equally."

Maybe in the school system as a youngster. But not as an adult at her own club.

❧ *Murder Threats in Orange County* ❧

Jan Bradshaw's lawsuit against the Yorba Linda Country Club in Orange County, California, evoked the darker side of some people's human nature. The hostile reactions began with threatening phone calls to her from a caller with a male voice. He said if she didn't stop her lawsuit, she would be killed. The calls continued for months.

Then someone began erasing her name from the sign-up sheets at the golf club, clearly an inside job. Her photo on the bulletin board was mutilated. Women at the club who had initially supported her efforts now ostracized her. She hadn't expected that. At one point the ladies' association even publicly denounced her. At a poolside news conference they said if she wanted to play during men's hours, she should "find a man" to play with.

She was stunned, she said, to find that wives and widows at the club viewed her as a troublemaker. "The women treat me as if I had leprosy. I am deeply ashamed of them."

Jan Bradshaw, interior designer, mother of three, newly divorced, was learning firsthand what happens if you file a lawsuit against your own country club. She had presumed civility. After all, civility is what country clubs are supposed to be all about. What she hadn't foreseen was the fierce emotions many men feel when it comes to defending their right to a weekend tee time.

The ostracism for Bradshaw began soon after her Los Angeles attorney, Gloria Allred, filed the lawsuit in Orange County Superior Court. Allred, a feminist attorney who herself integrated the Friars Club years before, is not shy about getting publicity for her cases. She took to the wires. Within days, Bradshaw's story about spending the same amount of money as a man to get a membership but being denied weekend tee times and the right to vote and run for office at the club was news in the *Los Angeles Times*. Everyone at Yorba Linda Country Club read it. The reaction was swift: "I couldn't find anyone to talk to, to sit with in the clubhouse. I couldn't get golfing partners," she said. "I was certain they simply didn't realize I was a full member." No longer could she play in a foursome. She couldn't get one. Only one woman, her friend Dee Scher, continued to play golf with her.

For Bradshaw the atmosphere was chilling. For the fourteen months the lawsuit lasted, she was persona non grata. Nonetheless, the publicity of the lawsuit promoted changes. The American Golf Corporation, which at that time operated 115 clubs, owned Yorba Linda. Loretta Singer, the corporation's general counsel at the time, said Yorba Linda was the only club with such policies. The rules were part of the purchase agreement. "We have asked them to change, but they refused."

As often happens over the course of a lawsuit, the parties were asked to find areas of agreement in order to settle the case. The club made changes. American Golf prevailed, and the restrictive weekend tee times were lifted. And whether the women at Yorba Linda wanted it or not, they also got the right to vote and to run for seats on the board.

What Mrs. Bradshaw accomplished helped women. It did not help her. After she settled her lawsuit, reportedly for her initiation fee of $14,000 plus legal fees, she moved on to another club.

"The level of hostility toward me at Yorba Linda was so intense that I said there was no way I could stay at that club," said Bradshaw. In 1991 she founded an organization, Fairways for Women, to help women fight discriminatory rules governing golf courses. "People who don't play golf don't realize this goes on," she says. "How can clubs take a person's money and then treat them differently just because they're a woman?" Good question.

✎ *It was the chicken wings that finally got to me.* ✎

—Jackie Neal, a lady member of
Newport Beach Country Club

At Newport Beach Country Club, also in Orange County, a very different kind of sex discrimination issue developed. On April 8, 1986, W. D. Ray, chairman of the board of the Newport Beach Country Club, wrote a three-page letter to the club's single ladies. The subject: the elimination of single-lady membership because it had been created on a sex-based discount and was therefore unlawful.

The single ladies, said Mr. Ray, could convert their existing memberships to one of two new memberships never before made available to women. To become a charter member they would have to pay an additional $3,000. To become a founding member they would have to pay an additional $12,000.

What Mr. Ray did not say in his letter to the ladies was that the club permitted single men to convert their existing membership to charter memberships without paying any additional cost and to convert to a founding membership at only $3,500 additional cost. Simple arithmetic showed that the ladies were being asked to pay $3,000 more than the single men to become charter members and $8,500 more than single men to become founding members.

Some of the women actually paid the amounts sought. Others did not. When they learned of the differences in the costs between men and women, they wrote numerous letters to Mr. Ray. "To no avail," said Jacquelyn G. Neal, the lead plaintiff in a lawsuit that ultimately involved twenty-eight women from the club.

In addition, the single women, about ninety in all, learned that male members often did not have to pay guest fees for female guests while single ladies had to pay guest fees for male guests. They also learned that men received free snacks.

"It was the chicken wings that finally got to me," said Ms. Neal, explaining her reason for coming aboard as a plaintiff. "Men get free snacks in their locker room, and women get nothing."

For the next three years, the women tried to work it out. When they could not, they sued, including several women in their sixties. It took far less time to settle. The club hired a top law firm to defend it against accusations of violations of the Unruh Act.

The basis of the lawsuit was that the club, acting as a business establishment, had discriminated against the women, charged them inequitable membership fees, and made no effort to change or correct those inequities, despite efforts by the women over a long period of time.

The lawsuit argued that the Unruh Act is aimed at businesses. The women reasoned that many private clubs fit the description because their bars, pro shops, and other facilities are open to the public and because members write off club expenses on their income-tax returns as business deductions.

After a year or so of haggling, the club ultimately agreed to reimburse the women a total of $30,000, a settlement the women toasted with champagne outside the club's entrance, much to the chagrin of club officials.

The club said it decided to pay the $30,000, which it described as minimal, in order to avoid an expensive court fight. As part of the settlement, the club also agreed to provide the ladies free chicken wings.

❧ Steve Kline in Ohio: A Man Fights for His Wife ❧

Steve Kline's long legal journey into the sexist world of country club life is unique because few men take on their club in an effort to end discrimination against their wives.

Steve Kline was different. For years he had experienced the discrimination against his wife, Deborah. And he wanted it to end. He wanted to be able to play golf with his wife on a Saturday morning. And he couldn't. So Debby had his complete support when, in June 1992 she filed a complaint with the Ohio Civil Rights Commission against their country club. Steve had been the club's regular member, and Deborah an associate, a spouse, for the previous six years.

Their story began when the Klines wanted to play a round of golf together one weekend day at the Terrace Park Country Club in Milford, Ohio, a suburb of Cincinnati. The starter gave them the go-ahead a little after noon that day, but minutes later they were stopped by the club's assistant pro. He could play, but she could not—at least not until the ladies' time began, a half hour later, at 12:30 P.M. The Klines were upset.

They had tried in previous years to get the tee times changed.

They talked to their friends. They wrote letters. And Steve was elected to the club's board in late 1991. Eventually a group of women led by Debby brought the problem to the Golf Committee in May 1992. The committee recommended to the club's board that it conduct an experiment: drop all weekend restrictions for the month of June. Perhaps once the club realized that the course would not be inundated by women golfers, it would eliminate weekend tee-time restrictions. To the committee and to the Klines, this sounded like a reasonable approach. The board rejected the golf committee's proposal on a vote of 7 to 1, with the lone vote in favor cast by Steve.

At that point, the women led by Mrs. Kline hired an attorney. One of the women who interviewed attorneys with Mrs. Kline in 1992 later abandoned the case. She told Mrs. Kline that she had encountered such opposition from her husband that she was left with a choice: her marriage or weekend tee times. She chose her marriage. Mr. Kline said another woman was threatened with the loss of her job if she continued to support the cause.

The complaint asked the Ohio Civil Rights Commission to find that the club engaged in discriminatory conduct. The women asked to be given equal tee times, the right to vote, and the right to hold survivorship rights. There were a number of factors that made the Klines uniquely qualified to bring the case: they were financially able to pursue the case, including hiring their own attorney. Even after the state attorney general's office took up their case against the club, they kept their own attorney, not an inexpensive enterprise. In addition, they joined another country club, with nondiscriminatory practices, while keeping their membership at Terrace Park. The case went through various stages at the Ohio Civil Rights Commission. Over more than two years, numerous legal issues were raised, and the commission sought to eliminate the discriminatory practices through conciliation. It failed. A finding of "probable cause" was issued against the club in 1993, and a four-day hearing was held in 1994 in which testimony was taken from club officials, from the Klines, and from others.

In December 1994, the commission issued a twenty-six-page opinion. The Klines won everything. The club was ordered to stop its discriminatory practices and to allow women—spouses, single members, and widows—to vote, to run for office, to play golf on weekend mornings, and to be treated equally as members. The hearing examiner found that although the club had, in 1989, eliminated "sexist language" in its handbook, it did not "equalize the rights and privileges of the spousal members."

Unfortunately for the members, the commission also ordered the club to end special events reserved exclusively for one sex or the other. In 1994 that included twenty-two gender-specific events, several men's stag days, and four ladies' tournaments. It's the kind of order those unfamiliar with golf but concerned about equal treatment might be expected to write, and is a prime example of why private clubs would do better to tackle these issues themselves than wait for the state to do it. Neither the Klines nor anyone else would have gone that far. If the club's officers had been responsive to the legitimate points raised by the women in 1992 and had worked with them when they had a chance, the club would have had wiser policies at far less cost. The club is considering an appeal.

❧ Wildwood: Saga of a Sinking Class ❧

In the lawsuits we've dealt with so far—those of Mary Ann Warfield, Jan Bradshaw, Deborah Kline—the women have been individuals making complaints against their clubs for various wrongs. This case illustrates the class-action lawsuit at work. Marcia Welch and her husband were members of Wildwood Golf Club near Pittsburgh, Pennsylvania. At least, she had thought of herself as a member. They had been there for twelve years when they divorced.

Her soon-to-be former husband requested that their joint membership be put in her name. Their divorce lawyer thought this transfer could be accomplished by letter. It turned out it needed a change in the club's bylaws. The bylaw amendment went down to defeat.

When the matter had come up for official discussion before the vote, only men were allowed to speak. After all, only men had the vote! Marcia Welch was there and she remembers it with a vividness that only the dispossessed feel. "I wasn't allowed to speak or to clarify. It was deemed out of order for me to do so. I was very upset and frustrated," she said. It also didn't help that, according to her complaint, the ballot box wasn't sealed properly; the actual vote count was not announced; only that the amendment failed; and the ballots were destroyed after the count but before any independent group could check the results.

The club saw the whole matter very differently. The board wrote Ms. Welch's attorney that if she wanted to become a member of Wildwood—and here she thought she had been a member for twelve years—then she should request an application. "Ms. Welch would be subject to the same review, initiation fees, dues, waiting requirements and vote of approval as with all new applicants." But this was not what propelled her into litigation. It was only when a club official later told her that there would be no changes made, and that if she didn't like it she could sue, that she sued.

Ms. Welch turned to a litigator who, with her husband and children, was also a family member of Wildwood. Deborah Iwanyshyn was aware that her client Marcia Welch was not alone. Other women at Wildwood, and at similar clubs around the country, faced the same problem. So, she thought, why not make this an action on behalf of all women in similar situations, not just Marcia Welch? This is the classic approach of a class-action lawsuit. As it was a civil-rights lawsuit as well, attorney's fees would be paid in accordance with federal law.

Ms. Welch sued in U.S. District Court in Pittsburgh in July 1990 on behalf of herself and all other female members of Wildwood. She sued under a section of the old Civil Rights law, section 1985 (3), that enabled a group of women to assert a private conspiracy to deprive them of due process. The lawsuit outlined discriminatory conduct in membership, voting, tee-time, and grill practices. More than two years later, a federal judge certified the class. By 1994, some 270 Wildwood women signed on to become members of the class.

Alas, they soon became a vanishing breed. In three cases, husbands had intercepted letters from the federal court and withdrawn their wives from the lawsuit without their knowledge. Each man signed his name to a document that requested his wife's signature. Two women in the class reported receiving calls urging them to withdraw, or opt out of the lawsuit. Apparently the club conducted a telephone campaign to get women out of the suit. When Mrs. Iwanyshyn learned of these activities, she was understandably upset, and she set in motion a process that was risky but necessary, she thought. In a class-action lawsuit, after a certain date, the defendants are not allowed to contact the plaintiffs to encourage them to change their minds. To do so would be judged intimidation. That date had already passed in this case. But by complaining to the court about potential fraud and interference by husbands, and seeking to explore the matter further for trial purposes, the plaintiffs opened the door for the country club to receive a new time period for women to opt out of the lawsuit.

Within a few weeks, the class of 270 shrank to a class of 106. Why? There are several possible explanations.

Economics: "The club will have to pay all the legal fees" is what many husbands apparently told their wives. In fact, the club was insured against this form of loss, but the declining women may not have known that.

Interpersonal dynamics: Joining the lawsuit was creating a rift in marriages. Many of these women did not work and were supported financially by their husbands. They did not believe that in this area they were entitled to basic rights—not if the husbands wanted them.

The plight of retirees: For senior citizens, women whose main activity in life was to meet their friends at the club and play golf, the club gave their life purpose. Why should they sue their friends? The movement created a shrinking class, but a class it remained. One hundred and six women of Wildwood arrayed against their own club for simple rights: to vote in club affairs, to hold memberships just as men do. Had the group shrunk much more—in fact, if it had gone down to under 100 members—it would have lost its standing as a class. But it held, barely. "I never expected so many wives to opt out. Why wouldn't women want to improve their rights?" asked Ms. Welch's attorney.

At this writing we can't know the outcome. The case will be decided in due course, either by settlement or by trial. Marcia Welch has joined a new golf club where she is not made to feel like an outsider, but that doesn't end the lawsuit. Her lawyer continues to feel that women are being hurt and that if she wins this case, then any woman in any state could go into district court and know she had a good chance of having her rights vindicated.

Lawyers live with such hope. Time will tell if the hope is justified in this case.

❧ Shunned in the Bay State ❧

Midge Martin is naturally upbeat. She speaks briskly and to the point. A financial planner in Springfield, Massachusetts, she is an energetic woman who has waged an eleven-year battle with her country club for golf course equality. She and her husband, Charlie, have been members of the Longmeadow Country Club for twenty-nine years.

But for the past four years, the Martins have not had a conversation with anyone at their country club. No one will play golf with them. No one will join them for a drink. No one will dine with them. No one will talk to them, even to say hello. Not at the grill. Not in the pro shop. Not in the locker room.

Members act no differently outside the club. The Martins live in a small town, Longmeadow, Massachusetts, population fifteen thousand. Everyone knows everyone else. If the Martins happen upon a club member as they are pushing their cart down the aisle of the local supermarket and they move to say hello, the club member turns away, hiding his or her head in the grocery shelf.

The Martins are being shunned.

What have Midge Martin and her husband done to deserve this sort of treatment? Their crime was pursuing Midge's desire for weekend-morning tee times, so that she could play early or invite clients to the club. The first female general agent for Connecticut Mutual Life, Mrs. Martin has spent most of her working life in an all-male world. But until she filed a complaint against her club and won the right to early weekend tee times, she could not play with clients at key hours or vote or propose a member for admission.

She had accepted this situation for more than twenty years. Always an independent person who privately cringed at the inequities at the club, she decided in 1984, at the age of fifty-nine, that she would take it no more. She began by working from within. First she asked the president of the club to meet with her. "Absolutely not," he said. ("And he was a friend," she said.) "We all know what you want," he added. Next she asked the board to listen to her. She wanted them to give "some consideration to career women." The board refused to meet with her.

Rebuffed, she decided to plead her case before the membership. At her own expense, she sent a survey to the five hundred members of the club to find out their views on women teeing off on weekends. She told the board she would share the results with them. The board said it didn't want the survey results. She wrote a second letter to the members, telling them that. At about this time, one board member approached her husband: "Charlie, can't you control your wife?"

"From 1984 on I wrote to the board each year. Every year I was getting nowhere. I was getting angrier inside. I was trying to do it the right way. In February 1990, I wrote my last letter. I said, 'Let's solve the problem.' I did not get a reply. In April, I asked the club president, 'Don, did you even get my letter?' He said he had, and he added, 'Be patient, be patient.'"

Before taking a further step, Mrs. Martin studied the tee-time operation at the club. She wanted to see just how heavy traffic was. "One Saturday in the spring of 1990 I arrived at the club at 10 A.M. I went to the pro shop, checked in, let the pro shop know I was there. I would tell them I was going to the ladies' locker room to change my shoes so that I would be ready to play at 1 P.M. Then I would sit near the window, looking out at the first tee and wait. And wait.

"I did this in April. In May. In June. In July. Don't you think that after a month, the guys would have said, 'We better do something'? Nothing happened. And by and large after 10 A.M., the tee was empty. That is, until 1 P.M., when women could tee off.

"There were many empty tee times. They knew that. One day in July, it was 100 degrees. It was so hot that my friends decided not to play with me. Since I couldn't play during the week, I played the eighteen holes alone in the heat. I came home. I had tried everything. I didn't want to go outside the club. I talked it over with my husband. He said, 'You've been more than patient.'

"On Monday I went to the Massachusetts Commission Against Discrimination. I almost didn't go in. What am I doing here? I asked myself. But I went in and I made my complaint. The next day the story was in the newspapers. I later found out that the reporters check the filings every so often to see if there's a good story."

Other newspapers interviewed her. She told one reporter, "I am trying to jar these medieval men off their thrones." The club reacted with fury. "We were getting ready to solve these problems," the club president said. Mrs. Martin still expected that the club would call her and work it out. Instead the club hired an attorney. When the club president finally called, he asked her to withdraw her complaint or run the risk that the board would not meet with her. "But they wouldn't meet with me for six years. So I said no."

Soon after the state attorney general's office intervened on her behalf and forced the club to change its bylaws to make them gender-neutral. The club also began working on the weekend tee-time problem, on integrating the grill, and on changing membership classifications. Many in the club opposed those changes. Soon after, the Martins began to receive harassing telephone calls in the middle of the night. One day they found golf balls with Longmeadow's logo on their patio. The balls had stopped short of hitting their big bay window. Next someone pulled up Mrs. Martin's lovely flowering crab apple trees and threw them away. Finally, a beloved Himalayan cat was poisoned. At her job, where she was a top insurance agent, she would receive nasty, obscene messages, telling her to leave the club.

"I have lived here all my life. All of a sudden these terrible things started to happen. This was very hard for my husband and myself to understand. We have no proof that these acts came from anybody at the club, but all these events happened only after I made my complaint."

In the fall of 1990, the state attorney general's office suggested that Midge Martin file a complaint against the club with the town selectmen, the town's elected governing body. The local selectmen had authority over the club's liquor license, and in Massachusetts a liquor license may be revoked if a private club is found to have practiced discrimination against a specific category of people. Two public hearings were held. Mrs. Martin said that the hearings produced an agreement to end discriminatory weekend tee times. But in the spring of 1991, when she went out to play, she found that the men at Longmeadow had decided to hold their own tournaments on weekend mornings. "From 1991 to 1994, the club consistently violated their own settlement agreement," she said.

This dispute could have been resolved easily, as events at a neighboring club proved. Two women members at nearby Springfield Country Club monitored Midge Martin's case, because they, too, wanted early weekend tee times. They are career women and could not play midweek. So they sent a letter to their own board. A committee was formed, and within a month or two the board voted to change its bylaws in order to open up the club's playing hours for working women. There was no animosity toward the women, no major upheaval, no fuss. It was just a different board—a younger, more progressive board. They may have learned from the Longmeadow experience.

Meanwhile, shunning continued at Longmeadow. It is remarkable to Mrs. Martin that the men engaged in shunning are many of the leaders in her community. They are the insurance executives, the bankers, the lawyers. "Their attitude toward women permeates our society. . . . If all these men have this mind-set in a recreational setting, can they really change that mind-set when they move from the club to the business location?" she asked. "What they are doing is telling their sons and daughters that it's tradition for women not to vote, not to hold office, not to tee off at a decent weekend hour. Their mothers seem to take the attitude that the men have been so good to them. Why make trouble?"

When the club finally changed its weekend tee times, it created a new category of membership for the golfing couple that wants to play early weekend mornings. The cost: after much wrangling, an additional $600 for a two-member weekend golfing couple. As things have turned out, the Martins are the only members in this group. All the other couples have chosen to stay in family memberships, at lower fees, with restrictive weekend tee times for spouses.

Mr. and Mrs. Martin are still members at Longmeadow because they won't be pushed out. She's accomplished much. Women can now vote, hold office, go to the men's grill, and choose a family membership with early tee times.

"For all of this, no one speaks to us, socializes or plays golf with us." She has one lawsuit outstanding. It asks for legal fees and damages from the club for the personal harm caused by institutional shunning.

⁂ PART III ⁂

Other Voices, Other Venues

10

Public Courses Today

Women who seek equality with men lack ambition.
—Bumper sticker on Patty Sheehan's car,
The Sporting News, 1983

When so many women have problems on the private playgrounds of America, it should come as no surprise that some consider the public course alternative. As noted earlier, public courses were once the poor cousins, markedly inferior in golfing layouts, overcrowded, lacking in amenities, rarely able to offer their players a truly rewarding round of golf. But the difference between private and public has been shrinking. It is now possible to stick with public courses and enjoy a happy and comfortable life with golf.

Public courses have been part of American golf almost from its inception. The course that gave public golf its start was Van Cortlandt Park Golf Course, in the Bronx, New York, and it soon had mates in Boston, Chicago, and other major cities. As public courses evolved, they came in three varieties: privately owned, municipal, and resort courses.

Privately owned public courses are sometimes called daily-fee courses, and there are some 6,800 of them in the country. They offer clinics, lessons, leagues, and, in some instances, even caddies. Then there are the municipal courses, owned by the town or city, and there are roughly 2,300 of them in the United States. They will sometimes limit play to town residents and their guests, and in this sense are not totally public. Taken together, these two types make up the vast bulk of the nine- or eighteen-hole public courses in the country. Finally, there are resort courses. As the name implies, these are typically scenic courses with excellent accommodations and high prices. Major resort courses are throughout the country from Sea Island, Georgia, to Pebble Beach in California, with many stops in between. These are meant primarily for vacationers, but they may have memberships for local residents.

Between public courses and those that are distinctly private lie the semiprivate courses. A good example of a course that combines features of the public and the private club is my home course in Manchester, Vermont. It was started by a group of savvy Vermonters in 1970, who realized they could use a federal rural-development grant to help attract business to their local area. It has a private membership like other private clubs, but its policies also require that it be open to guests of a number of local motels.

Variations on this type of course exist in many communities. One variant is the course that is part of a real-estate development. Such courses must accept memberships from persons who live in the development, and they often accept outside members to offset costs. Then there are a number of special courses with limited access. The main categories would include university courses, military courses, and occasional company-owned courses.

As public courses evolved, they were especially significant to minority golfers, who were excluded by rule or by custom from the world of private country clubs. This affected primarily the male players, who would hunt for public courses that would accept them. It is less well appreciated that there were minority female players who were similarly desirous of playing opportunities. One is Ethel Williams, a member of the first all-woman Negro golf club in America.

In 1937, when both private and public golf courses in Washington, D.C., existed for whites only, a group of Negro men would leave their wives every Sunday before dawn and set out to Baltimore or Philadelphia to play golf at courses that welcomed them.

The dozen wives left behind didn't like it a bit, and one of them, Helen Webb Harris, decided to form a golf club for the women left behind. Each was married to one of the golfers, members of an all-male club called the Royals. The chauvinists weren't about to let the women join the club, though when they gave a party, they wanted the women to do the work, remembers Ethel Williams wryly.

The women called their club the Wake Robin Golf Club, said Mrs. Williams, who is now, at age eighty-nine, the only surviving original member of the club. She related the club's history to me in the living room of her home in the nation's capital. The creed of the young women golfers was a simple one: "To perpetuate golf among Negro women, to make potential players into champions, and to make a permanent place for Negro women in the world of golf." Their first meeting was held April 22, 1937.

At first their husbands were opposed to the wives becoming golfers. "Mine criticized my early golf swings," said Mrs. Williams. "He said I was like an ironing board with arms and legs." But from such tentative beginnings came a champion. Mrs. Williams is now a member of the Negro Golf Hall of Fame and eleven times a senior club champion. She proudly displays her sixty trophies in her apartment.

The women could put up with the teasing from their husbands; what they found more difficult was finding a place to play. Washington public courses were closed to blacks, except for those who were caddies who could play on Mondays, the day courses are traditionally closed for repair. So these women followed their husbands' example. They would get up at 4 A.M., put on their purple culottes and yellow golf shirts, and go to neighboring states.

In 1939, when Franklin D. Roosevelt was president and Harold Ickes was the secretary of the interior, some members of the Royals met with Ickes to talk about getting a public golf course. From that discussion came Ickes's decision to build a nine-hole golf course on an old city dump. It was called the Langston Golf Course.

And that is when the Royals and the Wake Robin women began to play in their own city. It was quite an experience. "You could hit your ball and when you went to look for it, it could be in an old empty tin can that was exposed or somebody's old automobile tire," Mrs. Williams recalls.

Two years later, in 1941, Secretary Ickes ordered that the public golf courses in the nation's capital be desegregated. At one course, the East Potomac Park Golf Course, some of the Royals and Wake Robin members were stoned when they tried to use it. "White men and their children would come onto the course after we hit the ball, and they would pick it up and run with it. They kept taking our balls. Their dogs would run with them on the course. And the stones would come flying. But we kept on. We were taxpayers too." At times the men were forced to ask for a police escort to get them around the golf course.

In 1967 Mrs. Williams retired as a control clerk from the Bureau of Printing and Engraving, the first black woman on that desk, she says. She still plays weekly with the forty-strong Wake Robin women. She has never had a formal golf lesson, but likes to listen to the male golf announcers, particularly Ken Venturi, give pointers about how to play a shot.

"You know, one thing I like, it takes me out of the house, and it takes me out into the open. After the first hole, I give the cart to my partner. And I say, 'I'll walk. I'll meet you down the fairway.' "

The Jemsek family in the greater Chicago area are specialists in public golf. They run the golf course complex at Cog Hill Golf and Country Club in Lemont, Illinois, some thirty miles southwest of Chicago, with its four 18-hole golf courses, including Dubsdread, the championship layout used for the Western Open. Cog Hill offers a variety of lessons, clinics, and leagues for women to learn how to play and keep at it.

Joe Jemsek, who is known as the father of public golf, had a dream. He wanted to provide golf for the average man on courses that the wealthy played on. He was taken by Medinah No. 3, and he set out to create a course that would be as special for public golfers.

His son, Frank, who grew up on public golf courses, says public course growth was the result of two developments: the arrival of Arnold Palmer on television in the late 1950s, a man who looked like a regular guy, and the arrival of the golf cart. Golf carts cut down on the annual spring heart attack rate on the fairways, provided the time together for friendships to form and grow, and provided needed cash for the public club.

Women were part of that growth. "I've seen more and more women on the courses after the late 1950s," said Carol McCue, vice-president of Jemsek Corporations and a forty-year-long public golfer. "And now we have a lot more women at our courses who are career women. They play for social reasons, they play for exercise, they have a good deal of disposable income. There are also women who are picking it up again after they raised their families."

By now as many as 37 percent of all new golfers are women, and at least two-thirds of them are playing on public facilities. What do they find? I begin with places where the game is learned and then move on to the golf course.

❧ *Getting Started: Ranges, Par-Three Courses,* ❧ *Lessons and Equipment*

All golfers need to get started in the game, and for men and women alike the usual starting place will be a driving range. Even private club members are likely to want to begin in the nonthreatening world of a public driving range. Most will spend a lot of time at the practice range, certainly days, probably weeks, and, if they are wise, probably months. That is how it should be. You really do have to practice and to learn something about the game before setting foot on the course.

There are several good things about ranges: there are plenty of them, they are not hard to find, they often have equipment if you don't have your own, and they are relatively inexpensive—buckets of balls cost a few dollars.

Another good thing about driving ranges is that for any beginner, male or female, you get a chance to learn and to make mistakes without holding up people on a real golf course. Also, unlike golf courses, which over the years have accumulated all sorts of rules about etiquette and dress, driving ranges are mercifully free of such things.

The *driving* range is just what its name implies: you can drive the ball as far as you can hit it. However, at a driving range it is much harder to learn the *short game*, the pitching, chipping, and putting that are essential to the game of golf. The best place to learn that is a *pitch-and-putt* or *par-three* course.

One course in particular stands out in my mind, and the situation that led me to it is one that I believe many women have encountered. My husband, Stan, and I are members of a semiprivate golf club in Manchester, Vermont. Stan, who has played golf all his life and was the captain of his college team, gave me my first set of clubs at Christmastime in 1987. I assumed that come late spring I would play at our country club in Manchester. I took some lessons with our pro and went to a clinic the club offered for women. And then, out I went.

I stepped up to the tee and concentrated on all that I had learned.

I addressed the ball. I stepped back. Now to the grip and the stance. How did my knees move? And how should those shoulders feel? What did the pro say about the pivot and about swinging through?

I looked around. It was then that I realized that everyone was waiting to watch my swing, or so I thought. Just as I thought I had it, I heard my husband's voice: "Remember, keep your head down." Now I was getting edgy.

The next thing I noticed was that Stan was glancing back a lot. As I came to find out, he was doing what was natural for him to do under the circumstances; he was moving me along. When I asked him why he was looking back, he 'fessed up: others behind us might be *waiting*. Soon I began to glance back—every other second, it seemed.

Then I began to whiff the ball. When I whiffed it enough times to feel a blush on my cheek, Stan gently explained the concept of "picking up the ball." And so it went. I played poorly for about a month. I then faced a dilemma. I had a golf course to play on and didn't want to play it. I loved the idea of spending four or five hours at a beautiful course in the Green Mountains of Vermont. But I felt self-conscious. The reason was obvious: I was not yet playing golf. (I later learned that many husbands would not have taken kindly to accompanying their novice-golfer spouse on the golf course in the first place.)

By nature I'm not a quitter. But what was I to do? One night at dinner, I told my husband that I would not play at our club until I could consistently get the ball airborne. That was my minimum requirement. Now, where could I go to practice hitting the ball and not feel intimidated? I asked. We discussed driving ranges, but I had gone to driving ranges. I wanted to experience golf on a course.

"Why not try the par-three municipal in Arlington?" he asked. Par-three courses are usually nine holes with no hole longer than two hundred yards or so from tee to green. The next day we arrived at the par-three course in the next town. It was there that I finally relaxed. It was there that I finally got the ball aloft. It was there that I began to feel confidence. Soon I was going out alone or with friends. A few months later I took my young nephew to play. "Not bad," he said when I hit it straight (and airborne) eighty-five yards.

My par-three course is often filled with local women, men, and children. It is a great place to learn, and that's what women need, a benign place to learn. My little par three does not stop women at the door. There is no door. The official welcome, if you want to call it that, is a little box with a sign on it: IF IT'S NOT WORTH A BUCK, DON'T COME BACK. I cherish the Arlington par-three course.

Most ranges or par-three courses and almost all private clubs will have instructors prepared to give lessons for a fee. Over the years, I've taken a number of lessons with different male pros with varying results. One pro was indifferent. I paid $25 for a half hour of instruction, and after twenty minutes he was looking at his watch. Another pro was terrific with experienced golfers, but not terribly good with beginners. A third pro was extremely helpful and seemed to have a golfing rapport with women. It may be significant that he was the only one I found who had been recommended by a woman. "Consult your PGA professional," say the television ads, but it's clear that some male teachers are better than others for women players. There are still relatively few women teachers.

Another way to get instruction is to go to a golf school. These schools vary in expense and amenities, from well-appointed hotels with excellent meals to day camps with many local clientele. There are all kinds of packages advertised in magazines like *Golf Digest, Golf* and *Golf for Women*. A school provides closely supervised instruction and a chance to play on a real course. Students are divided into groups according to their skill. If the instructors care, as they did in my school at Sea Island, Georgia, the golfer learns a lot.

Some schools are geared for women, like the one at Pine Needles Resort, in Southern Pines, North Carolina, the site of the 1996 U.S. Women's Open. The resort is owned by Peggy Kirk Bell, a famous player of the 1940s and 1950s. Many women rave about the instruction there.

Instruction requires equipment. And while getting clothed and equipped does not produce the same sort of tension women often feel on the golf course, the buying of clothing and equipment often is not an easy or pleasant experience.

Women who are new to golf are often financially well-off. They have money to spend. But plunk them down in a golf warehouse or a pro shop and they realize that men are given a vast array of choice in equipment, while women are not. Yes, it's getting better. There are more manufacturers making golf clubs for women, but as for clothing, shoes, and getting served . . . well.

If a woman goes shopping for irons and takes her husband or male friend along with her, the salesman usually talks to him. At one golf store, a salesman addressed questions to the husband while his wife stood by silently. Finally, the husband turned to the salesman and said,

"Look, she's buying the clubs. Talk to her, ask her." The salesman looked dumbstruck, but did as he was told. If a woman is with a man, she will get waited on. If she's alone, she is often on her own.

❧ Playing on Public Courses: ❧ Starters, Rangers, and Tee Times

When players have a golf swing and an introductory understanding of the game, they head for a regular eighteen-hole golf course. After all, that's the point of learning: to play the game on a regular full-size golf course. Only in Japan does one find large numbers of players who are restricted to the driving range because of costs and overcrowded conditions at golf courses.

The people I've talked to who run public facilities say that clubs haven't always been attentive to the needs of their women players, but that they are getting better, largely because women are now a key ingredient in their businesses.

I believe they are right. But in doing research for this chapter I found that women from different areas of the country often had less than positive things to say—women who were working or nonworking, married or single, beginners or experienced players, housewives or career women. Though hardly statistically representative, their remarks seem to give a fair picture of what is going on out there.

The same themes kept cropping up in interview after interview. The main theme revolves around attitude and "climate." Certainly since the civil-rights movement of the sixties we expect public golf courses to be free of discriminatory rules and procedures, and for the most part they are. They rarely have anything like the gender-specific bylaws of the private clubs. Nonetheless, many women say they feel hostility in the air. What they seem to sense is a common male attitude toward women and golf: women may have to be tolerated on the course, but they needn't be encouraged.

Starters and rangers (sometimes called marshals) are key figures in the experience for women. A starter is the guy (and it is usually a guy) who controls access to the first tee. Golfers have to check in with him before they are allowed on the course. The starter takes the starting times that have been given out by the pro shop and checks the golfers against that list. He may also be able to fill in any vacancies that appear as a result of cancellations. At public courses, starters have long had the reputation of helping men and hindering women, both by what they do and what they say.

"I've heard starters apologize to a male threesome when they assign a woman to their group. But the same starter thinks nothing of assigning a ninety-year-old man to a woman's threesome—without any apology—when the women can play rings around him," said Maureen Sullivan, an amateur golfer from Westchester County, New York, who plays in a business league.

Many starters need an education in courtesy and respect for women players. Rachel Shuster, a sports columnist for *USA Today*, described it well in a column that appeared in the newspaper in August 1993: "I joined a threesome of women at a public course this summer and found them unnerved by what the starter said: 'You ladies are standing too near the first tee, and you're talking too loud.'

"Thing is, they weren't that loud, and they were a decent distance back off the tee. They weren't angry, though. 'That's the way we're always treated,' the ladies said."

The ranger is hired to patrol the course. Since the single most costly trait is slow play, rangers roam the course in golf carts pushing folks along, often singling out females. Many career women who play on public courses say the rangers, who are almost always male, need to be educated. They perpetuate the stereotype of the woman as slow player.

Jenny Elliott, of Arvada, Colorado, has a nineteen-handicap and plays golf a couple of times a week at public courses. "I see the ranger coming and I tense up. And I say to myself I have to hit the shot really fast. It really bothers me when a ranger stops and waits to see you hit. And that's when you really flub a shot. It puts pressure on and causes me to feel uncomfortable playing. That's where I've experienced the most discrimination."

Becky Powell, the owner of the Powell Group, a marketing and public-relations firm in Houston, Texas, says, "Marshals assume we play slowly. Last July 4th our foursome—and we were the only women on a daily-fee course—had an encounter with a marshal. Somebody hit the ball into the rough; a marshal came over and got all over us. We all shoot in the nineties and got done in the right amount of time. That sort of thing angers me. Just like any other discrimination, this has to do with preconceived ideas without any validity to them."

One woman from Connecticut, who has a twenty-handicap and plays primarily on public courses, says, "The rangers have a tendency to follow women more closely and speak to them more frequently. They tolerate more from a man than a woman. They watch us more. We have complained about slow male groups, but they don't do anything."

Sometimes novice women golfers may be partially to blame for their mistreatment because, like any beginner, they don't know enough about course etiquette, about picking up the ball, moving along, and being ready to hit the ball when it's their turn. Public courses emphasize pace of play, but many women feel singled out. One woman put it succinctly: "Marshals look at women and see if they are slowing pace, as opposed to watching pace and seeing who is slowing it."

Ms. Elliott, a communications executive, says she has such a fear she will be stopped by a ranger when she plays with beginners that she takes them out only on weekdays, when there are fewer rangers around. She said, "We are not what slows the game down. What slows it down are those who are looking for balls, those who take extra time on the green lining up a putt, those who are taking eighteen practice swings."

Getting a tee time on a public course requires persistence and fortitude. If you live in a town with a municipal course and want to play there on Saturday morning, you may well have to show up in person in the wee hours of the morning. Some of these courses don't take reservations, and they assign tee times on a first-come-first-served basis. The queue sometimes begins at 2 A.M.

A businesswoman I know waited in line a couple of mornings at a town course and then said, Enough. She asked a kid who worked for her if he would sit in for her. He agreed. He used his car, took along his girl-friend, and got paid twenty dollars. But then one day the other golfers in line got angry. The businesswoman wasn't waiting in the queue herself. She wasn't playing by the rules. So she stopped using the municipal course. Many town and county courses still operate this way. Waiting in line before dawn is not the easiest, most relaxing way to start your day on the golf course. But it allows the golfer to tee off early and even come back later on. Some people play thirty-six holes this way.

Increasingly, however, public courses have changed their tee-time system. It's now more civilized. Some have automated tee-times. Others have first-come telephone systems where weekend tee times can be set days or sometimes weeks ahead. Easy as pie.

Well, not always.

I know a foursome of women who take turns each week calling for a tee time at the public course where they are frequent players. Each begins dialing at 7 A.M., when the pro shop opens, the first moment they can make a tee time for the weekend. Each uses autodial, so that as fast as she gets her first busy signal, the call is repeated.

Never have they gotten through before 11:30 A.M. When they do get through, the first available tee time is for 11 A.M. or later. The course is very busy, they are told. Doris, one member of the foursome, said, "One weekend we checked out the course at an early time and found it filled with Japanese men—all executives." The women guess there is some sort of standing tee time for these men.

Another woman who also plays regularly at a public course and can supposedly get a tee time at any time, provided she can get through on the telephone, said, "But on occasion women have been told, 'No early tee times,' and the pro has been rude, and then subsequently we found that there were early tee times."

Connie Wheeler, a bookkeeper from Joplin, Missouri, has been playing for three years at semiprivate and public courses. She says that at her semiprivate club men have standing tee times. "The people at the pro shop fill in the names of the men. They don't admit it, but that's what goes on."

Not every golfer wants an early-morning weekend tee time. There are legions of golfers who prefer to play golf late in the day when the course is quieter and emptier. Jeanne Vivona of Jersey City, New Jersey, who has been playing for sixteen years, is an afternoon player.

"I'm not going to get up at 4 A.M. and wait in line. If you play late in the afternoon, it is not as crowded, you can play at your leisure, and you don't get as much pressure from men."

Can an informal group of men get tee times on a standing basis? At some courses, absolutely. Men who often play together, members of the men's association, say, have one of their group telephone, or better yet, go directly to the pro shop to make group tee times, say for Monday, Wednesday, or Friday at 8 A.M. They might get three consecutive times. That would enable twelve men to play. Enterprising groups of women may negotiate the same sort of deal, particularly if they make arrangements long in advance and bring in a large group or league for a specific date and time.

It is not unknown for golfers, of either sex, to pay the pro for a starting time. Many pros will refuse, but some don't. "Pre-tipping" is the polite word for it.

A number of women have complained about not being able to get early-morning tee times at public courses. Sylvia Garlowich, of Deer Park, Texas, described her experience in a letter to the *Houston Chronicle* in the summer of 1994:

> I have never played golf at any of Houston's country clubs, but I am an executive in a major retail firm and have found discrimination toward females at several public golf courses. I have golfed with several men in the past few years and have tried to call and place tee times for us. On several occasions I have been given tee times only in the afternoon. Later the same day, my husband would call and be given a tee time hours earlier.

The women's tee-time issue attracted national attention in 1993 when ABC-TV's "Prime Time Live" show did a brief segment on tee times, sending "testers" out to one public course in Cincinnati, Ohio, where they claimed to find that a male, arriving at the shop just after a female, got an earlier tee time.

One case proves nothing, of course. In this instance they may have picked a course that actually has a good reputation among women players. In fact, no one has done a thorough and systematic study of the issue, but the frequency with which women report tee-time problems suggests that there may be something there.

❧ Slow Play and Intimidation ❧

Women are often accused of slow play by men. And if there is one negative feeling frequently expressed by women players, it is the feeling of intimidation, a feeling within the women themselves. These two experiences are pervasive, and they are linked. As the reaction of women to starters and rangers indicates, the sense that men are predisposed to label them slow players is a prime source of their feelings of intimidation.

It is not unusual for a golfer to spend five or six hours completing an eighteen-hole round of golf. That's a long time for a round that should take four hours at most, and in Scotland might take two and a half. Who holds up play? Is it men? Is it women? Is it a combination of both? Is it beginners of both sexes? Do beginners go out on the course too early in their game? Are they unwilling to pick up their ball and move on? Does it take a new player six swings to get a tee shot in the air?

Slow play is not an issue only for amateurs. The PGA Tour, the organization that represents the best male golfers in the country, has had to set penalties for slow play. Indeed, nowadays there is a lot of anecdotal information that men are slower than they used to be because they have the model from television of very "deliberate" professional players taking their time lining up putts. Also, some golfers develop intricate betting schemes that result in slow play. For example, one game is called Bingo, Bango, Bongo: on each hole a player gets a point for being the first one on the green, another point for being the player closest to the hole when all are on the green, and a third point for being the first in the cup. It is the latter point that may require excessive ball marking and putting.

A study commissioned by the Women's Golf Summit showed that women play slightly more slowly than men on average, but well within a reasonable eighteen-hole time of four to four-and-one-half hours. Still, officials sometimes use women's slow play as a reason for their rules. One public course in Hermitage, Pennsylvania, run by a VFW chapter, banned women in the morning because it said they play too slowly. "It plugs up the whole course," said the course manager. The board's policy permitted women after 11 A.M. on weekends and holidays. And in one of the few court cases involving public courses, slow play was the issue as well.

Back in 1982, in Lawrence Village, Long Island, New York, two women golfers took the village to federal court, charging that village regulations at the public course prohibited mixed foursomes during prime-time morning hours on weekends and holidays. Until 1980, women were not allowed to play at all during the prime-time weekend and holiday morning hours. The reason? Village officials said they played too slowly. The judge ruled that the golf course was public and built with public funds, and ordered the village to obey the law against discrimination "as do all other public facilities."

The slow play issue is too important to be left to the world of perception and stereotype. It would not be a surprise to find that women, who on the average take more shots than men, will take longer to play a round of golf. But that's on the average. Any serious golfer knows that many women are good and fast players, many men are agonizingly slow. As Dr. Hanno said in her letter to Carrollwood Country Club, if slow play is a problem, deal with slow play, not with gender.

There are many things courses, public or private, can do to speed up play. One is to hold clinics teaching players timesaving strategies. Another is to distinguish more clearly between beginners, who natural-ly will need more time, and experienced players. The beginners may be asked to play at those times when they will least hold up play. A third, which many courses now employ, is to have an expected time of play and ask rangers or marshals to politely warn groups when they are falling behind. Another way is to do what they do in France: certify that golfers play at a certain level before they are permitted to play on a course. The problem can best be dealt with by dealing directly with the slow players wherever they are found, not by stigmatizing one gender or the other.

One reason women give for quitting golf is intimidation, and this is especially true of those who are still learning. Sometimes they are intim-idated by the game itself. As Ms. McCue, of Jemsek, says, "It looks so easy on television. And some come to take a lesson and then we don't see them again." Often they are intimidated by those who have played longer, sometimes other women, but usually men.

A recent study reported that a whopping 82 percent of the women interviewed in a golf survey identified male golfers as the most common source of their intimidation. One reason is that public courses are still a man's domain. Women, Ms. McCue believes, also feel the need to become perfect at the game very quickly. And that is not easy to do.

Men don't feel that way. One male executive of the DuPont Com-pany attended the women's golf summit in 1993. "In all the time I played business golf, a score of 140 or 150 was not uncommon with the men. There's no reason you need to feel intimidated. I really wish you would get rid of the word. Go out and play the game and enjoy it, and get better if you can. If you can't, pick the ball up when you're more than two over par."

Some instructors are trying to deal with the intimidation issue head-on. Frank Jemsek of Cog Hill learned how common were feelings of intimidation or embarrassment at a 1991 golf summit. So his public courses in the Chicago area now feature "No Embarrassment Golf

Schools," an explicitly nonthreatening environment in which to learn or improve your game. This attitude is very important to communicate to beginners, because continuing to play means they will become better golfers, and better golfers get respect. Getting respect generally means receiving less discriminatory treatment. Jemsek Golf is still learning: its brochure announcing No Embarrassment Golf Schools, and aimed at women players, features a man on the cover! But its heart is in the right place.

Jane Dally of New York City has a seven-handicap and is a fine player. She says she has never experienced discrimination at any public or private course. She started to play at age five and joined the boys' golf team in high school. When she walks out of the pro shop and onto the first tee, she carries herself like an athlete; she views herself as an athlete. And the fact is, men want to play with her. She does not view herself as a female golfer. "I have always considered myself a golfer, not a female golfer—a player and a competitor. I play with men. They enjoy my company, and I tee it up with the best of them."

The catch-22 is that women golfers, in general, can get better only if facilities allow them to work on their games. At the same time, the slow-play stigma makes them reticent. "Women don't have the confidence they as a paying customer should have to enjoy the game and to forget the stigma and the stereotype," she said.

Public courses ought to educate marshals and starters about slow play in regard to men and women. And all newcomers ought to learn about the etiquette, pace, sportsmanship of the game. It is an economically sensible thing for courses to teach these things; but few public courses do.

❧ *Public or Private* ❧

The choice of public versus private is a real one. The problems of gender bias are not absent from public courses, but they reveal themselves in the amorphous area of *attitude*. Only in the private clubs are they routinely found in the rules and bylaws. For some people that leaves little choice.

Arlene Resnick, the president of a Great Neck, Long Island, brokerage firm, tried for years to get a full membership as a single woman member in any number of Long Island golf and country clubs. She wanted a place to play and to entertain business clients. The answer was always no. It had nothing to do with personality or lack of love for the game. Discussions never got that far. What it had to do with was her status: she was divorced and the clubs she applied to had no category for single women.

Ms. Resnick knew country club life well. Her parents were founding members of Pine Hollow Country Club in East Norwich, Long Island, the club where she learned to play golf. When she married, she brought her husband into the club. When they divorced she was forced out. He stayed. Her daughter and son-in-law are now members of her old club.

For nearly four years, she tried to get into a club. She would call. "They would say, 'What's your husband's name?' And when I said there was no husband, there would be all this humphing on the other end." Then, quite by accident, in the spring of 1994 Ms. Resnick learned about the Hamlet Golf and Country Club, a development course in Commack, Long Island, for residents who live on the golf course. She called and asked if there were golf memberships for outside people. Before long, she was in.

"Here you are a citizen. You pay your money. You tee off when you want to. I was out there at 9 A.M. Sunday morning with three other women. I bring male guests and clients. It's the best thing I've ever done. It's wonderful. It's beautiful. It's new. I feel like a human being again. I can enjoy golf again as I have enjoyed it all my life. And I can entertain business clients, just like the men. But I had to go outside the mainstream to find a club."

For others, the choice is not so easy. Only a few expensive resort clubs can offer the full set of amenities available at many private country clubs. Some women executives are likely to find the same shortcomings in facilities that led Darwin Davis, a black executive with Equitable Financial Companies in New York, to seek a private club membership.

"I'm at a disadvantage with my competitor. If I want to take the state controller out for a round of golf because I want to talk to him about a bond issue, the best I can do is to take him to the public course I play in Stamford, Connecticut. The best I can feed him is a hamburger. My opponent takes him to his country club, where he has a great lunch, with a bar, and he gets to use a locker room with a shower, and afterward he has his shoes shined. . . . I have worked hard and that's the

American way. But one's efforts should bring rewards. I make enough money to do it; I'm a gentleman, a family man. I love golf. There is nothing about me except the color of my skin that keeps me from a club."

That was in 1990. Davis continued his quest and is now a member of St. Andrew's Golf Club in Hastings-on-Hudson, New York, the same club that was so snooty to women early in the century.

Though it is often lacking in amenities, there is something about the spirit at public golf courses that is captivating to those who experience it, men or women, and they look back on it with fond nostalgia if they make the shift from public to private. A few hours on the course can be fun, irreverent, sometimes raucous time spent with people for whom golf is often the highlight of their daily, weekly, and monthly round of life. Putting sports competition first, enjoying the spirit of the competition, deflating pretenders and status seekers is all a part of it, and this is more easily accomplished on public courses than on the more sedate setting of the private country club. But this romantic view shouldn't blind us to the other reasons women, in particular, may stay on the public side.

Ann Gravseth, a merchandising manager in Dallas with a twenty-one-handicap, has been an avid golfer for the last ten years. She comes from a golfing family and has taken the game up again for social reasons, then realized what a good vehicle it was for business. She has been to several four-day golf schools and with her husband and children has attended two U.S. Opens and other golfing events. Her family lives for golf. They and the relatives even have a family golf tournament in Minnesota, complete with a traveling trophy. All of her family's vacations are organized around golf.

Though she and her family could afford a private club, for now she is staying put. "I am not a feminist woman type. But I am absolutely appalled that we still have these arcane rules of not playing on Saturday morning. We play now in an old cheap club in Dallas, more like a public course. It's a social place, where women can play any time they want. I refuse to pay ten grand to join ninety-nine percent of the other clubs around here that won't let me play until noon on Saturday. Of all the things that I hear about, I still can't believe it. It's not that I want to play with my bosses on Saturday. I want to play with my husband or a girl-friend. I'd like to help get that changed, but I won't join a fancy club until I find one where discrimination against women doesn't exist."

Inventive Organizations
for Women's Golf

*The golf industry has not been attuned to the fact that
women are on the outside, looking in. . . . They don't realize just how bad it's been.*

—Nancy Oliver, founder of the
Executive Women's Golf League

In the space of three short years, from 1991 to 1994, Nancy Oliver's
Executive Women's Golf League has grown to seven thousand members
in thirty states and seventy-five cities and the District of Columbia. Virtually all of the women who join are career women. And they are now
enjoying golf for pleasure and golf as a way to make business contacts.
The Executive Women's Golf League (EWGL) is a young organization
that is making golf a "user friendly" sport for women. It is also the largest
of the new women's golf organizations that have sprung up.

The women in the Executive Women's Golf League now belong
to eighty chapters nationwide. They come from all kinds of businesses
and professions. They are bankers, lawyers, judges, writers, financial
analysts, and marketing and merchandising executives. They run their
own businesses or have high positions in organizations. They are now
becoming comfortable with leaving the office early to get to the golf
course midweek as their male colleagues have long done. Most are
beginners. They will spend money on equipment, on lessons, on food.
What they want is a comfortable setting. Nancy Oliver figured that out
one day when she was forced to confront herself.

Nancy Oliver's livelihood was golf. She ran her own golf marketing company. She counted a number of top golf and country clubs,
including the PGA of America, as clients, and she chatted routinely
with the best-known newspaper and television golf writers in the country. She lived it. She breathed it. She made good money from it. She also
had a dirty little secret. She did not play it.

"I knew all the golf writers. I would tell them I would join them
for the back nine. But I didn't. I got by with that one for quite a while. I
was doing rather well at it. I laughed at all the jokes."

All this is rather remarkable since she had made golf marketing
her career for thirteen years. Clearly she, more than most, knew the
benefits of an eighteen-hole round with CEOs and the like. And she
knew what it felt like to spend months drawing up events and tournaments for her clients and then not play. At the same time, she had a husband, four children, a house, and you know the rest.

Then a couple of things happened to Mrs. Oliver that made her
realize she had to learn how to play golf. Her career grew and she began
to mount more visible tournaments. Next she received an invitation to
play in a golf tournament that attracted all the state's top CEOs. "It used
to be you didn't get the invitation. Now I get it and I can't play. In the
past, I went to the cocktail party. Finally, some dear friends wanted me
to play, and I said no, and the friend said, 'How come?' and I said, 'I
don't know how.' And he said, 'You're kidding me.' "

She wondered, How do I learn to play golf? Do I go through the
Yellow Pages and call up a pro? Maybe I get a lesson or two, but then
whom do I play with and who will hold my hand through this process?
That planted the seed. Driving home one day in 1991, convinced she
had to learn how to play golf if she was going to hold her head high in
the golf marketing business, Nancy Oliver said to herself, "I'll be darned
if I'm going to do this by myself."

"So my brain began to go tick, tick, tick. And I typed up a memo
to the president of Emerald Dunes, one of my clients, and I proposed a
clinic once a week, every Tuesday. We would teach executive women the
terminology, the etiquette, we would give them equipment in the form
of rented clubs and range balls. We would charge twenty-five dollars.
And they would need clubs and they would need gloves, and they
would get them in the pro shop. I never mentioned I wanted to learn
how to play golf.

"He said, 'Fine, let's do it.' I knew the golf writers, so I wrote up a press release and sent it to them. They put the item in their stories. On July 10, 1991, we began. We had twenty-eight women. None of them knew where the bag-drop area was. When we were through, the women said, This is such fun, why not get together once a month to play golf? Some of the women were from Fort Lauderdale, an hour away, and they said, 'We want something nearer.'"

Nancy wrote a press release. Out it went. On the first day at the course, a local television station showed up and they were live from the putting green. What a novel idea, women wanting to learn how to play golf to develop business contacts.

The media propelled the whole thing. It just started rolling. And her golf game? "Not worth a hill of beans," she says.

Nancy Oliver wasn't yet out on the course herself. Instead, she was getting other women out there. Her idea to learn how to play golf had turned into an organization. She was on the phone. She was writing press releases. She was posing for photos as her new chapters opened. It was an idea whose time had come.

"I'm a good middle-ground-type person. But this was beginning to take its toll on my own business. I was a one-woman band.

"We had four groups up and running by November. So we charged dues and the checks were made out to the Executive Women's Golf League. I took the checks to the bank, but we had no company. So I had to get a company. I had to get a business license and a bank account. We needed a logo. We got stationery. We went to press. We looked official. Then our logo started showing up on things, and one of the attorneys I know said to me, 'Do you have that name registered?' and I said, 'Oh, gosh.' And he said, 'Don't you think you ought to form a corporation and register it with the state?' And I said, 'Would you do that for me?' And he did.

"Clearly there was a need for the leagues. But soon I didn't have time for my clients, for my public-relations campaigns, for brochures and golf marketing. My billable hours started going down dramatically, and so my husband and I sat down and we said either I have to take the phones off or, if I'm going to do it, I'm going to do it right.

"And that's how we began."

Leagues make it easy for women to grow in golf, to find friends, to feel safety in numbers, to work on their games, to take lessons, to learn the etiquette. Once they get confidence, they accept invitations they once rejected and they play with male colleagues at office outings.

Playing golf with clients makes a tremendous difference in the way they are perceived, they say.

As the previous chapter showed, women need a comfort zone in order to learn how to play. Obviously, the primary appeal is the game itself and a love of the outdoors. But in a sport traditionally dominated by men, "Women were crying out for a welcome mat," Mrs. Oliver says.

"The golf industry has not been attuned to the fact that women have been on the outside, looking in. The golf industry does not realize just how bad the situation has been for women. For the golf industry to thrive, it has to grow golfers," she said.

In the last three years, Mrs. Oliver has learned a lot. She has learned that each league has its own needs and style and that to work, a league needs an enthusiastic pro, a dedicated core group of professional women willing to give the time to organize events, and a golf course that welcomes women.

As for the new golfers, they've had some surprises.

Many thought they would begin by building up their skills so that they could play with male colleagues and compete for business. They have accomplished that. But to their surprise they also made new business contacts with the women they met through the league's clinics. The other surprise is that they are making friends.

That may sound strange, but for working women with children, husband, home, career, there is little time left in the day for adult friendship. At one end-of-season party, Mrs. Oliver recalls, women were asked to talk about their success stories in golf and business. And afterward each received a yellow rose.

One woman stood up to say her story was a little different. Mrs. Oliver recalls what she said: "'Alise and I were paired the first day and we just hit it off and since then it has been kind of a tough year for me, and she has been a wonderful friend. And I want Alise to know I have not had a close friend like this since high school, and I want her to know she means the world to me.' And the woman gets very teary, and they hugged each other and both got yellow roses. There wasn't a dry eye in the house. And I sat there quietly, like a fly on the wall, thinking, Good Lord, what have I created."

By the summer of 1994, the organization had grown up, even going so far as to establish a branch in New York City. But she needed more backing to take it to the next level, to corporate sponsorships of leagues, to further expansion in other cities, to tournaments and the like. The arrival of International Management Group of Cleveland was the next logical step. That partnership was formed in the summer of 1994.

IMG knows the economic potential of this group of women. A survey for the LPGA in 1993 shows that most women golfers are employed fulltime, often in professional roles, that their household income is over $60,000, that the golfer and her family own one home, sometimes two, and that she plays a pivotal role in purchasing major items and planning vacations. Often the woman is the sole decision maker.

Over the years, a number of women executives across the country have organized and operated executive women's golf leagues in their city. They share a common desire: all want to play golf, to meet other executive women and do business. In the process, each has helped transform women's amateur golf in their areas.

Susan Dunning, an account executive at Dean Witter, is a wife, a mother of two small children, and holds a full-time job. She left New York City in 1990, where she worked on Drexel Burnham Lambert's bond desk, and with her family headed for Cleveland, Ohio.

Once there, she wanted to meet people and to a find a sport she liked to play. "I worked at a public golf course as a kid, and I could never understand why people waited in the parking lot at 5:30 A.M. to get a tee time. Now I understand. I'm out there, too, at 5:30 A.M."

After meeting other women at a public course, she called Mrs. Oliver and started a league in Cleveland. She thought she would get thirty women for the first outing. But she got the story in the *Cleveland Plain Dealer* and she then received hundreds of calls.

"Many were the 'Who's Who' of Cleveland. All of a sudden we knew we had a major mega-tiger by the tail and we didn't know what to do with it. First we were overwhelmed. Then we went into full speed. In two weeks we put together the best kickoff party you ever saw." What began with 88 women at her first golf clinic in 1992 has now grown to three leagues and 250 women.

She has done what she can to have some impact on the private club world. She recognizes that women in the leagues are treated fairly, and then get to a private club and learn about discrimination. One businesswoman in her group wanted to join a private club only to find out that her non-golf-playing husband had to join for her and then she could not play on weekends.

So when a charitable organization called Ms. Dunning about inviting some women's league golfers for a tournament at a private club, Ms. Dunning replied she could not promote an event at a club that did not take women members. The tournament sponsors decided to look for another site.

Now in its fourth year, women in the leagues have learned the rules, are taking out clients, have learned the etiquette. They play at several public courses in the area, places where they have a standing tee-time date. "We are now honing in on the fine points. We are teaching them how to bet."

Chris Owens, an estates attorney in Maryland, started the Baltimore chapter in 1992. She put small notices in various legal newsletters, and the response was overwhelming. "Our kickoff dinner was in March 1993," she recalled. "It was the worst imaginable weather, a torrential rain that night. And yet two hundred and twenty women showed up. Many were newcomers."

Soon after, Ms. Owens found a public golf course, the Turf Valley Resort and Country Club in Howard County, which had the capacity (forty-five holes) for their group as well as dining facilities. "They couldn't have been more accommodating. They recognized the potential. The first season we had 330 members. Well over 50 percent were beginners. The club pro set up clinics for them." The cost at the course for weekly green fees and cart: $22. "Women are now going into their firms or businesses and saying, 'When you put together your tournament, I play golf, too.' "

Jane Shumaker, a native of Buffalo, New York, took up golf four years ago. She is the associate vice-president of operations for the Dean Witter office in Buffalo. She golfs for the pleasure of it; she golfs for business. She uses those public or semiprivate courses whose management understands that the women's golf market is just waiting to take off.

Like Ms. Dunning and Ms.Owens, Ms. Shumaker understands the marketing power of the EWGL. She calls up the management of a local public course. "I tell them, 'I am bringing you sixty women to play golf. Those women have come right from work. They're hungry. They're gonna eat somewhere afterward. Why not your clubhouse? But don't you think you need to give us a deal here? Don't you think that we should have a two-for-one drink special or something? I'm going to give a banquet when we close our events. We've been frequently to your pro shop. Would you want to participate in this? When these women think about lessons, aren't you somebody that ought to be considered?'

"We use our resources. We know how to do that. And maybe the golf pros aren't used to this breed of women. We're gonna call them and ask about getting a block of tee times. If we don't get them, we'll say, 'Thank you very much.' We'll call the next place."

Gloria Conway Jones, former president of the Washington, D.C., chapter of the EWGL and now the organization's regional liaison for the Mid-Atlantic region, picked up her golf clubs for the first time in twenty years in June 1992. She had retired as a corporate executive, she had started her own public-relations firm, raised her sons. Now she had time for golf.

As a black woman, she saw the potential for growth among black women golfers. "I get so tired of all these new organizations popping up and being exclusive to one culture or one race or whatever. What I really wanted to do with the Washington chapter of the EWGL was make it representative of the area itself. When I joined the league, I think there was one other black person in it. When I left as president, we had about forty-five minority women." Recruitment was largely by word of mouth.

Besides bringing in minority women, she also brought in men. "I did not exclude men from anything we did," she said. "We're just in it to have fun, enjoy golf, and benefit from the networking it brings. I don't care how you look at it, this is a man's world. I don't think you can exclude them totally. Some of our membership feels we should do that. I always say, they can make or break us."

In the past, she said, black women have not taken to golf because it takes too long to play. "A lot has to do with our culture; family has always come first. In a lot of black families, the mother is the dominant figure. She is tending the house, tending the kids, taking care of the husband. And now she's working, too. And I really don't think she has time for golf."

As more black women enter corporate life, and the statistics show there are more female black executives today than there are male, more will take up the game.

The idea of executive golf leagues has now branched out far beyond Nancy Oliver's substantial achievement. Over the years other groups have organized to accomplish many of the same goals. Two of these are the Businesswomen's Golf Link and the Professional Business Women's Golf Network.

Women golf pros or assistant pros also have started clinics at their own public courses for career women and other golf-business groups. Bridget Pendergast, the head pro at Honey Bee Golf Club in Virginia Beach, started a women's group at her club after a student who worked midweek complained she couldn't join the traditional ladies' midweek morning group. Honey Bee is a daily-fee course that caters to outings, tournaments, daily play.

At the outset she had to convince the club owner to give the idea a try. "I proposed Tuesday at 5:30 P.M., after work ended. We started with twenty-two. Now we have one hundred and fifty women. They play more and that has doubled my lessons and increased the revenues of the club by twenty percent. We have increased revenues at the pro shop because these women work. They have money. They buy good equipment, good clothing. We have a buffet afterward. Everyone loves it."

Who are her students? "Secretaries, teachers, doctors, judges. You name it, we have it." And why was her group so successful? Was there a secret?

Just the obvious. "Our course has been real user-friendly for women. They have no problem here. There is no one who doesn't feel welcome, regardless of her ability. They have the same tee times. They are treated like everyone else. They feel very comfortable. I think many women wanted to play the game and they were intimidated by it. Now that we have provided a nonintimidating environment, they feel free to come out, to play. They have a very good, very easy feeling about it. Four years ago they couldn't hold a golf club. Now they are organizing their own golf outings."

Is It Any Different for

Women Professional Golfers?

*We have the quality, talent, and ability to justify a level
of acceptance above what we've historically received.*
      —Charles S. Mechem, Jr., LPGA commissioner, 1994

Do the women on the LPGA Tour, the nation's best women golfers, face the same sort of discrimination that confronts women amateurs? Or are they treated differently?

The short answer is: Yes, they are treated differently, because for the most part they are taken seriously as fine golfers, but they also have to put up with many of the same stereotypes that plague women in golf generally.

Charles S. Mechem, Jr., commissioner of the LPGA since 1990, is struck by the discrimination tour women face. As he told Steve Ellis, then the editor of *Golfweek* magazine, in early 1994, "When I see great women golfers who literally can't go into certain clubs and play, or when I see tee-time restrictions at clubs that are based on nothing other than the desire of male chauvinists to protect their turf, I just find that unconscionable."

This chapter will describe briefly what women in professional golf have experienced as individual players, and how the LPGA is dealing with bias against women in professional golf.

❧ *The Developmental Years* ❧

The women who become golf professionals begin their golfing careers early, many of them in childhood and almost all by their mid-teens. It is rare to find a player like Elaine Crosby, 1994 president of the LPGA and a woman who earned over $340,000 in tour prizes in 1994. In her mid-thirties now, she began golf at the ripe old age of twenty! But she is an exception.

Audrey Wooding is a recent Stanford University graduate who is trying to make it on the LPGA Tour. She grew up in the State of Washington, where her parents were members of Fircrest Golf Club. Club rules allow youngsters to begin to play at eight years of age, so that's when she started. "It was a little bit of parents helping, junior clinics, and a busload of kids who would go to the course after school and pay a dollar and hit a tub of golf balls. A lot of fun. We had five kids. In summer our mom would drop us off at the golf course and say, 'Spend the day. See ya.' So that's how we started."

Audrey learned more technique and "mechanical stuff" in her teens, and it enabled her to win the 1985 Washington High School State Girls Championship. It didn't hurt that she competed as a member of the high-school team—a boys' team with girls on it if they could qualify. How would she describe the experience? "I liked it. The guys on my team liked it. We were good, we knew how to play. The guys on other teams did not like it—not any of our competitors—didn't like having to play against a girl and getting beat. A pride sort of thing. But it was fun. I always enjoyed being out there competing with guys."

I met Audrey Wooding when she was in Vermont last summer to play in the *McCall's* LPGA Classic at Stratton Mountain. She is a rookie on the tour and knows just how tough and competitive the tour can be. She went to Q school (qualifying school) and finished two shots below those who got an "exempt" card, which gives them automatic entry to any tour event, but she is still able to play in many tournaments. She made the cut at Stratton, which means she was in roughly the top half of the field and could play Saturday and Sunday and win prize money.

It's too early in her career to speculate whether she'll make it as a professional tournament player; 1994 was only her rookie season. Fortunately for her, she graduated from Stanford with an engineering degree and was an Academic All-American. But she is also a serious, highly competitive golfer whose early experiences with golf were virtually all positive. It will be interesting to watch her career take shape.

Carrie Wood is also a rookie on the LPGA Tour. Her experiences are in some ways similar to Audrey Wooding's, in some ways different. Her family wasn't involved in golf the way Audrey's was, although she had a grandfather who played the game. She actually learned to play while working on the public golf course near her home on Cape Cod, Massachusetts. Like Ms. Wooding's, her high-school experience was important in her development as a golfer.

"I played on the Dennis-Yarmouth Regional high school team. They didn't have a girls' team when I was there, though they do now. It was good. The guys didn't have any problem with it, as long as I could keep up with them. They did not disapprove at all. It was a positive experience." Indeed it must have been, because she was the state high-school champion in Massachusetts in both 1988 and 1989, and won the state's amateur championship in 1989.

After high school she wanted to go to college in the South, where she could play golf year round. She went to Mississippi State because they offered her a partial scholarship right from the start. It was clearly a winning experience for her. "The women's team wasn't really strong but I went on to do really well myself: three-time All-American, won the SEC [Southeastern Conference] once, and won four or five collegiate tournaments."

So she went to Q school and, like Wooding, fell a few shots short of getting an exempt card. So she, too, has to wait for events that are not filled. "In the first four and a half months, everyone was playing out here, so I couldn't play. It's something you have to get through." So she played mini-tour events.

Carrie Wood is looking for sponsors. She has a Callaway bag, wears Ping hats, gets free equipment. She tries to keep her expenses down by staying in private homes instead of motels, driving everywhere, taking local caddies. Still, "it's frustrating not making money or cuts. Eventually, if things don't get better . . . But you have to give yourself time. In about four or five years I'll know." She recognizes that she's still a rookie. "You see what other girls have gone through and you try to learn from that."

Wood and Wooding are from the newest generation of young professionals, and both have benefited from the movement toward gender equality that has been occurring over the last twenty years or so. They both had great success in their respective states as teenagers, both were allowed to compete on equal terms with males on their high-school teams, and both profited from the boost Title IX has given to intercollegiate varsity athletics for women. But some women professionals who started their careers earlier did not have such positive experiences or opportunities.

Betsy King, one of the great female players of recent times, was one of them. She told a group of children—gathered to meet her at an LPGA event in the summer of 1994—how she grew up in Pennsylvania and played field hockey and basketball in high school, but not golf. "In those days, because I was a woman, I was not allowed to play on the boys' golf team." Obviously, there was no girls' golf team.

Martha Nause is a veteran player who joined the LPGA in 1978, a year after Betsy King and some sixteen years before Wooding and Wood. Like Wooding, she had supportive parents who were members of the local Sheboygan, Wisconsin, country club. Indeed, her mother was president of the ladies' association, where "she was allowed to sit in on board meetings but wasn't allowed to say anything." Like the rookies of 1994, Nause had been a champion as a teenager in her home state of Wisconsin. But she reports a very different high-school experience.

"At the time I was in high school there was no girls' golf team. I could have played—I was competent enough to compete—on the boys' team, but at that time personally I was too shy to push things through and was told by some of the boys on the team that if I went out for the team, they'd quit." Nor did she receive support from coaches or others in athletics. "It was sort of understood that the girls didn't have the opportunities that boys did—not that you liked it, but that's the way it was."

Martha Nause has gone on to have a career in women's golf. When I interviewed her in early August of 1994, it had been three years since she had won on the tour. But shortly after our meeting I learned that her persistence had paid off. She had won the prestigious du Maurier Ltd. Classic in Ontario, Canada, one of the LPGA's "majors," and picked up a check for $120,000. She finished the year ranked twenty-second on the money list with $212,130 in official earnings.

Experiences similar to Martha Nause's have been shared by some other women golf professionals but not all. These women come from a wide variety of backgrounds and experiences, just like their male counterparts.

If there is a common thread through preprofessional life, it has to do with the importance of junior golf. On this theme I spoke to that veteran of veteran professionals Patty Berg. We talked about her growing up in Minnesota, and I asked her whether many girls were playing golf then.

"No, not like they are today," she answered. "Of course, they didn't have junior golf. . . . You see, junior golf leads into junior high, high-school golf, and then into college golf. And that's about nine years of your life. You have those nine years to determine whether you want to be a professional golfer, man or woman. And you know what it means to travel and everything. And then you also have had all the competition, so you also know how really tough it is. It's an education program, too."

These days junior golf may tend to serve as a buffer against discrimination. Audrey Wooding reported that the first time she encountered discrimination was as an adult at a private course with restricted tee times for women.

❧ The Women as Individual Professionals ☙

The typical women's golf professional, if there is such a person, can hit the ball more consistently and outscore the vast majority of male golfers. Further, she can outdrive most of them—not the really big hitters, perhaps, but the rest. And she is recognized by most people as the talented woman she is. She is invited to courses, appreciated for her good play, and enjoyed for her company. As professionals, these players generally do not experience the routine restrictions wives and daughters face in much of private club life. The tournament players among the professionals have moved far beyond that world, and even the club and teaching professionals are likely to find that the rules that normally apply to club women may be bent for them.

That is why it must be particularly galling when the old values are trotted out, the old rules invoked, and the very best players find themselves treated as though they are members of a lower caste and not worthy of the benefits bestowed on menfolk. Here are just a small handful of such incidents:

Dottie Mochrie, a native of Saratoga Springs, New York, could not play golf at her home club on Saturday mornings because that was when the men played. After she won the New York Junior Amateur and State Amateur, the club allowed her to play. "It's really unfortunate when it happens to junior players," she told *USA Today* in 1990, after the Shoal Creek incident.

Judy Rankin was the first woman on the LPGA Tour to earn a six-figure salary from tournament winnings, back in the mid-seventies. After a chronic back problem took her out of tournament play, she became a broadcaster for ABC Television and a popular member of ABC's staff. She is hardly a radical feminist; indeed, she reports having experienced very little discrimination in connection with golf and believes she's been treated fairly by her employers, partly because they are nice guys and partly because gender equity is company policy.

So she finds herself at the British Open at Royal Troon Golf Club in Scotland in 1989. "The fellows I work with called one day and said, 'You know, you want to go play?' And I was going to play, but they called me back a few minutes later and said, 'Whoops, women can't play here.'" So Judy was left behind. She's not bitter, doesn't have a problem with all-male clubs, and notes that she has played many tournaments at a nearby club that is quite male-dominated. But forget Judy's feelings for a moment. What would be wrong with letting her play? What valued principle would be violated?

Jane Blalock, now a television commentator and head of the Jane Blalock Company in Boston, a golf business enterprise, won twenty-nine tournaments in her years on the LPGA Tour. I caught up with her at the Women's Golf Summit in 1993 and I asked her if as a professional golfer she had experienced discrimination at the golf course.

"Recently," she answered. "At a grill." In the spring of 1991 she had just finished a round of golf with three male friends at the Wollaston Golf Club in Milton, Massachusetts. Afterward, they headed for the grill. It turned out to be a men's grill. "They would not serve me. I had to sit outside on the porch."

A life-or-death issue? No. Trivial? Undoubtedly. Deflating and demeaning? Certainly. But what cherished, long-held value was being maintained here?

Elaine Crosby relates a story about a club in her hometown in Michigan, "where they had a pro-am to raise money for a local hospital." (A pro-am is a favored form of competition in which, typically, three amateurs pay big money to play a round of golf with a touring professional, with most of the proceeds going to charity.) "One of the big car-racing people was putting it on, and Pepsi had sponsored a team. A member of the Pepsi team was a woman. When she went to register— her first name was a genderless name—and they found out it was a woman, they said, 'You can't play.' Why take something so seriously that you would take a co-sponsor like Pepsi, slap them in the face, and say, 'A woman? You can't have a woman.' "

These are a tiny sampling of the indignities that professional women golfers have either experienced or witnessed. They illustrate the extent to which those who organize country club life will go to maintain a policy of segregation by gender. One of the unhappy consequences is that the older women professionals are so accustomed to these patterns that they take them for granted. Charles Mechem, Jr., the current commissioner of the LPGA, reports that after four years of running the tour, this is one of his most depressing observations.

Renee Powell is the premier black woman in professional golf, and she can speak to what it means to be a "double minority"—a woman of color. She grew up on a golf course—her parents' golf course, in East Canton, Ohio. The story of how, as a young girl, she found golf begins with her father, William Powell, who loved golf and worked as a caddie, and could play on public courses in the East Canton area but found he was banned from tournaments elsewhere because he was a Negro. In 1946, he purchased an old dairy farm in the predominantly white East Canton area and designed a golf layout himself. His dream was to give members of both races a place to play. The course, Clearview Golf Club, opened in 1948, when Renee Powell was a toddler.

When Renee was three, her dad gave her a child's driver and cut down a putter for his little girl. She says she took to golf right away. She entered her first tournament when she was twelve and won it. By the time she was fifteen, she had collected over thirty trophies. Many of those early tournaments were sponsored by the predominantly black United Golf Association, an organization formed to give minority players a base from which to compete. Most other events were closed to them.

As a teenager she faced many forms of prejudice. She says that her parents interceded when they had to. She remembers the time when a major junior tournament in the Cleveland area attempted to institute artificial deadlines to keep her from getting into the tournament. Her parents threatened to expose the situation, tournament officials backed down, and she went on to win the event that year and the next.

When she was a teenager, she entered the USGA Girls' Junior Championship. The year was 1962, the same year that the PGA of America finally eliminated the whites-only clause from its bylaws. Renee Powell was a rare sight in the white world. She was the first black player to compete. Some of the players were terrific to her. Some were not.

After completing high school, Powell went to Ohio University in Athens, Ohio, where she became the captain of the golf team. She faced a turning point at the school when her coach told her she would not be able to play in the NCAA Championships because it was being played in the South and the hotel would not accept blacks. Rather than decline to play, the team went anyway. She was left behind. She remembers her feelings that day. "I was kept out of the biggest event of the year because of my race. It was unfair and cowardly, and I was angry and hurt." She transferred to Ohio State University.

In 1967 she turned pro. It was one of her father's proudest moments. For the first few years a young Renee Powell and an older Althea Gibson, the tennis champion, were the only two black women on the tour. When Gibson left the tour, Powell became the sole black female player. At the outset of her professional career, she said she experienced terrible racism, including death threats. Since she left the LPGA in 1980, there have been virtually no other black women players on the women's tour. This year, LaRee Pearl Sugg, a young rookie, will be eligible for some tournaments. (The absence of blacks among tour players is also found in the golf industry. In 1993, there was not one black sales representative in the industry, one source said. And in 1995 there are only a handful.)

Looking back, Ms. Powell said that as a teenager she encountered a lot more discrimination "from a race side" than from a gender side. "Of one thing I am sure. If my parents did not own a golf course, I would not have been playing golf. Because I would not have been able to get in at a lot of golf courses." She recently left as head professional at the thirty-six-hole Seneca Golf Course in Broadview Heights, Ohio, to take over for her father as head pro at their course. She knows that golf has a long way to go in the area of equal rights. "We all have a lot of work to do," she says.

🀧 *The LPGA Tour* 🀧

The women's tour has come a long way since the barnstorming days of the late forties and fifties, when Patty Berg, Babe Zaharias, Betty Jameson, and a few others knocked about the country giving exhibitions and playing in "Open" tournaments that had far more amateur entrants than professionals. Despite setbacks here and there along the way, the women's tour has grown into an established part of the American sports scene. It has an executive office and staff, many corporate sponsors for its major events, and appears on ESPN and sometimes on the national networks as well.

At the same time, many people feel that the LPGA Tour isn't as successful as it should be, especially in comparison to the two main tours for men. They are particularly concerned about the senior men's tour, which grew from nothing in 1980 into a highly successful venture and may be swallowing up corporate and television space that might have gone to the women.

The senior tour has going for it the name recognition built up over the years of leading male players such as Arnold Palmer, Jack Nicklaus, Lee Trevino, Ray Floyd and Chi Chi Rodriguez. Memories and nostalgia are a valuable hook for an audience, and they seem to be working for the senior men.

I'm not a corporate insider and I don't pretend to know how marketing decisions are made. Maybe the corporate world has reliable information that women's golf is not a great advertising vehicle, or that the "demographics" aren't right, but I worry greatly about what my sociologist husband has taught me about the "self-fulfilling prophecy."

By and large, if people *believe* something to be true, they will act in a way that will make it so, even though there is no underlying validity to their belief. If so, the women's tour will suffer because of the perception problem. On the other hand, maybe the product isn't as good as the men's. Maybe the women *are* getting their fair share, because their product isn't up to the competition. How *do* they compare to the men?

Just as I'm not a corporate insider, I'm also not an evaluator of golfing talent. The definitive word will have to come from someone else. But let's take a look at the published data, from the PGA Tour, the LPGA Tour, and the Senior PGA Tour, and see what they seem to be telling us, recognizing, of course, that even simple statistics are subject to a variety of interpretations. These figures all come from *Golf World* magazine and cover the 1994 playing season.

First, driving distance: The tours keep accurate data on who hits the longest ball. At each tournament, they take measures on two holes. To anyone who knows anything about either golf or gender, it will come as no surprise to find that the men outhit the women.

MEN'S TOUR	WOMEN'S TOUR	SENIOR TOUR
J. Daly 290.2	L. Davies 253.1	J. Dent 275.5

John Daly makes galleries ooh and aah with his thundering tee shots. Remember that the figure of 290.2 is his average drive, not his longest. And Jim Dent, though into his fifties, would be in the top ten on the regular tour in driving distance. Laura Davies, though remarkably long for a woman player, simply isn't in their range. It's worth remembering, however, that as good a male player as Corey Pavin is on the regular tour, he has a shorter average measured drive than does Laura Davies.

The real surprise to me is how similar the tour statistics are in measured golfing abilities other than driving distance.

Driving accuracy: The three tours report the percentage of tee shots that end up in the fairway instead of the rough. The most accurate drivers hit the fairways 82 percent of the time on the PGA Tour, 83 percent on the LPGA Tour, and 84 percent on the Senior PGA Tour. Maybe the women's fairways are a little wider.

Sand saves: The three tours also report the percentage of times players get "up and down"—out of the sand and into the cup—in a total of two shots. Here the men slightly outdo the women: Best man, 65 percent. Best senior, 63 percent. Best woman, 59 percent.

Finally, there is "greens in regulation": the percentage of times the player is on the putting green with two putts to make par. This is a pretty good indicator of ball striking ability and accuracy. The evidence: Best PGA Tour player, 73 percent. Best LPGA Tour player, 74 percent. Best Senior PGA Tour player, 76 percent.

Golf World figures also include putting skill, but it is measured in different ways on the various tours and so is not a meaningful comparison figure. Some men in the golf business feel that women may not be quite as good putters as men, but so far as I know there is no definitive evidence on the subject.

So the reality is that apart from length of tee shots, where the women clearly lose out to the men, the three tours are surprisingly similar. The women are competitors at a very high level. They are very good players in their own right, and needn't stand in the shadows of the men. The best ones can beat ninety-five percent of the males in the country.

Their ability shows in scoring averages.

MEN'S TOUR	WOMEN'S TOUR	SENIOR TOUR
G. Norman 68.81	B. Daniel 70.90	R. Floyd 69.08

The men scored better than the women, roughly two shots a round on the regular tour, a little less than that on the senior tour. The differences would have been greater, of course, if all three tours had played the same course, but the layouts are sensibly set up to reflect the natural differences in overall strength that are determined by age and gender. Accommodating to these differences, all three tours produced exciting, high-quality play, as demonstrated by Greg Norman, Beth Daniel, and Ray Floyd in 1994.

In my view, it's really beside the point to worry about which are the better players. What the figures suggest to me is that the women are fine players, and, even judging it conservatively, nearly as good as the men.

Since the women are almost as good, are they getting paid almost as much as the men? The same issues of *Golf World* that give us the scoring and the playing statistics also give us information on earnings. Here is what the earnings show:

	MEN'S TOUR	WOMEN'S TOUR	SENIOR TOUR
Best	N. Price $1,499,927	L. Davies $687,201	D. Stockton $1,402,519
Tenth	H. Irwin $814,436	M. Mallon $353,385	G. Archer $717,578

No one is going to claim any of these six fine players is in poverty. Indeed, most readers would probably settle happily for what Meg Mallon made playing a game she loves. But that's not the point; look at the differences. Nick Price made two and a half times as much as Laura Davies, and senior tour champ Dave Stockton made about twice as much.

The comparison of the tenth-place finishers is even more telling. Hale Irwin's tenth-place finish on the regular tour earned him far more than Laura Davies's first-place finish on the LPGA Tour, and senior George Archer earned more than twice as much as Meg Mallon. But the differential for women trying to make it on tour really shows up as one goes further down the ladder.

Comparing just the PGA and the LPGA Tours, the differential goes from roughly 2 to 1 for the top players to as high as 6 to 1 as we move to those just hanging on out there. Last year, Dennis Paulson, the 125th player on the men's tour (the highest number to get an exemption for the next year's tournaments), made $142,515. Connie Chillemi, in similar rank on the LPGA, earned $23,019.

These are only the official earnings, money from official tour purses. Both the men and the women have other possibilities for making money out of golf, of course. Exhibitions, product endorsements for clothing and equipment, appearances in pro-am events, and the like. Here there is less in the way of hard number comparisons, but it is obvious to those close to the industry that the men earn far more from those sources than do the women. So official money winnings almost certainly parallel unofficial earnings.

The point of comparing the money differentials and the playing and scoring differentials is just this: you can't explain the differences in money by the differences in performance. Laura Davies and Michelle McGann may not hit it as far as John Daly, but they're super-long hitters on the women's tour and they don't deserve to be making a third to half as much as their male counterparts. Nor do the other top women on tour. And those who are usually also-rans don't deserve to be making only a fifth or a sixth as much as the also-rans on the men's tours.

That is how it looks to me, but how does it look to the tour women themselves? One spokesperson is Carrie Wood, one of the two rookies you met in the early part of this chapter. A second is Martha Nause, a veteran you also met.

Carrie Wood: "Women's golf has improved dramatically, but I still think we are awfully far behind the men because of the purses, the sponsorships, and every aspect of it. The men are on [TV] every week and we are not. They play for purses of a million or more every week; we don't have that. The sponsors are guaranteed for them every week, not for us. Every person on the men's tour probably has some sort of sponsor—clubs, clothing, etc. But there are a lot of us out here who don't even have sponsors, myself included."

Martha Nause: "It infuriates me. It really infuriates me. Everybody who plays with us, and sponsors that are with our tour, they all say that we're so much easier to work with, more fun, more enjoyable, everything is better.

"So then my next question is: Why do we get half the money? We do twice the work! And we get half the recognition. I think that if there is one subject right now in my life that incites me more than anything, it is discrimination. . . . I mean, there's no doubt. There's not even a question in my mind that we are totally discriminated against."

The self-fulfilling prophecy, that women golfers won't sell the product, feeds on itself, particularly as Mr. Mechem says, if the decision makers are virtually all male. Prophecy becomes policy. If the corporate world generally believes the women's tour is an iffy investment, they won't invest. Women's tournaments and purses will suffer, the image of the women's tour will suffer, and the tour will lose out in the competition for TV ratings, attendance, and dollars.

If golf advertisers believe women don't sell golf balls or equipment, they won't use them in their ads. And guess what? In the last several decades women have rarely been depicted in golf advertising.

If golf's monthly magazines don't value women's golf, why would they put a woman on the cover of their magazine? And guess what? You can count on one hand the covers that have featured women.

If the major networks don't think they can sell women's golf as an attractive television package, they won't agree to show it. The result: women's golf on television has been fortunate to have occasional shows on ESPN, but aside from a few "majors" such as the Nabisco Dinah Shore, the U.S. Women's Open, and the McDonald's LPGA Championship, they seldom get on network television.

When they do, their ratings are respectable. In 1994, the U.S. Women's Open reached an average of over 2.5 million homes during its weekend broadcasts, not up to the nearly 4.5 million for the U.S. Open, but very close to the ratings for the British Open and the PGA Seniors' Championship.

Thus the tour faces a massive perception problem. After all, women have moved heavily into the labor force only in recent decades, and many studies show that they still don't get equal pay for equal work. Women executives face the much-discussed "glass ceiling" problem, the invisible barriers that seem to keep women from the very top positions. Counterparts of all this baggage exist in the world of sports, a world dominated by men's sports historically.

Finally there is that age-old problem already noted in connection with Dorothy Campbell Hurd and later Glenna Collett Vare: the restricting perception that one must be a woman first, a woman golfer second. The LPGA Tour still struggles with this one. It maintains a successful traveling day-care center for the mothers on tour and produces a list of LPGA Moms on Tour. The leading moms: Laura Baugh with five kids, Nancy Lopez with three, and many more with one or two.

This accommodation to working mothers is laudable. Still, there are some who feel that the stress on traditional female roles is another example of a media and "image" concern that won't let women be recognized simply for their athletic skills and golfing prowess. As one player views it, "most of the media people are male and they're threatened by a woman who is a good athlete, maybe better than they are. I don't think women's sports are really going to take off until those attitudes are changed."

Maybe attitudes *are* beginning to change. Other manufacturers are coming to the conclusion that Karsten Solheim, the founder and manufacturer of Ping golf equipment, came to long ago: it's right and good for business to support both men and women professionals. Karsten's company has supported women's golf in many ways. Among others, he has praised the women pros in advertisements, and since 1990 he and his wife Louise have underwritten the creation of the highly successful Solheim Cup, the women's version of the men's international Ryder Cup competition for men.

Other companies are now joining Karsten. In 1995, for example, Titleist, the country's largest manufacturer of golf balls, had a full-page ad featuring five women who had won tournaments with Titleist balls: Dottie Mochrie, Donna Andrews, Deb Richard, Kelly Robbins, Michelle McGann. The ad was the result of conversations that Mr. Mechem held with Wally Uihlein, the company's chairman and CEO. Other companies now featuring LPGA photographs of women tour players include Tommy Armour, Rolex, Maxfli, to name a few.

Strong tournament sponsors are also finding their way to the women's tour. Chrysler and others are signing on. The LPGA's philosophy is to turn the tour event into a warm and friendly environment that the fans and the sponsors will love.

LPGA former president Elaine Crosby says, "We're going to show them just how great we are as players and how much more we give than our counterparts." The spirit of giving is real. I personally saw Ms. Crosby put up with a brat of a kid as she was headed for her tee-off time. The child was obnoxious, but she was gracious beyond belief. The women's tour goes out of its way to please its customers.

At the LPGA Tour's pro-ams, the amateurs and the professionals play from the same tees, thereby allowing them to really converse and get to know one another. On the men's tour, the amateurs are separated from the professionals and the two don't get to know each other as well.

I've talked to men who reported having far happier times playing in women's pro-ams, where they are made to feel welcome, than in the men's version, where they sometimes get the feeling they are a nuisance from the professional's point of view.

The women's tour is finally getting more of what it deserves: more corporate sponsors, more television dollars, a full season of women's tournaments. The person trying to get the tour there is Charlie Mechem, Jr., who in 1994 was in his fourth year as commissioner of the LPGA Tour.

⅊ A Visit with Charles S. Mechem, Jr. ⅋

Charlie Mechem came to the tour from a very strong background in communications, having served as chairman of Great American Broadcasting Company, a TV network headquartered in Cincinnati, Ohio. A business entrepreneur and graduate of Yale Law School, he knows his way around the worlds in which the LPGA lives—television and corporate America.

Mechem believes the women's tour offers top quality. If it didn't, people could legitimately decide not to support it. "If they're not going to support us now, at least in the last half of the nineties, there's no reason for it, there's no justification for it. We have the quality, talent, and ability to justify a level of acceptance above what we've historically received."

How does Mr. Mechem go about the business of getting new sponsors, of getting more tournaments? I spoke with him late in 1994, and this is the sum and substance of what he said.

"Let's say you start with a clean sheet of paper; you're starting with someone who has not previously been involved in women's golf. I am absolutely confident that once we expose people to our product, we don't have to do a lot of selling. It really does sell itself. So the threshold issue is getting the customer to look at the product.

"One response is: 'Gee, I don't know anything about your product, but I am willing to take a look.' That's fine.

"The next response is: 'You don't fit our demographic model.' The problem with that is it normally comes from an [advertising] agency. The bigger the company, the more likely you're going to be put in the hands of an agency, and they are totally numbers-driven. You can appeal to seventy percent of the American public, but if you don't appeal to this, this, this, and this in their little demographic slots, you don't get into the room. I find this really ridiculous. This is not what we're all about.

"The next kind of response you get sometimes goes something like this: 'I really don't think your product's much good; they're not really as good as the men,' and on and on. The quick answer I give to that is 'When did you last see a women's event?' Well, you know, probably ten years ago. More often than not, it is a holdover from a day when I suppose you could legitimately argue that the women's tour suffered from a lack of depth. There were ten players, and then it sort of fell off the cliff of skill level. And probably at one point, maybe twenty-five or eighteen years ago, there probably was a time when that was a legitimate concern for a sponsor.

"But once you take the sponsor through and show him it is not true, they really change. My favorite response is 'Good, come out and play with me in a pro-am, and if by the third hole you're not convinced you're on the wrong track, the day is on me.' I know I am going to win that bet.

"The response that is almost impossible to deal with is grounded in a feeling that basically the women are either inferior or irrelevant. That's in some ways almost worse. That can take some very subtle forms. For example, if I am a CEO and I really don't have much respect for women, and the commissioner or one of his people comes in to see me and makes a pitch, I'm probably going to say, 'Well, it's too late in our budget cycle this year. We've already made our decisions. We really can't do that.' Or, and this is increasingly possible for a person to say, 'We're downsizing. We just laid off five thousand people and we just closed twenty-three plants, and we just can't now do a golf tournament.'

"It is that last and most subtle form of closing the door in our face that has been the most frustrating for me. Because, among other things, you can't look that person in the eye and say, 'I don't believe you.'

"I've gotten to the point now [that I] push the buttons before the other guy pushes them—and I talk about the depth of the tour, about the increasing crowds and the increasing purse levels. And then, something I have found to be very useful: I have now collected a list of all the companies that sponsor our events. I've taken the list, the number who have signed on in the last two years, and it's an impressive list in length and in the quality of companies.

"CEOs are just as prone to be influenced by peer pressure as the eighth-grader on the baseball team. If we start by telling them about Procter & Gamble, Anheuser-Busch, Chrysler, the resistance begins to melt. And then you take it a step farther, and you say, By the way, So and So, the CEO has told me, if you'd like to give him a call, he would be happy to talk to you about the LPGA. That approach is very helpful. You have to get into somebody's head."

These are the various approaches Mr. Mechem uses when he is searching for corporate sponsors who may be totally new to golf or golf products. It is a different matter when he is dealing with people already in the golf business. Mr. Mechem reports that more and more companies, like Wilson and Spalding, have women in decision-making positions, and that is helping. "I genuinely believe that ninety percent of the problem has been the result of guys being in the decision-making roles and not really knowing what to do. Because when we go to these new people, we've gotten sympathetic responses and now some results."

For sponsors, Mr. Mechem presents his case as a business matter, not a question of human rights. "The approach I've used is a basic business approach. I have said to equipment manufacturers, clothing manufacturers, club manufacturers, club owners, 'Look, I'm not going to argue with you about what you did ten to fifteen years ago. It's not productive. But look at the marketplace today. A low end and a high end, from twenty-five to thirty-five percent of golfers are women. That critical mass has now gotten too large for you to ignore. It doesn't matter if you like it, it doesn't matter where you think it is headed. When it was five percent, you could say, It is not my market. You can't do that at twenty-five percent.' "

It appears that Mechem is being successful. In an uneven economy he has managed to line up forty official tour events for 1995, an increase of seven over the previous year. As noted, many of the sponsors are solid, big-name companies. He thinks forty a year is about right, for many of the women don't want to be on the road for long stretches of time.

The real question is whether enough corporate and television dollars will flow into the LPGA to make it live on a par with the men's tours, or close to it. Only time will tell. The LPGA has been fortunate to have Charlie Mechem at its head.

❧ PART IV ☙

Turning Private Clubs Around

❦ 13 ❦

Golf's Governing Bodies

It was like Uncle Edgar always had this secret in the closet. Everyone knew it but never said anything about it, and once the secret came out, you had to deal with it.
— David Fay, executive director of the USGA,
on Shoal Creek

Though golf's organizations are in a position to help women, their track record leaves a great deal to be desired. Historically golf's major organizations, the United States Golf Association, the PGA of America, the PGA Tour, and the Ladies Professional Golf Association, stood for the status quo, representing the most conservative values in an arena conservative to begin with. These groups are essentially trade organizations; they are not crusading organizations. In the past both the men's and the women's tours have often held their tournaments at some of the nation's most private exclusive clubs, clubs that historically barred blacks, Jews, and women as members.

Whether a club was all white or all male made no difference to these organizations until the summer of 1990. And then in a flash the situation changed. What changed golf was not golf's governing bodies or its players or its press. What changed golf was corporate America, which, fearing the economic fallout from the publicized racial restrictions at a private golf club at Shoal Creek, pulled its television advertisements from a major golf tournament. As a result, corporate America emerged as far more socially conscious than golf's organizations or star players.

At issue were the social policies at Shoal Creek, in Birmingham, Alabama. The club was the host of the 1990 PGA of America's annual championship. It had hosted the PGA's national championship in 1984 without incident. But this year things were different. A local reporter was researching a series on membership policies at Birmingham country clubs. Hall Thompson, Shoal Creek's founder, admitted that the club discriminated against blacks and added that it "won't be pressured" into having any as members. He wasn't saying anything that wasn't also true at many of the nation's other most elite private clubs. But he had said it, and for print.

His comments set off a firestorm of criticism, which was totally unfathomable to many of the top tour players. Citing his comments, black groups effectively sought boycotts by television sponsors of the tournament. Protesters promised to picket outside the club gates. Some of the nation's top corporations, fearful of a planned black protest, eventually pulled more than $2 million worth of advertising from the telecast of the tournament.

The result was a stunning lesson to the PGA of America, and to all the other organizations that govern golf's world. The loss of big money threatened them to death.

With golf's golden egg about to disappear, golf's four major organizing bodies took action. Within months each formulated a new antidiscrimination policy. The policies of the United States Golf Association and the male and female professional organizations are virtually the same. Said the PGA Tour, which held 118 tournaments the year it announced its policy: "No PGA Tour, Senior PGA Tour, or Ben Hogan Tour [now Nike Tour] event will be held at any golf club that has membership practices or policies that discriminate on the basis of race, religion, sex, or national origin."

These guidelines affected nearly one thousand courses in the United States, clubs that host the tournaments (including qualifying tournaments) for golf's four major organizations. While the new policies were aimed at ending racial, religious, and gender discrimination simply on the basis of these categories, in fact what the guidelines have come to mean in the five years since Shoal Creek is that a host club had better get itself an African-American male member.

Enormous efforts have been made to find such males. But for the thousands of golfing women within the club membership little has been done. Until recently, with the exception of the LPGA, golf's three other organizing bodies, the USGA, the PGA Tour, and the PGA of America, have tended to view membership-policy, grill, or tee-time discrimination as "internal rules" of the club. Says David Fay, the executive director of the USGA, "The women's issue is a tricky business."

That's an understatement.

≈ *The United States Golf Association* ≈

Among all of golf's organizations, the United States Golf Association has a claim to leadership in the area of equal rights.

In its second tournament in 1896, at Shinnecock Hills on Long Island, New York, a Shinnecock Indian named John Shippen, who was part black, entered the Open. All the other men entered in the Open that year were white, and some said they would not play if Shippen was allowed to compete. Theodore Havemeyer, the president of the USGA, told the white men that it was their privilege to play or not. Shippen would play and the Open would be played without them.

It might well be said that the USGA peaked in 1896. From that incident came a significant USGA policy: on the week of the Open the host club had to adopt a nondiscrimination policy. The course would be open to persons regardless of their color for playing (if they could qualify) or for watching. What the club did the other fifty-one weeks of the year was its own business. Until the events surrounding Shoal Creek in 1990, that was the USGA's position. It lasted ninety-four long years.

Nineteen-ninety-five marks the 100th anniversary of the USGA's first U.S. Open, and it is appropriate that Shinnecock Hills has been selected as the host club for the centennial celebration. Long a benefactor to women, Shinnecock finally opened its doors to an African-American doctor in 1992, after it was selected as the centennial site.

The United States Golf Association, a nonprofit organization representing amateur golf in the nation, is the oldest of golf's major organizations. It sets the rules for golf tournaments and golfing equipment in the United States. Many clubs are honored to host one of its tournaments. Its procedure for selecting sites requires that a club must first offer its course to the USGA, which, in turn, selects one of the applicants as host to one of its thirteen annual men's, women's, boys' and girls' competitions.

Before 1990 the most famous of the tournaments sponsored by the USGA, particularly the men's U.S. Open and the U.S. Women's Open, have been held at some of the nation's most exclusive and, I have to add, racist, sexist, and anti-Semitic clubs. A major USGA event might well generate millions of dollars in revenues for a host club, but in the past a club's private policies were viewed as just that, private. Prior to the controversy over Shoal Creek, whether a club was all white or all male was not a relevant issue in the selection of the course for a national championship. Now the USGA automatically reviews a host club's policies and practices with regard to discrimination.

David Fay, the executive director of the USGA, says that the guidelines that came after Shoal Creek were directed toward admitting African-Americans. "Our policy was a direct result of Shoal Creek; in fact, Shoal Creek was the best thing to happen to this sport," Mr. Fay said. "Clearly the focus was on African-Americans. Let's face it, this country has a history of disenfranchising minorities in one form or another—Irish, Italians, Hispanics, Jews, and clearly women. But of all of those there's only one that was enslaved. This was a natural and proper policy."

The women's issue is tricky, as he put it. Once an African-American male, for example, gets into a club, he gets full access to the course. Once a woman gets in, she often does not have the same access: restrictive rules against women are considered "internal club policies." "That is our position," Mr. Fay says. Change is coming from legislation, from economic pressure, from government agencies, from the courts. But apparently not from his organization.

When the USGA held its U.S. Women's Open, the foremost golf event for professional women in 1992, it didn't seem to matter that Oakmont Country Club in Oakmont, Pennsylvania, had a long history of discriminatory rules against women, ranging from no single women members to restrictive tee times on weekends.

What makes the USGA's position even more incongruous in this case is that the executive committee of the USGA, which sets organization policy, did not select Oakmont for the 1992 Women's Open; the USGA *women's committee* did. The women's committee apparently has absolute control over site selection for all the USGA's girls' and women's tournaments. According to a committee member, their word is law.

Apparently, the executive committee of the USGA has no veto

power over the women's committee choices. It's not clear what would happen if the women's committee selected a host club that had no African-American members. "Had this come up before our executive committee, we would be very sensitive to taking the Open to a club with these discriminatory practices, yet when the women's committee made the decision to accept Oakmont for the Women's Open, that was their decision," said Reed Mackenzie, a member of the committee.

Not all forms of discrimination involving women are internal matters. The USGA pulled a qualifying tournament from Sharon Golf Club in Sharon Center, Ohio, when it belatedly learned the all-male club was still the site of a qualifying round. But unless it's an all-male club, the rule is: "Internal club policy."

Why are some forms of discrimination against women considered an "internal matter" when race discrimination apparently is not? Primarily because female relatives of male members have been around golf and country clubs in some capacity since the beginning. Unlike African-Americans, they have not been totally excluded. As guests, as WORMs, as "associate members," the women on the USGA's women's committee, for example, come from country club life; they are comfortable with the roles assigned to them, roles they have accepted.

Mr. Fay says these are issues that individual clubs must try to resolve. "The wives get up in arms. Working women have very little voice. They're outgunned; they're outnumbered. So the women's group may go back to the board and say, 'We want it to remain as is. We don't want to give up our exclusivity on Tuesday for exclusivity on Saturday. We have other things to do on weekends.' So now the working woman is left out in the cold. She has put down a lot of money, and she can't play weekend mornings *or* Tuesday."

The trend, he says, is to resolve these matters through legislation or the courts or by having the couples themselves choose a primary member who will have access to the tee on weekend mornings. "Some clubs seem more and more to be realizing that if they don't do something it will be imposed upon them." But he apparently doesn't feel that his nonprofit organization should take any position on these issues.

This is how the CEO of the organization that speaks for amateur golf in the United States understands the problem facing his host clubs. The USGA looks long and hard if a club has no African-American members and asks why. But no equity or voting memberships for spouses, no single women members, no decent tee times for working women, when men have all these things, that's okay.

But we should not put it all on the CEO. After all, he reports to a board that sets the policy in the first place. The USGA's need for demanding golf courses for its tournaments may come before whatever abstract beliefs in equality they may or may not hold. As a former high-ranking golf official said, as he readied himself to play at an outstanding all-male club, "When it comes to choosing between principles of equality and playing a marvelous golf course, we check our morals at the country club door."

The USGA is in a leadership position. It can take a stand and make a difference. It can help put an end to stereotypical thinking if it doesn't check its principles at the country club door.

❧ The Professional Golfers' Association ❧ of America

Unlike the USGA, the PGA of America, the first group to represent male golf professionals, began as an avowedly racist organization. Its constitution, adopted in 1916, at a time when segregation was legal, said its members must be of the Caucasian race. At this time the PGA represented tournament professionals as well as home club pros. This clause lasted until 1961, fourteen years after Jackie Robinson integrated baseball. Not that the PGA learned from major-league baseball. Far from moving on its own to adopt nondiscriminatory policies, the PGA of America was drawn into it kicking and screaming.

A year after Robinson entered baseball, Bill Spiller and Ted Rhodes, two well-known black golfers, and Madison Gunter, a local black golfer from Richmond, sued the PGA of America, asserting that the tour was denying them employment because they were black. They hired an attorney and the case would have gone to trial had their lawyer not been hoodwinked.

He agreed to a settlement of the lawsuit without requiring the PGA to drop the Caucasians-only clause. The PGA simply agreed not to discriminate against blacks. What the organization and its sponsors did instead, Spiller later said, was to call their tournaments "invitationals" instead of opens. And blacks were not invited. They were allowed in a few tournaments like the Los Angeles Open, and, of course, the U.S. Opens if they could qualify. But their opportunities were very restricted and the PGA leadership did nothing about it.

It took California's attorney general, Stanley Mosk (now on the California Supreme Court), to threaten to kick the PGA of America's tour off California's public courses, and even that wasn't enough. The PGA vowed to use private courses instead. So Mosk upped the ante. He wrote a letter to his fellow attorneys general, informing them of the PGA's position. In November 1961, seven years after the U.S. Supreme Court had ordered the nation's public school districts integrated by race, the PGA of America dropped its Caucasians-only clause.

The PGA's exclusion of nonwhites from membership had worked great hardship on Ted Rhodes, Bill Spiller, and the other players of tournament caliber. The most harmful effect of almost fifty years' exclusion was that minorities were not allowed to get on the PGA apprentice ladder to become teaching professionals and home pros for the thousands of public and private courses around the country. To this day there are only a few hundred apprentices and members of the twenty-four-thousand-member PGA who are Asian, African-American, Hispanic, or Native American. While minorities are overrepresented in our main team sports of football, basketball, and baseball, they are underrepresented in golf.

Today, the PGA of America is far removed from the world of the 1950s. When the tour players broke away to form their own group in the 1960s, the PGA was left with only one really major tournament: the annual PGA Championship. Ironically for the organization that began life discriminating against minorities, it was one of those tournaments—Shoal Creek in 1990—that has led every governing body in golf to change its policies.

The PGA continues to represent 90 percent of the male golf professionals in the nation and it represents some 703 female pros and apprentices, double the number of a few years ago, but this is minuscule in a male membership of twenty-four-thousand. The organization is conscious of how few female professionals it actually has in the nation's private clubs, although their numbers are slowly increasing. At the same time, more and more women are coming out of college as golf champions. The PGA is clearly aware it has to do more. It is recruiting African-American college players into the golf industry. It is also supporting junior golf among minorities and girls.

In 1990, after the PGA of America announced new antidiscrimination guidelines for tournament sites, a number of private clubs scheduled to host major tournaments bowed out rather than change their policies. The antidiscrimination guidelines were aimed primarily at eliminating racial segregation in host clubs. In the past, the PGA has tended to look the other way when it comes to how host clubs treat women. That policy appears to be changing. "We want a club that embodies the facts as well as the spirit of our antidiscrimination guidelines," said one top official who lived through the Shoal Creek crisis and learned from it. "We want a club to stand the test of time, we want clubs that we will go back to again and again. So what we are looking for is a demonstrably open policy, for both minorities and women." In short, the PGA of America is thinking in broad strokes, not narrow ones.

❧ *The PGA Tour, Inc.* ❧

As golf exploded in the 1960s, the interests of the touring professionals diverged more and more from those of the home-club pros, whose primary income came from running golf shops and giving lessons rather than from playing competitive tournament golf. A split was inevitable, and it came in 1968. Since then the tour has flourished. Today the PGA Tour, Inc., is an approximately $275 million nonprofit conglomerate, with three separate tours: the PGA Tour, the Senior PGA Tour, and the Nike Tour, which represents the young and up-and-coming professionals. Together, they conduct 125 cosponsored tournaments a year. The relevance of this for women is that these tournaments require venues, or country club sites, and these venues often have policies affecting women. Learning from the Shoal Creek experience, the PGA Tour, when choosing sites, enters into a contract in which the golf club must represent that its "membership practices or policies" do not discriminate on the basis of race, religion, sex, or national origin. Until recently, the tour, perhaps taking its cue from the USGA, waffled on gender. But that position has changed. Tim Finchem, the new PGA Tour Commissioner, says, "We do involve ourselves in cases where there are inequities in starting times and access to facilities."

In the past, they have ignored it. For example, as recently as 1994, Gregory Durden, chief of the Florida attorney general's civil-rights division, wrote to Deane Beman, then the PGA Tour commissioner, that his office was taking "very seriously" allegations of invidious discrimination at Cheval Country Club. (See Molly O'Dea's case in Chapter 6.) Mr. Durden reminded Mr. Beman that Cheval sponsored the Vantage Classic Pro-Am, as well as the qualifying round for the senior tour's GTE Suncoast Classic. Mr. Durden asked Mr. Beman if he wanted to be kept informed of the investigation. Mr. Beman "never called and never answered the letter," Mr. Durden said. This is hardly the way for a nonprofit, tax-exempt organization to respond to a government official.

The tour is now under new leadership, with some fresh faces on its staff and board. The Tour has instituted a minority training program for college students and has hired a few of its graduates. It has also become involved in helping shape the issues for the Women in Golf Summit, a national LPGA conference that addresses the issues of women's golf.

"We need solutions to some of the issues facing women in golf today," said John Morris, the tour's vice-president of communications, who says a significant percentage of the tour's television audience consists of women. Both he and Donna Orender, vice-president of the tour's television productions, plan to work on these issues at the 1995 golf summit for women.

The PGA Tour's involvement in women's golf is a positive step. Historically, the tour, like the PGA of America, has done little to bring about change in the area of discrimination. There are fewer men of color on the PGA Tour now than there were twenty years ago, and there are more on the senior tour than the main PGA Tour. This oddity is probably due to the decline in the use of caddies, as caddieing was traditionally a means of exposure to golf for those who did not grow up in country clubs. In any event, there are shockingly few blacks in golf compared with other professional sports. When given the chance to donate to programs to help minorities learn golf, the PGA Tour's contributions, judged against their vast earnings, have been minuscule.

The tour is an important force in helping corporate sponsors to search for tournament sites that are free of bias. They have lost a handful of sites as a result of their new antidiscrimination guidelines, including magnificent courses such as Cypress Point in California and those made famous by national television coverage, such as all-male Butler National in Illinois. But many of the golf and country clubs want the tournaments, and when they want them badly enough, their discriminatory practices against women will change.

❧ *The Ladies Professional Golf Association* ❧

One might think that since the Ladies Professional Golf Association represents women players, the organization would have taken a strong stand on gender discrimination at country clubs. It had not. And it had not even though some of the nation's top women players have experienced discrimination at private clubs, especially when they were growing up. Some still face it today.

As in men's professional play, women have depended on excellent private country clubs as sites for their thirty-five or more tournaments during the year. To make a big deal of restrictive policies regarding women might push a club to withdraw its invitation, and the LPGA has not been in a great bargaining position until Mechem's tenure.

Also, the LPGA, as well as the PGA Tour and the PGA of America, largely accepted the USGA's position that, as long as host clubs did not discriminate during tournament week, the clubs were entitled to make their own rules and that what they did "the other fifty-one weeks of the year" was of no concern. To have insisted otherwise might have had severe economic consequences for the LPGA.

That mindset at the LPGA has now changed. After Shoal Creek, the LPGA, like golf's other organizations, insisted on racial integration at the host club. But the LPGA, unlike its counterparts, did not view discrimination against spouses and single women at clubs as an "internal issue." The LPGA "reaffirms its opposition to discriminatory restrictions related to golf courses and club facilities" and "fully supports unrestricted memberships and equality in playing times."

The LPGA's guidelines have led to better conditions for women at private clubs, and each year more clubs are moving in that direction, Mr. Mechem said. For example, immediately after Shoal Creek in 1990, Wykagyl Country Club in New Rochelle, New York, site of the LPGA JAL Big Apple Classic, balked at changing its policies. One of the tournament's sponsors, *Golf* magazine, worked with the club.

The late Peter Bonnani, publisher of *Golf* magazine, said that the tournament was almost canceled three years in a row. "First the club was going to be picketed by the NAACP. The rules had to be changed regarding minorities. Then the LPGA's guidelines had to be followed. 'Shape up,' we said, 'or forget having the LPGA tournament.' The women in the club wanted equal rights and equal starting times.

"A week before the tournament, the membership, with great wisdom, gave complete equal rights for women. Now women will have equal starting times. And believe me, Wykagyl is among the clubs that you would write down as being inflexible," he said.

The LPGA has adopted the position that host clubs with discriminatory policies will not be rejected outright because at this point in history so many clubs carry these restrictions that to bar all who hold them would severely reduce the possible pool of host clubs. In short, the LPGA put its host clubs on notice and set out to work with them to change policies. Mechem is taking discrimination seriously, but he is also aware of the line between principle and organizational suicide.

❧ The Public Lessons of Shoal Creek ❦

The 1990 story of racism at Shoal Creek in Birmingham, Alabama, is important to women at country clubs today for two reasons. It is important because it shows how golf's staid governing bodies can be propelled to change decades-old social policies if economic pressure is brought to bear. And it is important because it shows the relationship of professional golf to the world of corporate sponsors, a world dependent upon public goodwill in marketing and advertising products.

What the public now knows is that many of America's largest corporations put up the bulk of the prize money on the professional tours: $111 million on the men's tours in 1994 and $24 million on the women's tour in 1994. Many of these tournaments are named after the sponsoring companies, and they believe it would be an advertising and public-relations disaster to support a tournament held at a private club that disdains blacks or Jews or women.

The corporate world was motivated not by altruism but by the economics of public goodwill; they understood what it would mean to hold a great tournament in a club that demeaned potential purchasers of their products.

Because golf has been its own social arbiter for so long, it tends to be unaware of how others see its way of life. From the vantage point of black leaders, golf was rewarding some clubs with revenues and prestige even though these clubs were practicing institutionalized racism.

The spectacle of wholesale corporate abandonment of a tournament put the social issue on a direct economic line that golf understood. They could see those title sponsors fleeing, those hospitality tents coming down, those pro-ams abandoned, even though corporate leaders belonged to some of these elite clubs themselves.

Though the issue at Shoal Creek was race, Shoal Creek is important to women because these new guidelines apply to gender, too. And while golf's organizing bodies have tended to enforce the guidelines differently when it comes to women rather than race, women seeking change now know that they can take their complaints to corporate sponsors of golf tournaments with some hope of success.

14

Bringing Outside Pressure to Bear

Do you pay dues or reimburse membership costs for your executives at a country club? How have you handled the problem that clubs will not extend membership privileges to your female executives?

—From a survey the Nassau County Women's Bar Association sent to three hundred Long Island businesses in 1990

Bringing outside pressure to bear on the inner workings of country club life is a risky business, an approach a member turns to only when efforts to work from within have failed. The risks include alienating fellow members, doing economic damage to the club, and potentially losing one's own membership.

Nonetheless, from what I've seen, outside pressure often gets the job done when all efforts to work cooperatively within a club have produced little or no change.

There are many ways outside pressure can be brought to bear, but they boil down essentially to two main types. The first is to use the mass media—newspapers, magazines, radio, television—to bring the glare of the public spotlight on the club's policies. Usually a well-placed story about the issue, without the member's name in the piece, is what is aimed for. There is nothing clubs want to avoid more than to have their dirty linen washed in public. Local newspapers, radio, and television will do just that, and if the wires or networks pick it up, it's even more effective. Of course, anyone who tries this runs the risk of being treated as an outsider at his or her own club if perceived as the agent who caused all the publicity.

The second method is to mobilize economic or political pressure from groups and organizations that use the club's facilities. These may include local businesses or professional associations that hold lunches, dinners, or outings at the club. Sometimes a local women's bar association will take a strong stand, as did the women's bar in Albuquerque, New Mexico, when they withdrew an event from a private club because the club discriminated against women. Sometimes a national professional group, such as the American Bar Association, will take a position—as when the litigation section of the ABA moved its luncheon from a Honolulu golf club that discriminated against women to one that did not.

Sometimes members or organizations seeking change take both steps, keeping a reporter apprised of developments as they occur.

❧ *The Media Before and After Shoal Creek* ☙

The story of Shoal Creek was a defining moment for the press, and surely for the golf press, because it was now forced to cover a story it knew intimately but had not written about. In general, the golf press—newspapers, television, and magazines—has defined its social role narrowly. Golf writers cover instruction, players, tournaments, equipment—usually as it pertains to male golfers. But the inequities of social policies at private clubs are not high on a golf writer's agenda. And one can understand why.

For one thing, many of the readers of golf magazines are members of exclusionary private clubs, as are many of the advertisers and many of the editors. In the past and in the present, the CEOs and members of the boards of the USGA and the PGA Tour have belonged to some of the nation's leading all-male clubs. The golf press has long taken the view that a private club is an extension of a person's home. The press is invited in for the tournament week. They play the course, they cover the event, they leave. It is thought that to comment on how the home is kept would be rude to the host.

Before Shoal Creek, elite private clubs did not publicly discuss membership policies. Some of these clubs were a century old, and many began with Caucasians-only clauses in their bylaws. Few reporters ever took on this story, in part because many reporters may have heard that their publisher was a member of the local country club. If a reporter dared to ask about membership policies, the club's officer said "No comment," nicely, and shut the door. After Shoal Creek, many private clubs continued that practice. Only now their conduct may wind up as the subject of a column, as happened to Winged Foot Golf Club in Mamaroneck, New York, when a *New York Times* sportswriter couldn't get the club to answer his questions.

I first went calling on clubs in the fall of 1989, before Shoal Creek broke. Jerry Tarde, the editor of *Golf Digest*, had the courage to take on the topic. He asked me to do a series of stories on discrimination and privacy issues facing private country clubs. Many clubs would not give me the time of day. Some spoke on condition of anonymity; some spoke after contacts were made through intermediaries, and then only guardedly. This was a world on which little outside light had been shed, and they wanted it to stay that way. But the stories were published and exposed a little of the hidden world of country club life. Score one for Tarde.

My two-part series was published in *Golf Digest* in May and June of 1990. When it first appeared, it attracted little notice. Efforts to publicize the series failed. Then, two months later, Shoal Creek happened. I suddenly found myself on network television, explaining the world of private golf and country clubs. Why me? Because few other journalists had written about it, and when reporters called the clubs they got the usual reception. "No comment."

One major effect of Shoal Creek was that the world of the exclusive private club now became front-page news. *USA Today* assigned a team of reporters to get the story and played it in a big way. They spent a month learning the membership practices for clubs hosting tournaments under the auspices of the PGA Tour, the LPGA, the USGA, and the PGA of America. *USA Today* wrote dozens of stories and put together a chart of club practices, reviewing the policies of scores of clubs. Each year the newspaper has done an update, although in 1994 the coverage was sparse because, like other media, *USA Today* was focused on the baseball strike.

The Associated Press did a survey of all upcoming tournaments through the year 2000 and sent it to thousands of subscribers. Everywhere you went the story was played from a local angle. In Washington, in Chicago, in Denver, in New Haven, among many cities, stories began with how local private clubs fared on the discrimination scale: "A survey of the area's 22 clubs showed that . . ." Newspapers loved the story.

Local television arrived at the clubhouse gates, ready to roll. When they were ordered off the premises, they really had a story.

Before long the idea behind the story spread. What if the local private club up the road held no tournament? Did it discriminate, too? Who were its members? How did the club select people? Were whole groups of people simply out of the loop? Editors began to think about policies at country clubs. They assigned reporters to find out about them. This was new. Soon the story became one that newspapers and television could revisit. And they have. That is the big difference. There is now public awareness of how country clubs conduct themselves.

Country clubs, for their part, generally continue their policy of not commenting on these issues. When Mrs. Dorothy Moller, the widow we met in Chapter 5, sued Paradise Valley Country Club near Phoenix, Arizona, in January 1995, the club observed that the lawsuit had indeed prompted stories in newspapers and on television. But it said in a letter to its members, "We feel that no useful purpose is served by discussing the membership matters of a private club with members of the media, and our attorneys have advised us not to do so."

Despite these policies, women now know how to attract the media to the story. If a club hosts a professional golf tournament, the press will be on the scene. Any member determined to put his or her club in the spotlight—and few members would take this route—doesn't have to do much to make it happen. Put up a picket line or threaten to put up one and coverage will follow, if not from television reporters then from the print press.

If an advocate for change simply wants a forum, it is easy to borrow a tournament for a day. Sharon Keil, a former Ohio amateur golf champion, is an expert at this approach. She has fought for a bill now pending in the Ohio legislature that would give women equal access and membership rights at Ohio private country clubs. In May 1994, when she wanted to promote her views, she held a press conference at a local fire station that was just a three-wood away from the PGA Tour's Memorial Tournament, in progress at Muirfield Village Golf Club in Dublin, Ohio.

At the press conference, she said women faced restricted tee-time hours at most of Ohio's 160 private clubs. Reporters from the Associated Press and other news organizations wrote stories that appeared across the country. Press conferences that coincide, as this one did, with the public interest created by major golf events often get extra attention.

Here the women's problem was highlighted, whether it was an issue at Muirfield or not.

❧ *Conflict in Kansas* ❧

Diane Graham's tee-time case against the exclusive Hallbrook Country Club is a classic example of how to use the media to change a club's tee-time laws. In less than a month, she hired an attorney, filed a complaint against the club, and took to the airwaves across the country.

Robert Stephan, then the Kansas attorney general, evaluated her case under a recent Kansas law barring discrimination at private country clubs and found the club to be in violation of the law. The club quickly changed its tee-time policy, just as Ms. Graham was readying for a debate on Sunday's "Good Morning America".

Ms. Graham is chief executive officer of Stratco Inc., one of the state's leading chemical engineering companies. She and her former husband purchased a house on the Hallbrook golf course in Leawood, Kansas, in 1989. She said that on several occasions over the years she had been denied weekend tee times because she was a woman, a fact that caused her embarrassment with business clients. To overcome the tee-time restrictions, she joined another golf club in Kansas City that had none.

On one occasion she had been given a tee time apparently in the belief that she was Mr. Graham, not Mrs. Graham. When she arrived at the club with a male client, she was told she could not play. "There must be a mistake," she said, because she could see a "Graham" on the book. "I was very embarrassed. I thought, This is unbelievable."

She quickly moved into high gear. First she moved from Kansas to Phoenix, Arizona, in part, she said, because she wanted to protect her children from adverse publicity. She did this in January 1994, before she filed her lawsuit. She knew early on, she said, that hers would become a nationwide cause.

Mistakenly believing the case to be the first of its kind in the nation, she took to the airwaves. She hired a public-relations firm to set up broadcasts, and she traveled to the nation's capital. In one day alone in Washington, D.C., she had sixteen radio interviews and two television interviews. The shows went to households in Denver, Cincinnati,

St. Louis, Richmond, "all over." She also gave newspaper interviews. Her case received page-one coverage in the *Washington Post* and on the wire services, and she and her attorney, Gail Hudek, did well on local radio shows and in local papers.

The case came to a quick resolution. Mr. Stephan let it be known he wasn't happy with Hallbrook. (For his official letter to the club, see Chapter 12.) Mr. Stephan said, "On the surface it is amazing to me in the 1990s or eighties or seventies this would even be an issue. I thought matters such as this had been answered long ago." He then declared discriminatory men's and women's tee times to be unlawful. He ordered the club to comply within ten days, and the club did.

It didn't hurt that the Kansas law had been passed after Tom Watson, whose wife is Jewish, quit the Kansas City Country Club, a club he had known since childhood, because it denied a membership to Harry Bloch of the famous tax firm H&R Block because Bloch is Jewish. From start to finish the case took about two months. The law moves more quickly when the media is on the scene.

❧ *Nancy Saunders, Westchester Country Club,* ❧ *and the PGA Tour's Buick Classic*

Many women assumed that tournament officials meant it when they said a private club that discriminates by race or gender will not be permitted to host tournaments. They have often been dismayed to learn that their club thinks its discrimination problems are solved once it admits one or two African-American men.

Westchester Country Club, host of the PGA Tour's Buick Classic each year, admitted its first two minority males shortly after the PGA Tour announced its Shoal Creek guidelines. It moved quickly when it came to race. Not so when it came to women.

After Shoal Creek in 1990, Nancy Saunders (the real-estate executive you met in Chapter 5 who lost her full voting membership at Westchester when she married David Saunders) wrote a letter to then tour commissioner Deane R. Beman and to Edward Mertz, general manager of Buick Motor Division of General Motors. Her purpose was to inform them of the club's then gender-biased bylaws and tee times and to get them changed.

Beman, she says, did not reply, but Buick responded quickly, talking to her and to her attorney. Buick spokesmen also talked to the club's president, who convinced them that the club was working on the issue and informed Buick that the club had opened up its second, shorter course to women on weekends. She sent copies of her correspondence to me at *Golf Digest*, because I had been writing about these issues. That was in 1990. Owing to events that followed, she has become more circumspect.

The club's next step was to order David Saunders to appear before the club's executive committee. Club officers told him to stop his wife's letter-writing campaign. He said, "Talk to her, not me." At the next meeting, the club president said Nancy Saunders's behavior was "detrimental" to club life. She was told she and her husband would be out if she didn't stop her campaign.

By year's end, the club changed its bylaws to permit a married couple to decide which spouse would be the member of the club. If David Saunders wanted to be the member, then Nancy Saunders would have to spend roughly $50,000 for her own membership in her own name in order to play the championship course. Westchester also eliminated the practice of requiring a woman member to transfer her membership to her spouse upon marriage.

But they didn't make it retroactive to include Ms. Saunders.

The moral of this story is that while Nancy Saunders took some heat, she also got some changes. Buick helped by asking questions. And even though the company did not threaten to abandon Westchester at this point, their concern prompted club officials to act sooner rather than later. When Buick found out about the men's grill, it added this form of exclusion to what it already knew and threatened to pull the tournament altogether. (See Chapter 7.)

❧ *Calling in NOW* ❧

The National Organization for Women is no stranger to the private clubs dispute. It was active in changing admission policies for private luncheon clubs in Washington, D.C., and New York City that had long discriminated against minorities and women. It recognized the impact of excluding women from those places where men regularly met to conduct business and to socialize. NOW has often geared up its legal staff to present friend-of-the-court briefs in cases involving private clubs.

After Shoal Creek and its publicity, NOW decided it would use its political clout when necessary. Since 1990 it has appeared or threatened to appear outside country clubs that discriminate against women in one form or another. These threats have been publicized and NOW has claimed small victories, both in getting internal membership practices changed and in keeping companies from holding tournaments at clubs that discriminate against women.

In 1993, for example, the NOW chapter in Nassau County, Long Island, New York, forced the Grumman Corporation, Long Island's largest private employer, to cancel its annual summer golf outing for more than 100 suppliers. NOW had threatened to picket corporate-sponsored events at country clubs that did not allow women as members.

The event had been scheduled to be held at Deepdale Golf Club, in Manhasset, the site of the Grumman event since 1981. After learning of NOW's planned protest, Deepdale decided to pull out. Grumman went next to Cold Spring Country Club. Told of NOW's planned protest, it, too, pulled out.

Gloria Freund, executive director of the Nassau chapter, was pleased with the results. She told the *New York Times*, "A company that is willing to use a restricted club implicitly if not explicitly subscribes to its bylaws and supports its objectives by the payment of thousands of dollars in fees for the use of the segregated premises."

Were NOW's efforts worth it? There was never a charge that Grumman had discriminatory policies. The charities attached to these sorts of tournaments didn't benefit. Nor did clients or employees. Does the public benefit by greater exposure to the issue? Perhaps, but these possible gains are not cost-free.

Do women members or potential members at clubs where protests have occurred tend to fare better in the long run? The anecdotal evidence is that they do. Clubs have changed when exposed to the glare of publicity. And private clubs that lose economically may well decide to take a long look at their policies. Grumman may have to take its business to a club with more equitable policies or decide to entertain its clients in some other way.

≈ *Of Judgeships and Clubs* ≈

Besides the media, outside pressure has been brought to bear on private country clubs and their members from a variety of groups—the Senate Judiciary Committee, the American Bar Association, the local men's or women's bar group in a city or a state.

For more than twenty years, the Senate Judiciary Committee grappled with a political albatross: nominees to federal judgeships or to top posts in the Justice Department who belonged to discriminatory private clubs but who would resign from the club on the eve of their nomination, and then be appointed to a post where they would pass judgment on legal or policy issues regarding discrimination. In 1990, the committee enacted a resolution that, although nonbinding, served to unite the views of both Democrats and Republicans on the committee. Essentially it says that membership in discriminatory clubs is incompatible with the goals of the federal justice system, and it warned lawyers seeking federal judgeships and posts to the Justice Department not to belong to such clubs.

The issue of membership in these clubs arose most notably when Justice Anthony M. Kennedy was nominated to the Supreme Court in 1987 by then president Ronald Reagan. Justice Kennedy had been a longtime member of The Olympic Club in San Francisco when the club had no blacks and no women members (see Chapter 3), and he kept his membership when he sat on the Ninth Circuit Court of Appeals. He resigned from Olympic the day before he flew to Washington to discuss his Supreme Court appointment with President Reagan. He had done little to change the club's policies before his nomination to the U.S. Supreme Court.

More recently, Eleanor Dean Acheson resigned from The Country Club, in Brookline, Massachusetts, rather than jeopardize a top appointment in the Justice Department. At The Country Club, long the enclave of Boston Brahmins, women have gone from nonvoting adjuncts of their husbands to having full voting and golfing rights. But the club, which now has Asians and Jews as members, still did not have a black member when Ms. Acheson was nominated to her post in 1993.

When Ruth Bader Ginsburg was nominated to the U.S. Supreme Court in 1993, the public learned that she and her husband, Martin, an attorney, had dropped their memberships at two golf clubs because they excluded blacks and women. One club, the Cold Spring Country Club on Long Island, was not unfamiliar with prejudice. Otto Kahn, the turn-of-the-century Jewish financier, built the course because he was turned away at others on Long Island. Martin Ginsburg's father was among the founders. According to the *Washington Post*, the couple also resigned from the Woodmont Country Club in Rockville, Maryland, after the club changed its policy and ordered federal circuit judges to pay a $25,000 initiation fee. The Ginsburgs felt that policy was directed at one of Judge Ginsburg's black colleagues on the D.C. Circuit, Judge Harry Edwards, an avid golfer, whom they had brought into the club. So both judges Edwards and Ginsburg resigned.

The idea of resigning from a private club whose rules they felt barred or degraded people began for Mr. Ginsburg in the 1960s when he resigned from New York City's Harvard Club because the club had a separate entrance for women and his wife became uncomfortable using it. He rejoined when the club later opened its doors to any Harvard graduate regardless of gender or race or creed.

Over the years, the American Bar Association has gotten tougher when it comes to membership in private clubs that discriminate on the basis of sex or race.

It has required its officers and board of governors, in all about thirty members, to resign from discriminatory clubs unless the club changes discriminatory bylaws as of a certain date. It has also barred committees, at midyear and annual conferences, from holding professional or social functions at clubs whose membership does not include women and minorities.

Recognizing the special damage this sort of discrimination can hold for its minority and women members, the ABA has recommended that law firms not hold functions at discriminatory clubs and not pay such club dues. It has also urged its thousands of members to work for reform from within and, if that fails, to resign from the club.

Local bar associations can be especially effective if they launch a campaign and attract media coverage.

❦ Women Attorneys and the Private Country Club ❧

In the weeks after Shoal Creek, the Nassau County Women's Bar Association in New York went on a tear. In the space of a few short months, the group pushed on twin fronts to expose discriminatory club practices against women in wealthy Nassau County. They did it by writing letters, conducting surveys, and pressing reporters to write stories. They had the clout of their own organization, the ability to devise an effective campaign, and the contacts to carry it out.

Norma Grill, a tax attorney from Long Island, whose husband held the membership at Cold Spring Country Club, the one from which Justice Ginsburg and her husband resigned, chaired her bar association's gender-bias committee. From that perch, she directed events that eventually led the New York State legislature to enact a law against private country clubs that discriminate on the basis of race, gender or religion.

The association, with its three hundred women attorneys, began its work by targeting judges and other public officials as well as businesses on Long Island. They conducted surveys to find which individuals and organizations supported discriminatory private country clubs, and they began a move toward an economic boycott of those clubs. They succeeded in getting newspapers to publicize their findings.

At one point, for example, the association conducted a survey of three hundred Long Island corporations:"Do you have a corporate membership at a club? Do you pay dues or reimburse membership costs for your executives at a country club? How have you handled the problem that clubs will not extend privileges to your female executives? Do you sponsor outings or tournaments or hold events at a country club?" The bar asked for names of clubs and then aired the results at a public forum. Coming from women attorneys, some in the tax trade, the message was inescapable.

This case illustrates that organizations have economic power and can bring about change, but it takes the energy and commitment of individuals to mobilize the organization and to keep it focused on the target.

Sometimes smaller leads to larger. From her experience with the local bar group, Mrs. Grill learned about the role of lobbyists and which groups and legislators might oppose a statewide bill to end discrimination at private country clubs. She set out for Albany, the state's capital, in 1991, and found that a bill that would open the doors of the country club to women and minorities had been languishing there for thirteen years—since 1978. She and the women's bar targeted former State Senator and Republican majority leader Ralph Marino, a member of the Nassau Country Club, for repeatedly blocking the bill. By July 1994, New York State had a new private-clubs law.

❧ *Your CEO and His Country Club* ☙

If a committee from Congress and the ABA and the local bar association can mount a campaign against discrimination at private country clubs, what is the role of the executive and his corporation?

Corporations interact with country clubs on a variety of levels: to note just three, CEOs may have private club memberships, their companies may pay for memberships for other employees, and they may sponsor professional tournaments or business conferences at the club. Often the clubs in question exclude top female and African-American executives.

Each one of these raises separate issues. The company with women and minorities in its labor force, which will necessarily include virtually all large companies today, or the company whose products are advertised and marketed to women and minorities, may not wish to sponsor major events at clubs with discriminatory policies. To do so sends a terrible message to their employees and their customers. That is the lesson of Shoal Creek.

Should those companies pay for the costs of their male executives when business entertainment requires it but the male belongs to a club with exclusionary policies? Consider what message is being sent to female and minority staff, let alone what tax complications might arise.

The toughest questions may concern the CEOs' own country club membership. When Paul H. O'Neill became chairman of the Aluminum Company of America in 1987, he learned that one of the perks of running Alcoa was membership at Laurel Valley Golf Club in Ligonier, Pennsylvania. According to the *Washington Post*, when he inquired if the club admitted women and blacks as members, and was told, No, he refused to join. But he didn't stop there. The company adopted a policy that it would not pay dues for any of its executives to organizations that discriminated, or reimburse expenses incurred at such clubs. O'Neill's order was viewed "as a first step in what has become a total reshaping of the company's corporate conscience," the newspaper said.

Some corporate executives do push hard for changes regarding access and membership. Often they work from within. But sometimes that doesn't succeed.

In 1994, John F. Smith, Jr., president and chief executive of General Motors, resigned from Bloomfield Hills Country Club in Michigan, long an exclusive bastion of the auto industry's top executives, because Roy S. Roberts, a black vice-president, was rejected for membership. This was not racism, the club president said. But he offered no other reason for the action. The club has one black member, Leroy C. Richey, a general counsel for Chrysler and an outside lawyer for the USGA.

Usually if a candidate is rejected—and often one blackball will do it—club officials inform the sponsors, who then withdraw the candidate's name. But instead of withdrawing the name, Roberts and his sponsor, J. Michael Losh, GM's chief financial officer, insisted that Roberts be formally considered. He was then turned down. That Smith and Losh pressed instead of withdrawing says something about whether they believed it was racism or something else. When Mr. Smith resigned from Bloomfield Hills, the story landed in the *New York Times*, the *Wall Street Journal*, Reuters and CNN's "Moneyline."

John Smith backed his belief with action. Many corporate officials have not. They consider their public, corporate role to be one thing, their private leisure activity another. But public and private aren't so separate, especially for top corporate officials in position to exercise leadership.

As Reed Mackenzie, the lawyer who helped Minnesota arrive at an equitable tee-time policy, put it, the corporate attitude is perplexing. "The most difficult issue for me to understand is the case of somebody who heads a big company. You say to him, 'You know, the things you do at your club you wouldn't stand for for a minute at your job. Why is this any different?' "

He raises a good question. Will these men take a leadership role in bringing women into their own clubs? Ultimately, they may meet themselves coming around the corner.

15

Going for Legislation*

*I don't think we necessarily want the government in on
every area of our social and recreational life.*
—Kaye Brooks Bushel, former general counsel to the
Maryland Department of Assessments and Taxation

Some women take their clubs to court. Others use the media. Still others
seek out state legislators. Going to the legislature is often attractive
because it moves the issue away from confrontation with one's own club.
It says that the problem is a larger one and offers a solution that will apply
to all private clubs in the state. In taking this route, women are making
formerly hidden private club practices visible to public officials.

For the nearly 135 years since they began in the U.S., private golf
and country clubs had been accountable to no one except their membership. They typically answered to no outside group, let alone the legislature of any state. Indeed, the most sweeping piece of social legislation of
our times, the Civil Rights Act of 1964, expressly exempts all private
clubs from its sanctions. Only public accommodations may not discriminate. Private clubs and fraternal organizations assumed that they were
subject to guarantees of rights of association under the Constitution.

But that protection has slowly begun to give way. As of 1995

---

* This chapter looks at a few aspects of legislation. For a fuller explanation of laws
pertaining to private clubs in the fifty states, please see the Appendix.

some fifteen cities and ten states have adopted laws that prohibit discrimination in private country clubs under one form of law or another. In enacting these new laws, state legislatures have wrestled with a major issue, one never before asked about private clubs in America. Is the need to eradicate discrimination in private clubs more important than a club's privacy rights?

The use of state legislation to end discriminatory practices takes two different forms. In the more indirect form, the state's power to tax or to license may be used. If the state is conferring a benefit, those enjoying the benefit should abide by state public policy on matters of race or gender discrimination. In Chapter 3, we saw a good example: Burning Tree Club lost a great tax break from the state of Maryland's "open spaces" law because of its insistence on keeping women out.

In its more direct form, cities or states may aim specifically at private clubs, passing rules prohibiting discrimination by category if the clubs are of a certain size and used for business purposes. The line here is a narrow one: if the club serves meals to nonmembers, has a liquor license from the state, permits business and trade, and acknowledges corporate tax deductions for memberships as business expenses, is it a purely private club or should it be treated as a public accommodation? Increasingly, states are putting private clubs under public-accommodations laws and their sanctions.

In looking at these issues with the golfing needs of country clubs in mind, it is important to raise the further question: how can the legislation be written to end gender discrimination without also destroying gender-specific sport competitions—men's tournaments and women's tournaments—that are a staple of country club life?

❧ *Open Spaces Laws* ☙

One answer is that it helps to have golfers close at hand. In Minnesota, Reed and Jane Mackenzie were much involved in golf life, so much so that in the mid-eighties each was scheduled to assume the presidency of their respective men's and women's state golf associations. They were members of Hazeltine National Golf Club, and Reed, who is a lawyer, was later chairman of the U.S. Open when it was held there in 1991.

Thus when a Minnesota legislator received a complaint from a woman constituent in 1985 about limited tee times at her private club, the Mackenzies were there to help educate a number of legislators. The lawmakers were incensed that clubs receiving lucrative tax benefits under Minnesota's sixteen-year-old Open Spaces Law were discriminating against women.

"For example, the original bill would not have allowed a men's club championship or a women's club championship because those were gender-specific," said Mr. Mackenzie. "It would not have allowed a women's guest day or a men's guest day because those were gender-specific.

"We had to educate the legislature that the women really wanted to have their own club championship and there had to be room within the legislation to allow those things to take place, that that wasn't really the evil they were bound to correct," he said.

Unlike many legislatures—which press these bills into committee, from whence they rarely emerge—Minnesota's legislators, wary of special privilege, were bound and determined to go forward. So the Minnesota Golf Association took a position endorsing the change but pressed for legislative language that would enable traditional golf competitions to remain.

Mr. Mackenzie and his wife next sold the bill to the 100 or so private golf and country clubs in the state, urging them to support it. "Some followed the spirit of the law immediately. For some it was a long and painful process," said Jane. By 1988 all but one club—Stillwater Country Club—had complied, and in 1994, faced with the prospect of very stiff tax penalties, it, too, gave in.

In its most critical part, the new amendment to the Minnesota statute requires that "a private golf course not use gender as a selection criteria for membership" and that women be given access to the golf course on weekends. The statute does recognize the desire for single-sex golf tournaments and permits clubs to hold women's- or men's-only play twice a week during weekdays and one weekend each month. Otherwise, every private club in Minnesota has open tee times for all members on weekends.

At Hazeltine, Mr. Mackenzie said, "we really had gone as far as we could by 1985, short of equal tee times. We had historically taken the position that regardless of whose name was on the membership certificate, either spouse could vote the share and either spouse could hold office, although not at the same time. So we had women on our board;

we had women members. Only the weekend tee times were an issue.

"We then made the decision that as a club that was going to host the U.S. Open, we should be free of any taint. So we simply said that effective in 1986, we are not going to have any gender-based tee times. Period. And it worked so well for us. The fears of club members that there would be lines on the first tee simply didn't came true."

Why? Because people are creatures of habit. Many women continued to play on their old days, Tuesday and Thursday. "Now I can go out there those days if I want to and also play," said Mr. Mackenzie, "and those women who need to play on weekends do so too."

The Minnesota legislature has continued to keep a weather eye on private club life. It mandated integration of club grills in 1993, and most recently it required clubs to treat widows equally or face the loss of the tax deduction. Women in Minnesota now have access to the golf course on a fair and equitable basis, a result of responsive legislators guided by fair-minded people who understand golf.

Mr. Mackenzie, now a member of the USGA executive committee, predicted in 1991 that private clubs in the United States would most likely be gender-neutral within five years. He and Jane have given lectures about the issue before various golf groups. "I am very much wrong. It's taking much longer than I thought it would," he said. One reason is that resistance to change has been stronger than he anticipated. Another is the need for more people like him to speak out.

When the State of Maryland enacted an open-spaces law to encourage private country clubs to maintain their land rather than sell it to a developer, the legislation was silent on the issue of discrimination. The year was 1965; the legislation was the first of its kind in the United States. Many of the grandest country clubs in the state were on the rolling hills of what were once some of the state's oldest and most beautiful horse farms.

In exchange for keeping its property open space and not selling it to developers for high-density projects, the state gave its private clubs a lucrative tax break. It assessed the property as undeveloped land rather than at its "best use" on the marketplace.

Clubs flocked to the tax abatement program. For example, one 281-acre golf course in Montgomery County paid taxes on a $14 million assessment—not the $61 million that was its full market value. In 1974 the legislature amended the statute to say those private country clubs that discriminated "in granting membership or guest privileges based on race, color, creed, sex, or national origin" would lose their preferential tax treatment.

Enter Kaye Brooks Bushel, who in 1990 was counsel to the Maryland Department of Assessments and Taxation. She conducted an inquiry into tee-time and membership practices at thirty-two clubs that had accepted Open Space designation and whose tax abatements were substantial.

Ms. Bushel, a lapsed golfer, found that virtually every one of these clubs denied women equal access to the course as a result of segregated weekend tee times. In less than a year, the clubs changed their policies, including some prominent clubs such as Congressional Country Club. Only Burning Tree Club fought it.

"Many made whatever changes were necessary. Others needed a little bit of prompting from me," she said. "It was common sense. Women who work will play on weekends; women who don't will play on weekdays when they usually played."

As a tax officer, Ms. Bushel tended to keep things strictly gender-neutral, including eliminating single-sex tournaments.

"Once you get government involved, then they've got to draw these lines and everything has to fit into a category. . . . I felt badly about it, because I thought the presence of the state in this whole operation did not achieve the best results. It went in with the best of purposes, I suppose, but the results were sort of ridiculous. We got rid of harmless things, like ladies' and men's days." As Minnesota showed, it didn't have to be that way.

"We met a lot of resistance from very angry, older, often widowed or retired females who really thought we had rocked the boat to their disadvantage, because they liked their Ladies' Days, they liked their ladies' tournaments; whereas the younger group of working women were pressing to have some ladies' tournaments on weekends so they could play. "

As she looked back on that inquiry now, from the vantage point of a partner in a Maryland law firm, Ms. Bushel said private clubs should learn that they are far better off working together to get things changed than leaving it up to government officials. Legislation can be a blunt instrument. On the other hand, many women in Maryland are enjoying golfing freedoms they did not have until the law was applied to their clubs.

❧ ❧

Maryland and Minnesota are the only states in the nation that have an environmental law directed specifically at golf courses. Other states have more routine tax benefits. Golf courses are often assessed at extremely low taxes because they are classified as farmland or unimproved land or recreational land. Some states, like Massachusetts, give certain nonprofit private clubs a tax break in order to prevent the commercialization of large tracts of golf property. Selling to a developer means more houses, more people, more schools, more taxes. Better to preserve the land, say the policy makers who justify the tax benefits, because development brings with it other costs. Besides, private golf property in winter is used by the public to sled or to ski or to ice skate.

Private clubs also receive a form of public financial support because as nonprofit organizations they are exempt from paying federal income tax and state income tax. There is, however, nothing to stop state legislatures from making these sorts of tax benefits conditional on nondiscriminatory practices.

❧ *How About Lunch at the Club?* ❧

The law that has made the most significant impact on country club life in the United States began in Manhattan, a New York City borough that had no exclusive private golf and country clubs but did have a deep concern about segregated luncheon and dinner clubs.

The time was 1984. Some New York City women and minority groups wanted access to the city's rich assortment of private luncheon clubs, places where men daily congregated to initiate and renew professional contacts and to conduct business. Women sought admission to these clubs, among them the New York Athletic Club, the Century Club, the University Club, and the Friars Club. Some were older women established in their professions but facing glass ceilings; some were younger women who had broken the barriers at Yale and Princeton and were up-and-coming bankers, lawyers, and businesswomen.

These women and their attorneys proposed a new amendment to New York City's Human Rights Law. The city council of New York held hearings, took testimony, and ultimately adopted the new amendment, which presented a revolutionary new approach to gain access to a world traditionally closed to outsiders.

The proposed ordinance said that if a club had more than four hundred members, served lunches to members and nonmembers during which business was conducted, and received payments or fees for use of space or facilities in furtherance of trade or business, then it could not discriminate against classes of people such as minorities and women.

The city council also recognized that employers paid for the club dues and expenses of their employees because employees' club activities helped develop valuable personal contacts for the employers' businesses. In these circumstances, the council concluded, denial of access to club facilities constituted a significant barrier to the professional advancement of women and minorities.

It was a radical step. Its repercussions were immediate. Shortly after the mayor signed the bill into law, the New York State Club Association, which represented some 125 private clubs in the state, went to state court to challenge it, arguing that the ordinance was invalid because it violated a club's right to freedom of association. But because no specific club argued the case, the courts had no detailed facts to work from, and when the case was finally appealed to the U.S. Supreme Court, it ruled that the ordinance on its face was not unconstitutional. In other words, the ordinance might be constitutional when applied to some private clubs, unconstitutional when applied to others.

As the court ruling put it: "If a club seeks to exclude individuals who do not share the views that the club members wish to promote, the law erects no obstacle to this end. Instead, the law merely prevents an association from using race, sex, and the other specified characteristics as shorthand measures in place of what the city considers to be more legitimate criteria for determining membership."

Before you could say golf, five other cities, including Los Angeles, quickly adopted their own version of New York City's ordinance. That enabled the city attorney of Los Angeles to bring a lawsuit against Brentwood Country Club. The issue: gender discrimination in tee times, grills, and membership. Other cities followed, as well as other states.

At the same time, federal judges are making new law in this area. In the spring of 1994, a federal judge in Louisiana, examining a New Orleans ordinance modeled on New York City's, ruled in favor of three historically white New Orleans men's dining clubs, among the most prominent in the city. The judge ruled that the three clubs were entitled to their free-association rights, and permanently enjoined the city of

New Orleans from investigating a complaint by a black businessman that he was denied admission to all three clubs. These clubs were small enough, intimate enough, social enough to qualify as a private club, not as a public accommodation. Judge A. J. McNamara said, "The members of these private clubs have the right to be free from government prying into their private affairs. . . . The First Amendment does not permit such governmental intrusion." He ordered the city not to hold a hearing into club membership practices.

The city of New Orleans appealed to the Fifth Circuit Court of Appeals, and in January 1995 that court upheld the lower court. So it's not over yet. A decade after New York City began to desegregate its private clubs, some private dining rooms in New Orleans have been held off-limits to public investigation. The U.S. Supreme Court is far from completing its work in this area.

❧ *A Michigan Legislator Gets Angry* ❧

The State of Michigan passed the most sweeping piece of social legislation ever to hit private clubs. It began when a woman attorney whose salary was helping to pay for her family's membership at the Travis Pointe Country Club in Ann Arbor received a bill from the club.

The bill outlined her family's share for construction of a new nineteenth hole, the proverbial men's grill. Why, she wondered, should she help pay for a new grill from which she was barred?

Eventually that question landed on the desk of then State Senator Lana Pollack (D-Ann Arbor), a feisty woman with a quick wit and a determined way. She grabbed the issue and wouldn't let go.

It would take two years, and then, one fine morning in the spring of 1992, on the eighteenth fairway at the Walnut Hills Country Club in East Lansing, at an LPGA tournament, Michigan's Governor John Engler signed Senator Pollack's bill into law.

The new law was actually an amendment that placed private clubs under Michigan's Elliott-Larsen civil-rights law. The new amendment was aimed at ending discriminatory rules against women who were entitled to use the club by virtue of their spousal relationship. The thrust of the law was to give women equal access to all facilities—on the golf course, in the grill.

Its language said: "If a private club allows use of its facilities by one or more adults per membership, the use must be equally available to all adults entitled to use the facilities under the membership." Overnight, the new law opened the clubhouse door to all members. And that was a revolutionary step.

When Lana Pollack's staff first began to gather information about clubs, they quickly learned that women might want change but were terrified of the consequences. The complainant, for example, refused to tell her grill story in a public forum. At first, Senator Pollack was unsympathetic. Some women would have to show courage. But she soon learned that few women were interested in being courageous, not when it might lead to social ostracism. Once the senator understood the complexity of the issue, she exerted the leadership herself.

Before any legislation was mounted, members of the senator's staff visited a number of the editorial boards of influential newspapers in the state. "We learned to get the press early. Before any legislation was even introduced, we spoke to editorial boards, to the place where tone is established. We found out they agreed with us," said Alma Smith, Ms. Pollack's former chief assistant.

The law was enacted over two legislative sessions and after conservative senators offered up a compromise that was defeated. Its sanctions were simple: any club, regardless of the number of members, that practiced discrimination in permitting women access to a club's facilities faced the loss of its liquor license. Gone were tee-time restrictions that made it difficult for professional women to meet clients to generate business. As Ms. Pollack had said, "That amounts to economic discrimination."

"Country clubs would never dream of putting up a sign that says no African-Americans before 3 P.M. But that's exactly what they've been doing to women," said Ms. Pollack.

The Michigan law is remarkable for its scope and breadth. Many in the private-club world are still shaking their heads in amazement. It is also remarkable that it met so little resistance from the ever-vigilant, well-organized National Club Association. The Michigan law does press the privacy issues to their limit. Gone are the usual requirements of a public-accommodations component: sheer size or commercial involvement.

The law has been challenged by a group of single male members from the Detroit Golf Club (see Chapter 2) and by the Elks, a fraternal organization, that bars women from membership. A federal judge hearing the Elks case has ruled that the new amendment applies only to equal facilities. If a woman is in the club, she must get equal access. So far the Elks has not invited women in as members.

Enforcing Legislation: *Investigation and Demand Letters*

It's one thing to pass a piece of legislation, and it is another to get it enforced. A law at the state level is usually enforced by the state attorney general's office, usually the division of civil rights. The process begins with a complaint and is followed by an investigation. If the attorney general's office finds the country club to have violated the law, the office will send the club what is commonly known as a demand letter. This letter orders the club to comply with the law within a certain period of time or face further action.

Three cases in this book can illustrate these processes. The first involves the investigative process, the second and third the writing of demand letters.

Remember Lee Lowell, the woman in Chapter 6 who was chased around Cedar Brook Club on Long Island by a posse of male golfers?

The New York State Division of Human Rights investigated whether Cedar Brook was "distinctively private," as the club claimed. First the division sought financial information. When the club refused, the division went undercover. A state representative, whom the division described as a "tester," called the club to ask whether they rent their facilities out. During the conversation, the club manager made arrangements to show the facilities and discussed financial terms of a rental agreement. When the tester visited the club, the manager "made it clear that the club acts as a catering hall and also rents its recreational facilities to non-members. The tester made it clear that he had never been to the club and that he was not a member," a report describing the inquiry said.

"Notwithstanding those representations, the manager drew up a rental agreement and gave it to the tester. In light of these facts, and the fact that the club would not respond to the division's request for revenue ledgers which would show sources of its income, it is clear that the club does not limit the use of its facilities and services to members and bona fide guests of members." So undercover investigation showed what Cedar Brook was all about. The club, the state found, fell under the state's public-accommodations law and had engaged in discriminatory practices against Mrs. Lowell. Clubs invite this sort of investigation when they stonewall their own members and outside agencies.

Diane Graham is the businesswoman who filed a complaint with the state asserting she was denied weekend access to Hallbrook Country Club's golf course in Kansas because she was a woman family member. Robert T. Stephan, then the attorney general, provided the first analysis of the law in his letter to Hallbrook's attorney.

Mr. Stephan's letter is reproduced on pages 210–211.

Molly O'Dea's case against Cheval Country Club near Tampa, Florida, was the first test of Florida's new private-clubs law, enacted in 1993. (See Chapter 6). Reproduced on pages 212–213 is the demand letter from Gregory Durden, chief of the civil rights division of the Florida attorney general's office, to Cheval's attorney.

❦ Federal Taxes and Private Clubs ❦

What can the federal government do about discrimination in private clubs?

As it turns out, the government has a good deal of economic clout. Its powers lie primarily in the Internal Revenue Code. But enforcing the code when it comes to nonprofit country clubs has rarely been an IRS priority.

Under the IRS code, private recreational clubs face a loss of their nonprofit tax exemption if the club's bylaws or other written material provide for discrimination against "any person on the basis of race, color or religion." In the aftermath of Shoal Creek, Representative Charles Rangel (D-Harlem) submitted legislation that would add gender to the IRS private clubs section 501(i) of the tax code and would bar a private club from getting a tax exemption if it was determined by a court or federal governmental agency that the club engaged in discriminatory practices.

Three years later, in September 1993, he held a hearing before the House Subcommittee on Select Revenue Measures. The testimony from both sides is instructive.

On the one side were women who supported the legislation, women such as Lee Beard, a Pennsylvania bank president. When she became the bank's chief fiscal officer, in early 1993, she expected to be a member of the local country club. The bank's board had the same expectation. The club agreed that Ms. Beard would have a membership in her name. There is no other club in the area.

In her testimony, she said, "The club has become the primary place for businesspeople to meet, develop business contacts, and entertain. Membership by the CEO for my financial institution is important as a part of the business community." She testified that although she expected she would get full membership privileges, the club's board would not lift onerous tee-time restrictions that kept Ms. Beard and her clients off the course on weekends until after 1 P.M. The club has offered to let her skirt the tee-time rule when she has guests. "But I pay the dues and write the checks. I want the same access as any other full member." She still hasn't gotten it .

Ms. Beard argued that by allowing federal tax exemptions for clubs like hers, where the bylaws do not exhibit gender discrimination but the rules and practices do, "the taxpayers of our country are providing a financial benefit for discrimination." She urged the subcommittee to deny nonprofit status to country clubs that engage in gender discrimination.

On the other side was the National Club Association, the prime lobbyist for some one thousand private clubs in America. They argued against the bill, saying it would violate the constitutionally protected right of freedom of association and the privacy of private club members by utilizing the tax code to coerce them into modifying their club's membership practices. "It would be an abuse of the tax laws to use them to achieve such unrelated social objectives."

Congress, the NCA argued, should not confuse *exclusivity* and *selectivity*. "A private club has the right to be selective to ensure prospective members will be compatible with existing members."

The NCA said it was fallacious to think that tax-exempt private clubs pay no taxes and are subsidized by taxpayers, saying clubs pay employment taxes as well as taxes on unrelated business income.

Its last words put a special twist on the meaning of diversity. "How much more lively, interesting, diverse, and democratic our lives

STATE OF KANSAS

OFFICE OF THE ATTORNEY GENERAL

2ND FLOOR, KANSAS JUDICIAL CENTER, TOPEKA 66612-1597

ROBERT T. STEPHAN
ATTORNEY GENERAL

March 15, 1994

MAIN PHONE: (913) 296-2215
CONSUMER PROTECTION: 296-3751
TELECOPIER: 296-6296

Ms. Rosalee McNamara
Gage & Tucker
2345 Grand Ave.
27th Floor
Kansas City, MO 64108

Re: Hallbrook Country Club

Dear Ms. McNamara:

I appreciated the visit today from you and Mr. Bluhm. After considering your points supporting Hallbrook's tee time policies, I again reviewed the law and have reached a number of conclusions.

First, it is abundantly clear that K.S.A. 44-1002 (i) (2) applies to Hallbrook. Payment is received for use of facilities, space, meals, and beverages from members on behalf of nonmembers.

More serious is the meaning of the term "any discrimination in regard to membership . . ." found in K.S.A. 44-1002 (i) (2). During hearings on the Bloch Amendment, the Kansas legislature was provided with the text from a New York City law which stated:

> The government has a compelling interest in
> providing its citizens an environment where all
> persons, regardless of race, creed, color, national
> origin, or sex, have fair and equal opportunity to
> participate in the business and professional life of
> the city, and may be unfettered in availing
> themselves of employment opportunities.

This law was the basis of K.S.A. 44-1002 (i).

Page 2

I conclude that the language "any discrimination in regard to membership" covers a broader range of membership issues than you asserted at our meeting. I cannot find any evidence that the legislature intended to allow clubs to circumvent the nondiscrimination laws by interpreting the phrase to apply only to admission to membership. Under that interpretation, clubs could admit Mr. Bloch to membership, for example, yet restrict his access to use of facilities based solely upon his religion.

Finally, I do not believe that a policy which excludes a protected group from the use of facilities solely because of their status as a member of a protected group is minutiae beyond the scope of the KADD.

In order to comply with the law, Hallbrook should eliminate any policy on tee time availability or preference which discriminates against a group protected under K.S.A. 44-1002 (i). Thus, men's or women's designated times are unlawful. Please let me know within ten days of the date of this letter whether you would recommend to the Board of Directors that Hallbrook change its current tee time policy to one which complies with the law. If such a recommendation would be made, I expect the Board to revise the current policy within thirty days from the date of this letter; otherwise, I will file a complaint with the Human Rights Commission.

Thank you for your cooperation.

Very truly yours,

Robert T. Stephan
Attorney General

RTS/bls

OFFICE OF THE ATTORNEY GENERAL

DEPARTMENT OF LEGAL AFFAIRS
THE CAPITOL
TALLAHASSEE, FLORIDA 32399-1050

ROBERT A. BUTTERWORTH
Attorney General
State of Florida

Reply to:

Office of the Attorney General
4000 Hollywood Boulevard, 505-South
Hollywood, Florida 33021

April 11, 1994

William E. Sizemore, Esquire
Thompson, Sizemore & Gonzalez, P.A.
Suite 200
109 North Brush Street
Post Office Box 639
Tampa, Florida 33601   <u>BY FACSIMILE AND U.S. MAIL</u>

Dear Mr. Sizemore:

In light of your response to our letter of March 31, 1994, this
office has completed its initial investigation of Ms. Molly
O'Dea's complaint against Cheval Country Club, Inc., et. al.
Based upon the factual information we obtained and the prevailing
law, the Office of Civil Rights has determined that your client
is in violation of Section 760.60 and Section 509.092, Florida
Statutes (1993). We disagree with your position on the issue of
jurisdiction.

First, it is clear that Florida Statute 760.60, applies to
Cheval. The purpose of the statute is to provide access to all
facilities of a club, including Saturday morning tee times and the
Men's Grille/Card room, notwithstanding any member's gender.
Furthermore, under Section 509.092, Cheval is a public food
service establishment; therefore, the club cannot refuse service
based on a member's gender. There is little doubt that the
Florida legislature intended to eliminate the type of invidious
discrimination Cheval, its officers, directors, and parent
companies are practicing.

In order to comply with the law, Cheval should immediately
eliminate any policy on tee time availability or preference that
discriminates against a protected group. It is our position that
men's or women's designated tee times are unlawful. Also, Cheval
should immediately open the "Men's Grille/Card room" to all
persons using the club. Accordingly, this office requests the
Board of Directors of Cheval Country Club, Inc. to revise the
current policies, within twenty (20) days from the date of this
letter, including the addition of the requisite amendments to the
bylaws of the corporation.

Mr. William E. Sizemore
April 11, 1994
Page Two

In the event your client declines to comply with this request, the Office of Civil Rights may avail itself of any and all applicable remedies, including but not limited to filing a public food service establishment complaint with the Florida Commission on Human Relations. As you know, each violation of Section 509.092, Florida Statutes, carries with it possible punitive damages of up to $100,000.

Your attention to this matter is requested.

Sincerely,

Gregory Durden, Esquire
Chief of Civil Rights

cc: Rosemary Armstrong, Esquire

GD/cjh
File No.   93-900296
CHEVAL.demand

are because we can and do belong to a wide range of single sex, single race, single ethnicity, or single interest clubs, rather than being forced into government-regulated and mandated diverse membership associations." The NCA asked the legislators to reconsider the proposal.

As fate would have it, the Clinton Administration removed the deductibility of private club dues in Clinton's first year in office. According to an aide, Representative Rangel felt he had accomplished his point, even though the issue of tax exemption is different from tax deductibility. The bill is now dead. Left for another day and another congressman is getting the word *gender* into section 501(i) of the tax code and finding ways to enforce the code when the IRS has neither the manpower nor the funds for enforcement.

❧ *The National Club Association* ❧

The NCA wields tremendous influence in the world of private clubs. From its elegant offices in Washington, D.C., this trade organization, which ironically is now led by women executives, represents the nation's most prestigious private clubs, with an estimated one million members. The clubs include country, golf, city, tennis, yacht, and athletic clubs.

Well versed in virtually every legal, legislative, tax, and political issue facing the club world, it has a sophisticated staff with keen lobbying skills. Its considerable expertise, by way of staff and board and former board members, is easily mobilized to fight issues. It has lost some big battles in recent years, however, on the statehouse front.

When necessary, the NCA goes to court, and it fought hard for four years against the New York City ordinance. That case was a soul-wrenching experience, a real loss. To this day, the NCA continues to put out legislative fires across the country. It helps organize its members in the vast array of legal and tax issues clubs face. For example, in 1995 the Association plans to mount an intense lobbying campaign in the new Congress to restore the business entertainment deduction that Congress had reduced from 80 percent to 50 percent.

It keeps in direct contact with its membership, guiding clubs on a vast array of subjects. The NCA publishes a yearly legislative and legal guide, tracking bills aimed at curtailing the rights of private clubs. One of the association's great accomplishments is the publication of a vast periodicals index, which provides member clubs with policy approaches to everything from admitting members to managing the media.

In the last decade, Supreme Court decisions have whittled away rights that private clubs long took for granted. As a result, the NCA has told clubs to adopt gender-neutral bylaws, eliminate corporate payments of memberships and dues, keep smaller memberships, and articulate specific criteria based on "selective membership."

"Joining a club is not a rejection of those who do not belong. Rather, becoming a member of a private club involves a joining together of people with similar likes, interests, and purpose," the NCA says.

The NCA believes that clubs should be allowed to be formed on the basis of gender. To bar women's clubs because they are gender-based would be contrary to the views of society at large and would deprive the club of the single-mindedness and common purpose that have been so important to women's clubs. In the NCA's view, what applies to women applies to men.

The organization is now headed by two women. Sue Wegrzyn, its new executive director, does not play golf, but its legal and legislative specialist, Elizabeth Kirby Hart, has begun to take lessons. Neither knows firsthand the experiences of most businesswomen golfers in the Washington, D.C., area.

❧ Going After Individuals Versus Clubs ❦

So far all the legislation we have described has been directed at discriminatory private clubs. There is another possibility: sometimes the tax collector goes after the individual members of such clubs.

As you can imagine, going after individual members is even more problematic than going after the clubs themselves. It may be perceived by the members as being even more invasive than a subpoena requiring the club's financial statements.

Often administrative agencies have powers to impose change. When they push for equality, they can make themselves felt. In California, the champion for the women scorned by the country club has not been the courts, but the California Franchise Tax Board, an agency few outside California have ever heard of. One of its functions is to enforce the law that says a club member may not take a business tax deduction if his club engages in discriminatory practices.

To find out if a club acts in a discriminatory manner, the board uses its broad subpoena powers to seek membership rosters for the purpose of reviewing members' tax returns. In 1988 and 1989, the board targeted some fifty clubs across California.

Most clubs refused to turn over their membership rolls. One club fought back hard. The tax board took on the Pacific-Union Club, an exclusive, all-male organization whose mansion is located atop Nob Hill in San Francisco. No doubt the board believed it had a good case. The club was all-male. The board sought the club's membership list, seeking to conduct random audits of club members to check for illegal tax deductions.

But the club mounted a terrific fight. In July 1991 the State Court of Appeals ruled that the club could keep its membership list secret. In describing the Pacific-Union Club as purely private, despite its 958-plus members, the court noted that the club's "doors do not open from the outside; members and guests must identify themselves and be admitted by security staff. No member may bring the same person as a guest more than four times a month. . . . The proceedings at the Club facility may not be described or photographed and members may not talk to the press. This atmosphere of privacy recalls the Central Intelligence Agency, not the open doors and windows of the Rotarians." (A reminder that the Rotarians were all-male until a U.S. Supreme Court decision in 1987.)

"It is worth noting that the specter of a tax audit solely because of membership in a private group is chilling," the judges said. The board appealed to the California Supreme Court, but lost.

It was an important victory for private country clubs in California. The NCA would say that in an era of government intrusion, maybe the courts are just protecting the underdogs—the private clubs—from a political-correctness onslaught. Meanwhile the California legislature, one of the most progressive in the nation, has not been indifferent. It has repeatedly enacted a new bill that would prohibit issuing any state license to discriminatory clubs. But progressive legislators sometimes have conservative governors. Governor Pete Wilson has repeatedly refused to sign any private-clubs bill into law. He sides with the clubs.

❦ 16 ❧

Public Concerns and Private Lives

Miss Collett typifies all that the word "sportsmanship"
stands for.
—Bobby Jones, in his introduction to Glenna Collett's
Ladies in the Rough, 1928

The stories in this book are vivid evidence of the gender discrimination deeply rooted and thoroughly institutionalized in American golf. It is conspicuously present in private country club life, and found in less visible forms on public golf courses and in professional golf.

In a world that has become so much more conscious of civil rights, it is truly astonishing to see such blatantly discriminatory practices against women continuing in the country club world. Many of the women in this book have been demeaned, rejected, treated with indifference or contempt. When a club has been central to your life, it's crushing to be told you must leave it just because your marital status has changed. This is perhaps the most damaging form of disrespect, but even the less painful forms are galling, frustrating, debilitating. It is an insult to be treated as a second-class citizen, and it is especially damaging for business and professional women who seek and deserve the same membership and playing rights as men.

The male privileges embedded in club rules, bylaws, and practices are leftovers from the time when males had a virtual monopoly on institutional power, when women were systematically excluded and in some cases disenfranchised. The rewards to men from this period have come to be viewed as entitlements. The men won a lot of chips from a system they had rigged in their favor. It is a small step to the belief that they have these chips because they are more worthy of them than anyone else.

Yet the men who run country club life certainly don't see themselves as exploiters of women, as the agents and messengers of disrespect. The pattern of privilege is thoroughly natural to them. It has been their way of life. "Me, a sexist? Surely not. My wife enjoys the club, is happy with the tee times, and isn't complaining." So when country club women of long standing like Midge Martin in Massachusetts or Dorothy Moller in Arizona, having experienced unequal treatment for decades, bring their grievances to the board, often their clubs behave stubbornly, refusing compromise, only to find that the state may well order far more severe sanctions than had the men acted reasonably at the outset.

And the problem is not only the men. Often the WORMs—the wives of regular members—fail to follow their conscience and support those seeking change, and not because they think these other women are wrong. Often they agree with them. But they don't want to make waves, don't want to be perceived as troublemakers, don't want to displease their husbands.

Nonetheless the world is changing. Many private country clubs, quietly and without fanfare, have changed their bylaws to make them more accommodating to women. Their world has not collapsed. Golf's organizations are beginning to wrestle seriously with these issues. Public golf facilities, aware of the women's market, are increasingly thoughtful about how they introduce newcomers to golf. Women's business leagues are helping them move in the right direction. And in the world of professional golf, more sponsors and advertisers have found the LPGA Tour, which in 1995 will have more tour events—forty—than ever before. So there is reason for optimism.

It would be better for everyone if the issues of private club membership and access were settled in our hearts and consciences, rather than in the courts or by the legislature. But in order to have the kind of discussion among members that would bring understanding to a new level, clubs need to learn to keep talking, not to draw hard and fast lines, and especially to listen carefully and with compassion. Some of the clubs described in this book never even got to the talking stage, or if they appointed a committee to look into the problem, they rejected the committee's advice.

The message from legislators and human-rights commissioners around the country is that if the clubs don't act in a responsive manner, the officials will. Already, populous states such as New York, Florida, and Michigan have adopted laws restricting discrimination by private country clubs, as have some cities. The premise of most of these laws is that serving meals to outsiders or leasing facilities or providing business tax deductions or receiving special tax or property benefits as nonprofit organizations, gives the clubs a public side that invites government regulation.

But what if a golf club is "truly private"? It doesn't rent its facilities, is open only to its carefully selected members and their personal guests, and, aside from providing food for members and their guests and operating a proshop only for their convenience and not as a "profit center," has no taint of commercialism. This fairly describes some private family country clubs. Should we be concerned about their practices?

In my view this is a moral issue. Whatever the legality of the situation—and the U.S. Supreme Court will surely have more to say about a private club's right to freedom of association—it is really an issue of fairness. It simply isn't fair, especially in this day and age, to deny women equality of membership rights. If a woman executive is invited to join a club, and she pays a $25,000 initiation fee for a private club membership, she should get all the privileges that a male executive is entitled to. No more, but no less. And a club's bylaws should reflect that policy.

The argument that is sometimes given—that when WORMs have been asked about these issues many, even a majority, may prefer life as it is in their club—really isn't an answer at all. In most of the instances I know of, when women have been given a full understanding of the situation, they have voted for a more equitable sharing of privileges.

The reality is that people are creatures of habit. Most men aren't going to invade the Tuesday ladies' group, and most women who can play at other times aren't going to rush to the tee on Saturday mornings; only those who work during the week and can't play or entertain guests during weekdays. That's been the experience in states, like Minnesota, which passed legislation on the matter.

If clubs are genuinely in doubt, they can experiment with change for a month or two until they find the right formula for their club. But the moral and fairness issue should remain paramount: restrictions can legitimately be placed on members who can play anytime relative to those who work, or on golfers who play slowly. Restrictions should not be based on gender.

What then of the all-male clubs, where gender issues don't arise because one gender is missing? To me, it's again a moral rather than a legal issue, in which the principles are those of scale and business opportunity. If a tiny club is genuinely used purely for golfing pleasure, with no effect on business or commercial contacts, then who cares? But as these clubs become vital in the corporate life of the nation, they take on an enlarged significance and, in some sense, a public responsibility.

When Augusta National was proposed as the site for Olympic golf competition in 1996, how could anyone, including its own members, have seriously considered it? The Olympic movement has its own problems of elitism, but in competitive sport it draws thousands of men and women of all colors from around the world. To have them come to Augusta and compete at a place that took in its first black member only after Shoal Creek and still has no women members could be seen by the rest of the world as a cynical act of hypocrisy. Yet the idea was endorsed by all the leading golf organizations without apology.

Augusta is a magnificent golf course and a national treasure, made the more so by more than a quarter of a century of nationally televised coverage of the Masters every April. Its members are a national corporate elite. Being a guest of an Augusta member may symbolize close, warm friendship; it may also be a reward for successful corporate dealings.

Now, corporate elites may need and deserve their own private spaces, their own well-appointed oases. But think what it means when these oases exclude women entirely from membership. It's not that business deals are actually signed and delivered at Augusta or any other all-male club. That is probably a rarity. But contacts are made, networks and relationships are established, a common culture is being created, persons are being recruited and enticed with the promise of a "tee time at Augusta" or rewarded for their achievements. Yet some of the brightest, most deserving persons in the world are being kept out, solely because of their sex.

As a pure golf operation Augusta deserves its national ranking. But if it wishes to continue in its prestigious position, it ought to be genuinely open to the corporate elite of all races and both sexes. Bobby Jones, the spirit behind Augusta and its "president in perpetuity," was by all accounts a man of fine values. He played golf with the finest female players of his time, Joyce Wethered and Glenna Collett, and he wrote the introduction to Collett's book, *Ladies in the Rough*. I'd like to believe that were he now contemplating a new Augusta National, he would see to it that membership was based on achievement, golfing merit, and being a "kindred spirit," and that he wouldn't restrict kindred spirits to males.

And similarly for the thousand-member Pine Valley and other nationally ranked all-male clubs, clubs whose courses are held up as perfection in the golf rankings. How much would it really hurt them to allow in women members who are corporate or national leaders? Given the prominent role of these clubs in golf and in the corporate world, they should rise to the occasion.

Some of the corporate leaders who are members of all-male clubs rose to the occasion and protected their company's interests by disassociating the company from Shoal Creek. But while I want to acknowledge this role of corporate America, I also want to raise a question. Aren't most of the men who run corporate America also members of the very clubs that are engaging in some of these discriminatory practices?

These persons, these vice-presidents and general managers, to say nothing of the CEOs and chairmen of the boards, are active in virtually every private club in the country. They have typically acted to end discrimination that has an impact on their company. Have they acted to end it in their own clubs?

Their own clubs, they would probably argue, are a different matter. Their corporations, and particularly their marketing departments, had to oppose discrimination for good, solid business reasons or to comply with law. Country clubs don't have that burden—unless they are located in states with laws applying to them. Corporate leaders should not favor equal treatment of women in their clubs because it is good for business; they should favor it because it is the right thing to do. It restores to the women in their lives the respect they are due.

There is another point: the line between public and private is becoming blurred. The same women may be executives on the job and members of the club off the job. Can responsible corporate officials grant them equal rights in one world and only diminished rights in the other?

The heads of golf's governing organizations and other leaders in the golfing world face these issues even more directly. Do we allow a double standard when the staff and board of the United States Golf

Association, authorities for all the men and women who take amateur golf seriously, enjoy the special privileges of all-male or discriminatory country clubs? The women who have risen to positions of power and influence in golf face a special challenge. They are in positions of real leadership. But some of them are where they are because they've been willing to go along, to play by the men's rules, to accept second-class citizenship. They have been reluctant to use their positions to help the male leadership in golf move forward.

The fear when these issues of social responsibility are raised—either for corporate leaders or leaders of golf's governing bodies—is that responsible officials, already often donating their time, will simply withdraw from their more visible public roles and retire behind the private country club gates. We should at least have open dialogue about where to draw the line between public and private and what to expect from those in leadership positions.

Whatever the issues in golf, women are joining the game in increasing numbers. They are part of the growth of women in competitive sport, a development from Title IX programs that force universities to take women's sport seriously. And since Shoal Creek, private clubs hosting tournaments have been required to open up their doors.

One example of the new world is Kim Green, an African-American businesswoman in New York, who is president of her insurance brokerage firm. She and her husband, Sy, an executive of Chubb & Sons, are the first black members at Westchester Country Club, and their thirty-one-year-old daughter Jennifer is now a junior member, with the right to become a full member. The Greens will be able to pass on their golf membership to the next generation, "and a black female at that," Mrs. Green says.

There are now two black couples at Westchester and a third is going through the admissions process. There is the danger of tokenism, of course, that a club will rest after getting a single black member, or perhaps even a single woman member. In either case, one just isn't enough, although especially with minority memberships it has sometimes been deemed enough.

And as a journalist, I'm happy to see that even staid old British clubs are finally allowing women golf writers to interview the players in the locker room during the British Open. In Great Britain, reporter Liz Kahn has been covering golf for decades. It took nearly twenty-two years before she was able to get into the men's locker room. The occasion was the British Open at Muirfield and the year was 1992. She was taken inside by Michael Bonallack, secretary of the Royal and Ancient Golf Club of St. Andrews.

Generally the male golfers welcomed Kahn. However, in 1994, when the British Open was played at Turnberry, and when Bonallack did not escort the women journalists in, there was difficulty. Kahn was in the locker room with other golf writers, in an area traditionally used for interviews. "Jack Nicklaus knows me," Kahn described later, "and he says, 'What are you doing here?' And I said, 'I'm a journalist, Jack. I'm working.' He said, 'I don't care what you are. You're a woman,' just like that, to the locker room at large, and marched off." This from Jack Nicklaus, our country's greatest gift to professional golf. So we still have a way to go.

In some ways discrimination is easier to understand when it is aimed at faceless strangers. It is less easy to understand when people practice it against those they say they love and respect.

It's for the men in country club life to explain why they find it so easy to put their wives or daughters in a second-class position. Most of these men are reasonable, sort of, and would never concede that they are depriving their female loved ones of anything truly important. But by making such a big issue of tee times, or the right to vote in club affairs, men are converting practical concerns into a conflict between genders. Why? Is it really worth it when they could give a couple a half vote each and end weekend tee-time restrictions without much ado?

The men in these clubs are intimately connected to the women. So in the world of private country clubs, there is a special call to fathers to cherish their daughters and to honor their efforts to succeed in life, whether in the corporate world, the country club world, or both. These fathers should also remember that daughters come in all marital categories: single, married, divorced, widowed. Whatever their category, they deserve equality and respect.

This year a woman from Nutley, New Jersey, Sally A. Goodson, is leading a legislative campaign for equal access to the private golf course. The evening of the day on which the first story about her campaign appeared in the *Newark Star Ledger*, she was having dinner with her husband at their club, Forest Hill Field Club. A member of the club sent a bottle of wine to their table. His note read: "Thank you on behalf of my daughter."

☙ Appendix ❧

State Legislation, City Ordinances, and Private Clubs

These notes are meant to help those who want to know what their own city ordinance or state laws may say about private clubs and discrimination. Readers should check with lawyers in their own state as to whether there have been recent changes in legislation or whether there are additional areas of law that govern a club's situation.

☙ Public-Accommodations Laws ❧

A public accommodation is generally defined as a facility of any kind where goods and services are offered, sold, or otherwise made available to the public. In general, these laws say a facility may not discriminate on the basis of category—that is, race, religion, gender, ethnicity, among others. Not every area's law includes gender. Arizona and the Virgin Islands, for example, do not include gender in their public-accommodations laws. The public-accomodations laws of many states specifically exempt or do not mention private clubs.

The following states have public-accommodations laws that do not include private golf and country clubs:

Alabama, Alaska, Arizona, Connecticut, Delaware, Hawaii, Idaho, Illinois, Iowa, Louisiana, Massachusetts, Missouri (except when club caters to public), Nebraska, Nevada, New Hampshire, New Jersey, New Mexico, North Dakota, Ohio, Oklahoma, Oregon, Pennsylvania, Rhode Island, South Carolina, South Dakota (except when club caters to public), Utah (except when club is open to the public), Vermont, Virginia, Washington, West Virginia, Wisconsin, Wyoming.

The states of Missouri and South Dakota define a private club as a public accommodation only when the club's facilities are made available to the public.

The following states adopted laws similar to New York City's (see New York City ordinance below), redefining private clubs as public accommodations if they fit a variety of conditions: Florida, Kansas, Maine, Michigan, Montana, New York.

In some states, efforts have been made to pass New York City-type legislation, but the efforts so far have failed. The following are those that have come to my attention: Alabama, California, Connecticut, Indiana, Illinois, Kentucky, Massachusetts, Ohio, Pennsylvania, Texas, West Virginia, Wisconsin.

The following states do not have a public-accommodations statute or any other statute addressing discrimination in private country clubs: Arkansas, Georgia, Mississippi, North Carolina, and Texas.

❧ City Ordinances ❧

In 1984 a New York City ordinance was enacted that provides that private clubs with at least four hundred members, serving meals, and receiving payments for dues, fees, use of space, facilities, services, meals, or beverages for the furtherance of business or trade, are considered places of public accommodation, business arenas no longer entitled to constitutional protection as purely private clubs.

The following cities have enacted ordinances modeled after New York City's law: Atlanta, Georgia; Buffalo, New York; Chicago, Illinois;

Cincinnati, Ohio; Denver, Colorado; Los Angeles, California; New Orleans, Louisiana; Roanoke, Virginia; San Francisco, California; Shaker Heights, Ohio; Washington, D.C.; and Wilmington, Delaware. Some cities have reduced the minimum membership threshold to far below four hundred. Sometimes, as in Atlanta and Chicago, the law applies throughout the county in which the city is located.

Tax Statutes

Minnesota and Maryland provide tax benefits to those clubs that qualify for open space property tax benefits as long as the private club does not discriminate in membership and access to facilities on the basis of category.

California, Colorado, and Kentucky bar the taxpayer from taking as state income tax exemptions expenditures incurred at a private club serving alcohol that restricts membership or use of facilities on the basis of age, sex, marital status, race, religion, color, ancestry, or national origin.

Liquor Licensing

Virtually every state in the nation has a liquor or food licensing rule. Some states require that the license be dependent upon a private club's maintaining nondiscriminatory policies. In Connecticut and Arizona, lawsuits have been brought against private clubs under this rule, even though these states did not have a specific statute addressing discrimination in private country clubs.

The following cities and state enacted laws to prohibit the issuance of liquor licenses to private clubs with discriminatory membership policies: Atlanta, Georgia; Annapolis, Maryland; Boston, Massachusetts; and the State of Massachusetts.

❧ Corporation Law ☙

Each state has a body of corporation law that may have language barring a private club from discriminatory practices if the club is a nonprofit corporate entity, which most private clubs are.

❧ Public Funds ☙

Tennessee: No state organization may purchase membership for employees of the university to a private club that discriminates on the basis of race or sex.

South Carolina: The use of state funds at a function at a private club that discriminates on the basis of sex is prohibited.